AGATHA CHRISTIE:

The Woman and Her Mysteries

AGATHA CHRISTIE:

The Woman and Her Mysteries

Gillian Gill

G.K.HALL &CO.

Boston, Massachusetts

1992

Published in Large Print by arrangement with

The Free Press, a Division of Macmillan, Inc.

G. K. Hall Large Print Book Series

ISBN 0-8161-5558-5

Library of Congress Cataloging-in-Publication Data

Gill, Gillian.
  Agatha Christie : the woman and her mysteries / Gillian Gill.
    p. cm—(G.K. Hall large print book series)
  ISBN 0-8161-5558-5 (lg. print)
    1. Christie, Agatha, 1890–1976. 2. Detective and mystery
stories, English—History and criticism. 3. Authors. English—20th
century—Biography. 4. Large type books. I. Title.
[PR6005.H66Z655 1992]
823'.912—dc20   92-7518
[B]

For My Mother
Esme Scobie
and in Memory of My Grandmother
Mabel Croft

CONTENTS

PREFACE

Writing tends to be a lonely business, but not when you are writing about Agatha Christie. Unlike most people who have written about Christie, I did not start out as an aficionada of the detective genre, and I first began reading Christie as part of preliminary research for a book on later British women detective writers. As it turned out, I never got any further because Christie simply won me over. In her detective works I found an unusually spacious fictional universe that spanned almost six decades and began to catch glimpses of a fascinating mind. From her autobiographical writings I developed an empathy with the woman known as Agatha Christie — an empathy which is at the heart of this book.

When I had read all her published work, I was left with feelings of respect, admiration, and even affection. With her energy, her enthusiasm, and joie de vivre, her sense of comedy and good humor, her many loves — of husbands and books and ancient cultures, of architecture and music and landscapes, of tennis and bridge and crossword puzzles, of interior decoration and food and pets — she seemed the kind of person I should like to keep company with.

When I came to look at the secondary literature on Christie, another surprise awaited me. Had I taken the easy route and relied on Christie's critics rather than immerse myself in the writer's own work, I should probably have done no more than skim one or two of her novels that were featured in the many "best detective fiction of all time" lists.

I should certainly not have got any sense of what Agatha Christie was like as a person. Even the critics who claimed admiration for her fiction could barely stifle a yawn when discussing Christie's life and personality. Only one event in Christie's life — her eleven-day disappearance in 1926 — ever caught the public's attention. Christie possibly dead by her own hand or another's, Christie amnesiac, Christie enacting an hysterical fugue — this was the woman the public wished to find. Yet as all the ample biographical information now available about Christie proves, no event was less typical of this woman than the disappearance. Christie was to spend the rest of her life endeavoring to live down the reputation she had earned in 1926. Whereas the events linked to the disappearance connote passion, despair, failure, betrayal, madness, Christie's life as a whole is a model of equanimity, happiness, success, control, and sanity.

Everyone writing on Christie, whether friend or foe, agrees that she is very famous indeed, the most famous woman writer ever, perhaps the most famous writer, period!

It is claimed on good authority that Agatha Christie has sold more copies and earned more in royalties than any other writer. The author of seventy-eight crime novels, approximately 150 short stories, six "straight" novels, four nonfiction books, and 19 plays, she is estimated to have sold 2 *billion* copies in 104 languages, outselling even William Shakespeare. The annual earnings of Agatha Christie Ltd. (the trust set up in 1955 and owned partly by Booker plc and partly by the daughter, grandson, and great-grandchildren of the author) were reported by the *Daily Telegraph* of September 16, 1989 as two and one-half million pounds.

In April 1989, paperback rights to thirty-three of Christie's works until the year 2000 were acquired by Harper & Row for $9.6 million. Agatha Christie Ltd. refuses to even try to calculate total Christie earnings since the first book. Agatha Christie's most famous play, *The Mousetrap*, has been seen by seven and one-half million people since it opened in November 1952, and its box-office takings amount to 14 million pounds. Virtually everything Agatha Christie wrote is still in print in English, and television and film versions of her novels and stories have recently created a new generation of fans all over the world.

There is agreement that she was extremely successful during her long lifetime, ending her days as Dame Agatha, chatelaine of the beautiful Georgian estate of Greenway in Devon as well as of lesser properties, martyr to the British tax system, matriarch of a burgeoning and prosperous family. It turns out, however, to be Christie's very success that has made her uninteresting to critics. A woman writer who fails to go mad, have "interesting" lovers, bear illegitimate children, commit suicide, or die in poverty is simply no fun. It is Christie's relentless productivity over almost sixty years, her accelerating sales and ever-increasing fame, her personal inviolability to misfortune and disaster, that have made her so unrewarding a biographical subject.

It is perhaps only in the light shed by recent work on women's lives and by current ideas of women's writing that a coherent account of Agatha Christie's life, personality, and reputation can begin to emerge. Far from being the Mrs. Average Conservative Housewife inexplicably producing international best-sellers whom traditional critics have portrayed, Agatha Christie was above all a committed writer and a dedicated professional. Writing offered Christie a way to define her sense of self and a means to conquer the world. It afforded her an effective and essential form of self-therapy, a way of both hiding and revealing the self, a mask to hide behind as well as a starring part to play on the stage of life. Writing was almost as necessary to Christie's well-being as eating and sleeping, yet her attitude to her work was a mass of ambivalence, doubt, and uncertainty. She is a stellar example of the "anxiety of authorship" that afflicts all women writers to some degree. At the same time, her life and career offer rousing evidence that it may indeed be possible for a woman of talent to have fame, fortune, and happiness, books and babies, to marry her personal ideal of happiness with the world's idea of success.

Many people helped in the writing of this book. The Alliance of Independent Scholars provided me with a writers' support group that has been of great importance; Margaret Storch, Polly Kaufman, Jean Herbert, and Grace Vicary, to name only a few, were always enthusiastic, encouraging, and knowledgeable. Nadya Aisenberg was my most careful and demanding reader in the early stages, and she and Mona Harrington, both of the Alliance, gave me practical advice as well as theoretical insights. My old friends Ellen Peel, Margaret Ittelson, Christopher Lenney, and Willem Malkus read different chapters, offered suggestions from very different perspectives, and urged me, above all, to keep going. My editor, Joyce Seltzer, has been the soul of tact and cooperation from the outset, always able to see the wood for the trees and holding me to her own high standards of writing. The final shape of the book and the tone of the writing owe much to her influence. My husband, Mike Gill, has been enthusiastic about my Christie project from the start. He has not only encouraged me, and zealously read every page of the manuscript, but served as my computer consultant and word-processing instructor. This book could not have been written without him. I should like to thank my mother-in-law Dorothy L. Gill for her zealous search for Christie photographs, as well as Raymond and Margot Gill who provided me with some valuable information. Above all, my gratitude and affection go to my parents, Esme and William Scobie, who made incisive comments on my early draft, scoured book sales and the shelves of friends for copies of Christie's work, Xeroxed articles, sent off parcels, set up BBC Radio interviews, and generally acted as a combination of unpaid research assistants and public relations experts. Agatha Christie has proved a wonderful link between my American present and my British roots.

INTRODUCTION

The Hidden Author

The cultural legacy of Agatha Christie, the originality and brilliance of her craft, the importance of her message, as well as the meaning of her life, are subtly undervalued. Christie has won enormous fame but has never had the reputation for intellectual chic enjoyed by other detective fiction writers of her generation such as Chandler, Hammett, and Sayers. Ironically, Christie's low standing in the annals of culture is in part her own work, an outcome of her consistent and successful strategy of concentrating the reader's attention upon her fictional characters and plots while she herself remains silent, masked, unnoticed, the hidden author.

Readers of mysteries look for an absorbing puzzle, a well-paced plot, and a brilliant denouement. They are not much concerned with an author's biography or self-analysis or ideological speculations. As a creative yet opaque literary medium, detective fiction was perhaps uniquely fitted to the character of Agatha Christie, a woman obsessively concerned to avoid self-revelation. From early childhood, Agatha Christie sought to hide and protect her inner world even from those closest and dearest to her. As her fame as a detective novelist grew, far from emerging from her shell, Christie went to ever greater lengths to avoid personal notoriety. She communicated with the public only through her work and exercised an iron control over her personal domain which she tried to extend even after her death. Christie's hidden author strategy worked well in the sense that it earned her the creative space to produce an extraordinarily compelling fictional universe. Millions of fans have enjoyed her work and have not cared much about the woman behind the words. Nonetheless, the very self-effacement that led Christie to devote herself to mystery fiction, to limit intimacy, and to withdraw from public scrutiny have produced a persona for the author that has proved to be deceptive and demeaning.

One of Christie's major themes in her posthumously published autobiography is how shy she was, how slow, how chronically incapable of expressing her feelings. From her earliest years, she tells us, she was considered "the slow one" of her family, the child who hated to "part with information" and refused to allow anyone to enter unbid into her beloved secret world. At seven, at her first dancing class, she is so tongue-tied she cannot respond to a boy who asks her to dance, even though she very much wants to. Things are not that much better when she is seventeen. Her mother begs her to let people know that she is having a good time, and to say something, anything, however silly, to the young men she dances with. Frustrated by the profound malaise she feels as a speaking subject, Agatha turns first to music as a way to express herself, but this strategy is a failure. Whereas when alone with her piano Agatha displays real talent, if faced with even a small audience, she becomes again stiff and inept, her musical performance mirroring her conversation. Writing, however, unlike speaking and playing the piano, is an art of solitude and silence and Christie's failure with speech and with music leads her to the written word. "Inarticulate

I shall always be," she writes. "It is probably one of the causes that have made me a writer."

Agatha was shy and silent but, perhaps paradoxically, she was far from lacking in a social confidence grounded in strong sex-appeal and proven popularity with peers. Although a "scrawny chicken" of a child, Agatha grew up to be tall, slim, and blonde, and she had that elementary sense of well-being customarily experienced by a girl who never lacks for a partner. As at home in the world of the senses as she was alienated from the world of speech, Agatha was very attracted by and attractive to men. In her social world as in so many others, beauty was more important in a woman than wit, and there were rewards for a girl who was lovely, graceful, friendly, and zestful, and left other people to do the talking. Physical self confidence did not desert Christie early. As a divorcee in her late thirties, she found that there were still men anxious to flirt and propose and women to offer help and moral support. Indeed, at forty, a new life opened up for Christie, with new friends and rich cultural opportunities, when she began her exceptionally happy relationship with a husband fourteen years her junior.

In her life and her fiction Christie attached unusual importance to physical beauty in both men and women and a not inconsiderable part of her sense of self was bound up in her physical appearance. She had great difficulty in accepting her later self as, in her own words, "thirteen stone (182 lbs) of solid flesh and what could only be described as 'a kind face.'" Unfortunately, Christie did not start her career as a writer when she was a golden-haired girl and the time of greatest fame, and therefore of greatest demand for visual images of her, came when she was over sixty. The famous pictures of Agatha Christie do not show her as she liked to think of herself. Uneasiness with her appearance in later life led her to become even more silent and self-effacing in public. Thus, the rare photos we have of Christie are matched by a small set of unsatisfactory interviews between uncomfortable reporters and an evidently reluctant subject. Few people managed to meet the writer at the height of her fame and those who did agree that Agatha Christie said little, never gave speeches, and preferred to merge into the background.

Lack of conversational ability, social ineptitude, these are the Christie traits described by friend and foe alike, and in her autobiographical writings the novelist herself leads the pack of her critics, offering self-mocking anecdotes to illustrate her own inadequacy. A striking example of this self-criticism is Christie's account of the party organized to celebrate the tenth anniversary of her hit play, *The Mousetrap*. In November 1962, an exclusive and stellar group from London's West End had been summoned to the anniversary party at the Savoy at which the reclusive Christie was to be the guest of honor. The occasion was designed as an evening of triumph, a tribute to Christie's exceptional achievement as both novelist and playwright. Characteristically, however, Christie herself in *An Autobiography* writes the party up as a trial and a pitiful failure. Things started badly, she tells us. When she arrived, alone and a little early as requested by the organizers, the doorman refused to let her in. Amazingly, instead of protesting and brushing the man aside, Christie turned meekly away, sad, confused, chagrined, and yet in some strange way acquiescent in her own humiliation.

The mystery is *why* this famous and successful woman

was so wretchedly timid. Why did she dread public occasions so much? Why did this prolific writer — who was known to develop her plots in dramatic scenes that she "talked" to herself out loud — feel incapable even of writing a speech for herself and reading it to a live audience? Why did her conviction of inadequacy grow more and more disabling, as the public acclaim and official accolades were showered upon her? Could it be that "shyness" is just a convenient label stuck over the complex reasons for a chronic form of agoraphobia, that disabling fear of public occasions which so often afflicts women?

Agatha Christie was always peculiarly susceptible to fairy tales, and the *Mousetrap* party was to her a kind of cruel and nightmarish story in which Cinderella is turned away from the ball. Even when the door to the Savoy ballroom was held open for her, Christie perceived herself not as a heroine or a star but as a passive object, a joyless puppet. The Agatha Christie turned away by the doorman was playing almost a caricature of the neglected old person role so common in real life: as Miss Jane Marple remarks, no one takes any notice of an old woman. Christie is quite open about her reluctance to serve as a foil to the beauty of young actresses, and to be confronted later with front page photographs which proved how little her physical image now coincided with her inner self-image. However, it was probably Christie's fear and suspicion of the press, rather than the simple vanity she admits to, that made occasions like the *Mousetrap* party so painfully difficult.

Newspapers were permanently linked in Christie's mind to the period in her life when she had suffered despair and disillusion. In December 1926, Christie abandoned her car by the road near Guildford in Surrey and disappeared for eleven days, the victim, her doctors claimed subsequently, of amnesia. The dramatic national newspaper campaign waged around the already famous crime novelist's disappearance left a wound on Christie's psyche that never entirely healed. As *An Autobiography* makes clear, she never forgave the press for what was printed about her at that time. Christie drafted her autobiography almost forty years after her disappearance, yet she was still too traumatized to give any account of the last part of 1926. Instead, she refers to the event obliquely, in terms of the press coverage. "From that time, I suppose, dates my revulsion against the press, my dislike of journalists and of crowds. It was unfair, no doubt, but I think it was natural under the circumstances. I had felt like a fox, hunted, my earths dug up and yelping hounds following me everywhere. I had always hated notoriety of any kind, and now I had had such a dose of it that at some moments I felt I could hardly bear to go on living." This reference to almost suicidal depression must be taken seriously since throughout her life Christie's religious views led her to a strong condemnation of suicide. Furthermore, the dark emotions evoked in the passage are in contrast with the lighthearted, even-handed, self-deprecating serenity which Christie habitually chose for her autobiographical narrative.

From 1926 on, even after she had come to enjoy not only personal happiness and fulfilment but also success beyond her wildest dreams, Christie's public interactions were governed by a determination to keep her life strictly private and to allow the press and public no possible hold over her. Famous she might become but the journalistic hounds would always be kept at bay and the Christie haven would remain inviolate. Given Christie's imperative need for privacy and for total control of her personal life, the tongue-tied, slightly dim-witted persona the elderly novelist projected in her rare post-war public engagements may have hurt her vanity but it had its uses. Large scale personal popularity was something she neither cared for nor missed, and as long as people bought her books and left her in peace to write them she preferred to seem uninteresting and unworthy of attention. In one sense, Agatha Christie exploited her natural diffidence and lack of small talk to develop a strategy for self-presentation analagous to that of her famous character, Jane Marple. Miss Marple becomes the nemesis of murderers because she conceals a razor-sharp mind and sea green incorruptibility beneath old-maidenly flutter. Similarly, Christie was a brilliant, strong-willed, ambitious woman, easily bored and exceptionally unwilling to suffer fools gladly, who was ready to seem boring if the world would let her be.

Natural reticence and reserve, vanity, learned suspicion and revulsion toward the press, an insistent need to be in control over one's life, all were important factors in Agatha Christie's "shyness." However, the shyness issue is a question not simply of individual character traits or personal pathology but of an anxiety of authorship Christie shared with many other women writers. In her discussion of the *Mousetrap* incident, Christie says that on such occasions she is haunted by a feeling of being a fraud, of having no right to the name of author, of merely playing an authorial role, and making a mess of it in the bargain. On some deep level, Christie did not perceive herself as a writer and, given the dissatisfaction she felt with her personal appearance in old age, this self doubt may in part be explained by an inability to relate to available contemporary images of what "the writer" might look like. One image was of a person of her age and girth, but always male, a Grand Old Man of Letters such as Alfred, Lord Tennyson, Charles Dickens, or Conan Doyle, suave and distinguished, secure in the gift of the gab as well as the services of a good tailor. Who, except perhaps for Dame Edith Sitwell, has successfully created a powerful and popular image of the Grand Old Woman of Letters? Another problematic image available to Christie was of a young, charming, fragile, doomed woman, such as Virginia Woolf, Jean Rhys, Renee Vivien, or Katharine Mansfield, the kind of woman Agatha had indeed once almost become, but whom she had managed to exorcize.

Christie's insecurity as a writer and her failure to create a strong and positive public image during her lifetime is an interesting fact of literary biography but it is more than that. Christie's "shyness" matters because it has had an influence on the critical appreciation of her work. Just as Dame Agatha/Lady Mallowan was perceived as a conventional, old-fashioned, boring woman with nothing to say, so her books have commonly been referred to as badly written, stilted, stereotyped, and unaccountably slow to die a decent death. The congruence between the public image of the woman and the literary reputation of the work is striking.

To understand Agatha Christie, to develop both an accurate narrative of the events of her life and a coherent portrait of her inner reality, it is necessary to get past Agatha Christie's complex and fascinating defences and masks. Christie was not the simple or ordinary woman she claimed. Gifted with unusual energy, intellectual brilliance, and drive, full of sensual delight in the physical world, Christie was attractive, charming, and sociable, a passionate lover of men, a trustworthy friend of women. She was also, however, silent, reserved, hesitant of intimacy, haunted by solipsism, forever doubtful and insecure in her human relationships, seeking to be invulnerable. The least confiding of women, Christie did confide in The Reader, a distant, anonymous, unknown and therefore unthreatening person, with whom she felt she communicated on her own terms. It is, thus, not so much in her autobiographical works as in her fiction that we can find the hidden Christie. As the novelist V. S. Naipaul has written, "An autobiography can distort, facts can be realigned. But fiction never lies. It reveals the writer totally."

Christie allowed herself to be most self-revealing in the six novels which she published under the pen-name of Mary Westmacott, and which she tried fervently to prevent being traced back to her. In the period 1928 to 1944, writing her pseudonymous novels seems to have been a kind of catharsis for Christie, a successful form of therapy, a crucial mechanism whereby she worked through the important issues in her past and present life by recreating them in fictional characters, plots, and dramatic scenes. The second Westmacott, *Unfinished Portrait*, perhaps has most to tell us since it contains the best portrait of Agatha Christie that exists and also affords crucial testimony to what happened to Christie in 1926, the year of her "disappearance." The post-war Westmacotts, notably *The Rose and the Yew Tree*, are more mellow, reflective, and metaphysical than the earlier ones, and they offer the best expression of Christie's core values, of her outlook on politics, religion, and human relationships. All in all, the Mary Westmacott books, whatever their "aesthetic" merit may be, contain the key to unlock the inner world of a woman whose passionate need for fame was balanced by an obsessive need for privacy.

Why is it that Agatha Christie is so phenomenally popular? The answer cannot lie simply, as others have claimed, in her uncontested genius for constructing complex plots. Many other Golden Age novelists offered equally good puzzles. Christie's unique contribution was to create an original fictional world that is both totally convincing and highly unrealistic. Though Christie was certainly a very observant woman, as a novelist she sought to create fictional correlatives for her inner world of fantasy rather than to offer a mirror to her time and her social caste. Tapping into the unconscious, she developed a range of characters who follow neither the statistical norm nor the conventions of fiction. In Christie's fictional world, intellect and sensibility, weakness and strength, drive and inertia, sexuality and morality are not simply factors of gender or age. In a Christie novel, young men are often frivolous sex objects, and appreciated as such, while young women are the solid breadwinners. A woman over sixty can not only dominate the life of her family and community but also seek to promote her personal happiness through marriage to a much younger mate. Christie's heroines — as also her murderesses — do not easily toe the patriarchal line. Handsome, hard headed, and ambitious, they desire money and men, and are active in their pursuit of both. Furthermore, Christie is a pioneer in the fictional presentation of gifted active older people, particularly older women. The unusually rich opportunity for actors over sixty offered by a Miss Marple TV production is indicative of everything that the Gray Panthers owe to Agatha Christie. Hercule Poirot, Jane Marple, Tommy and Tuppence Beresford, Mr

Satterthwaite, are all formidable and fascinating characters who see retirement as an opportunity to start again on a new and freer life of active social commitment.

Just like everyone else, Christie was the product of a specific time and place, and she was certainly no revolutionary thinker. Nonetheless, Christie was significantly less enslaved by the ideology and structural prejudices of her culture, time, and class than such contemporaries as John Buchan, John Dickson Carr, E. C. Bentley, R. Austin Freeman, William Mole, Margery Allingham and Dorothy L. Sayers. The racism, the classism, the sexism that make the huge majority of popular novels written in the thirties and forties unreadable today are relatively unimportant in Christie's work. Christie was unusual in the deep cynicism she felt toward organized politics and political ideology of all kinds. This cynicism is at the heart of her delight in upsetting the reader's preconceptions and in confounding established scenarios. It is this originality that has made her as interesting to the American teenager in the late eighties as she was to the retired British Army colonel of the twenties.

The following pages offer a new evaluation of Christie the woman, as well as a careful analysis of Christie's craft as a writer of detective fiction. They are addressed very especially to an Actively Detecting Reader who wants to investigate how Agatha Christie builds her plots, lays her clues, and directs our attention *here* when all the important things are happening *there*, and who will appreciate some hints and strategies for discovering "whodunnit." It comes as a bonus that once you get the hang of Christie's plots and structures, you are in excellent shape for actively reading later writers like Ruth Rendell, P. D. James, and Robert

Barnard, who develop complex variations on Christie's melodies.

This book will, I hope, please all of Agatha Christie's many fans, will satisfy detective fiction buffs, and will speak to those who care about women's lives and writing. Mystery lovers can be reassured. I give the solutions to only five murder mysteries — *The Mysterious Affair at Styles, The Secret of Chimneys, Cards on the Table, The Body in the Library*, and *Nemesis*. Seventy-three more Christie mystery novels, as well as many short stories, still remain to be solved by the Actively Detecting Reader.

CHAPTER
ONE

Agatha Miller
Life Before Crime

The story of Agatha Christie begins at Ashfield, the house where she was born — a large Italian-style stucco villa on the outskirts of Torquay, an English seaside town in Devon. Agatha Christie loved houses almost more than she loved people, and she loved Ashfield with quiet intensity. Only her mother, Clara Miller, was more important to Agatha than Ashfield — but then Ashfield was her mother's house.

In 1879, soon after the birth of Madge, her first child, Clara Miller was deputed by her husband Frederick to look about the resort town of Torquay for another short-term house rental. Frederick Miller was absent in the United States and had by no means decided to spend the rest of his life in Torquay, rather than New York, London, or Manchester. But when Clara saw Ashfield and its two acres of gardens, she fell instantly in love with it. Told by its Quaker owner that Ashfield could only be bought, not rented, Clara impetuously agreed to purchase without consulting Fred. Ashfield was bought with Clara's own money, with the small legacy she had inherited from her father-in-law, and thus it was from the beginning Clara's house.

Ashfield cast its spell over Agatha, the third Miller child, just as it had over Clara. Agatha's life and her fiction were both marked indelibly by her passion for her family home. In 1921, when Clara and Ashfield fell on very hard times, Agatha was to turn to mystery writing as the one way she knew to earn money and thereby help keep the house in the family. In 1926, when Clara died and it seemed unavoidable that Ashfield be sold or at least rented, Agatha Christie would suffer a severe nervous breakdown as she painfully cleared the house of forty years' paraphernalia and memories. Two of Christie's early novels, *Giants' Bread* and *Peril at End House*, hinge on the protagonist's obsession with keeping the family home unsold. Only in 1939, when the house had been swallowed up by ugly urban sprawl and its trees and lawns were no more, would Agatha Christie agree to sell Ashfield and purchase the glorious Devon estate of Greenway in its place. Greenway too was special because it had associations with Agatha's mother. Agatha visited the house with her mother when she was a girl, and stored away in her memory Clara's remark that Greenway was the most perfect of the estates in the Dart area.

All her life, in rented London flats, suburban pseudo-Tudors, and gracious country mansions, Agatha Christie worked to recreate the mellow beauty, shining comfort, and old-fashioned elegance she had known at Ashfield. Finding the house that felt like home, redecorating, redesigning, planning the garden, maintaining a household — these activities were a primary pleasure and preoccupation with Agatha as they had been with her mother. To them she dedicated a great part of her royalties as well as her time and energy. To them she invited three generations of enthusiastic family and friends. But the houses that Agatha Christie made were not so much for others as for herself. She was actively forming for herself an environment of freedom and creativity. Virginia Woolf said that every woman writer needs a room of her own, and Agatha Christie may have had Woolf in mind when she insisted that she had no room of her own, wrote on any surface that carried a typewriter, and only once set up a place in England with her work table, her books, and her grand piano. But Agatha Christie did not need a room of her own — she was used to having whole houses. She was one of those rare women who can buy property at will, and buy it with money earned by their own work, not inherited or received from husband or lover.

So Frederick and Clara Miller's third child was born at Ashfield and was christened Agatha Mary Clarissa. Every name has a story to tell, and Agatha Christie had more names than most — three Christian names and, in the end, three surnames as well — Miller, Christie, Mallowan. Born Agatha Miller, she changed her name to Agatha Christie on the occasion of her first marriage to Archibald Christie, and was to retain that name even after her traumatic divorce and subsequent remarriage to Max Mallowan. Through one of the ironies of marriage, the mystery writer Agatha Christie made famous the name, and even the initials, of the person who caused her more unhappiness than any other.

The choice of a child's first, or baptismal, names often tells us a great deal about that child's parents and social milieu. In the case of women, who have traditionally changed their surnames when they marry, first names tend to be especially valuable clues to heritage. The first

3

names that Frederick and Clara Miller gave to their third child already tell us something about their family history and values. According to Christie's account, the first name Agatha was chosen by chance, having been suggested at the last minute by one of Clara's friends, who liked the name. This afterthought name seems fitting for a child whose birth, respectively eleven and ten years after her sister, Margaret Frary Miller, and brother, Louis Montant Miller, was something of a postscript. Several times in her career, Agatha Christie was to be tempted by male pseudonyms such as Martin West or Nathaniel Miller, but Agatha, that strange and memorable first name, triumphed, a permanent marker of the femaleness of the world's most popular author.

Mary and Clarissa, Christie's second and third names, point to a strong matrilineal tradition, since they are the names of her maternal grandmother, Mary Ann West Boehmer, and of her mother, Clarissa (Clara) Boehmer Miller. Mary is the name Christie retained for the pseudonymous non-mystery novels that were to be so immensely important to her. She combined Mary with her grandmother's maiden name of West, and perhaps with the name of the author of beloved children's classics Louisa May Alcott, to form the name Mary Westmacott. Agatha's older sister had been named Margaret after Clara's aunt and adoptive mother, Margaret West Miller. Agatha would in turn name her only child Rosalind Margaret Clarissa. The freely chosen first name of Rosalind, with its echoes of Shakespearean androgyny, suggested the idea of the child as an individual within the family unit, while the other two names, Margaret and Clarissa, continued the family tradition by commemorating Agatha's sister, her mother, herself, and her maternal great-aunt and surrogate grandmother.

The story of the sisters Margaret West and Mary Ann West, Agatha's maternal great-aunt and true grandmother, respectively, was part of the family legend Agatha grew up with. These two ladies played an important role not only in the life of Agatha's mother but also in that of Agatha herself, and themes from their lives were to be woven into Christie's fictional world. Margaret, born in 1827, and Mary Ann (usually known as Polly, as was customary in the Victorian era), born in 1835, were two of ten orphaned West children brought up by elderly relatives after their parents' untimely death. In her largely autobiographical Mary Westmacott novel *Unfinished Portrait*, Agatha Christie records some of her surrogate grandmother Margaret West Miller's memories of her own parents and siblings, the Wests. Christie's character Grannie fondly celebrates the family Eden of her childhood, and says that her youth was made happy above all by the obvious love and devotion of her parents — a theme that will recur again and again in Christie's fiction. Grannie remembers how much her busy Victorian mother enjoyed her month in bed after each new baby — "the only rest she got, poor soul." This Eden ends when the mother dies at the age of thirty-nine and her heartbroken husband soon follows her. Tuberculosis seems to have killed the West parents; in a quaint refinement of terms, Mrs. West is said to have gone "into a decline," while her husband died of "galloping consumption."

The parental tuberculosis happily seems not to have affected the West children, since Grannie attests that three of the children died in young adulthood (of yellow fever, in a carriage accident, and in childbirth) and the seven others all lived to a ripe old age. When Miriam (alias Clara Boehmer Miller), the mother of the heroine in *Unfinished Portrait*, recalls her own courtship, she refers to an "Uncle Tom" who gives her wise advice. This is presumably a West uncle, but of the six other West siblings who lived to old age, only one, Margaret, seems to have been known to their youngest great-niece, Agatha Miller.

Mary Ann (Polly) West, Agatha Christie's grandmother, at age sixteen married Captain Frederick Boehmer, an officer in the Argyll Highlanders twenty years her senior. At twenty-seven, Polly found herself a widow with four children, Frederick, Ernest, Henry, and Clarissa, to care for — not a very uncommon Victorian story. Polly's older sister Margaret West had followed a different pattern. In 1863 when she was thirty-six and the same year that her brother-in-law Captain Boehmer died — she married a wealthy American widower, Nathaniel Frary Miller, who had one child, Frederick Alvah, by his first marriage. Margaret and Nathaniel Miller had no children of their own, and thus it came about naturally that Margaret should offer to adopt one of the children of her widowed and struggling sister. Polly Boehmer accepted her sister's offer eagerly, and little Clara, aged nine, was sent from Jersey in the Channel Islands to live near Manchester (where Nathaniel Miller had business interests) with her aunt and uncle. Margaret West Miller thus became Clara's adoptive mother.

Living out a story of childhood unhappiness that has been told over and again by women writers — Johanna Spyri in *Heidi*, Jane Austen in *Mansfield Park*, Dorothy Wordsworth in her journals and letters — little Clara Boehmer was deeply miserable and upset by the separation from her brothers and what seemed an exile in a strange house. The fact that her elders deemed she would have a better chance in life in a new home did not make things better at the time. Agatha says that her mother Clara never quite forgave grandmother Polly for agreeing to the adoption and that Clara's deep melancholy and lack of self-confidence were due to this early experience of loss and self-devaluation. Maureen Summerhayes, a character in Christie's 1952 detective novel *Mrs. McGinty's Dead*, expresses the author's doubts about benevolent adoption with some poignancy: "My mother parted with me and I had every advantage, as they call it. And it's always hurt — always — always — to know that you weren't wanted, that your mother could let you go." The intensity of Christie's response to this early experience in her mother's life indicates that such a rejection by *her* mother would indeed have been unbearable.

Life in Manchester with her aunt and uncle Miller was sweetened for Clara by the occasional visits of Nathaniel's son by his first marriage, young Fred Miller. Falling in love with the romantic, older son of her adopted home was another fictional pattern for heroines that Clara Boehmer displayed in real life. Just as the adopted and semiorphaned Fanny Price in Austen's *Mansfield Park* fell in love with her cousin Edmund, so the teenaged Clara fell secretly and passionately in love with Fred. Like Fanny's, her love was improbably and romantically returned after some important hurdles had been cleared. Whereas Clara was a penniless young woman, living on the charity of her aunt and rich uncle. Fred was a very eligible bachelor, listed in the Social Register, and reported to have flirted with Jenny Jerome, the future Lady Randolph Churchill and mother of Winston.

The Millers were an old established New England family who could trace their lineage back to "Great New England ancestors of royal descent." Furthermore, Nathaniel Miller, Fred's father, had been a very successful businessman with the New York firm of H. B. Chaflin, and on his death in 1888 was to leave his widow and his son very comfortably off.

These objective obstacles were doubled by the subjective obstacles in Clara's mind. When the handsome, eligible Fred returned from sowing his wild oats and proposed marriage to the little "cousin" eight years his junior, she, like a true romance heroine, refused him. Brought up by her aunt "to be very diffident about myself," convinced she was terribly plain and "dumpy," Clara was unable to immediately seize her own happiness and risked, as it were, deferring it to the next chapter. Fortunately, Fred proposed again, and this time Clara followed her wise old uncle's advice and said yes. That her parents' marriage was a real-life version of a romantic women's novel had great significance for Agatha Christie's own adult attitudes to men and marriage.

When Fred and Clara were married in April 1878, Margaret Miller became Clara's stepmother-in-law, as well as her aunt and adoptive mother. This very complicated relationship between the two women was to be indicated by the title "Auntie-Grannie," which Clara and Fred's children, Madge, Monty, and Agatha, were to use when speaking of Margaret. The children's biological grandmother, Mary Ann Boehmer, was referred to as "Grannie B." She seems to have played a much smaller role in the lives of her daughter's children than did Auntie-Grannie.

Agatha Christie describes her father Frederick Miller as an unusually affable, easygoing, affectionate man, who loved society and was good at living the comfortable, leisured life of the gentleman. Madge and Monty, though different in many ways, seem to have inherited their father's outgoing personality and easy wit, but Agatha had a diffidence, a reserve, a verbal hesitancy that made her seem slow to her lively family. Only Clara, who knew what it was to lack self-confidence and the ability to express the inner self, understood Agatha, and acted almost as her translator to the world.

One incident in Agatha Christie's early years illustrates this unusually strong line of communication between mother and daughter. When Agatha was about six and living with her family in Pau in southern France, she was given a very special treat. Agatha's father and sister had planned a daylong muleback excursion into the Pyrenees, and they allowed her to go along. Agatha was totally happy at first, interested, amused, and not at all scared by the antics of her mule, who insisted on walking on the very edge of the trail and stopping on the brink at all the most perilous spots. All was wonderful until lunch, when the family's kind French guide, thinking to give a child pleasure, pinned a live butterfly to Agatha's hat. Tormented by the flutterings of the dying insect yet unwilling to seem ungrateful to the nice guide, Agatha could only relapse into hapless weeping. Irritated, her father and sister arrived back at the hotel to complain of Agatha's stupid tears and above all of her stubborn refusal to explain what was wrong. Clara Miller looked hard at her still silent and weeping child, correctly diagnosed that Agatha was crying about the butterfly, and unpinned it from her hat. Agatha remembered the "glorious . . . wonderful relief" she felt at that moment, as she was released from "that long bondage of silence."

Silence, an almost pathological aversion to "parting with

9

information," as the Miller family laughingly said, was at the heart of Agatha's nature. Already at the age of three or four, she had been "upset to the core" to realize that her Nursie was listening as she talked aloud to her imaginary friends the Kittens. She determined never to talk aloud again: "The Kittens were *my* Kittens and only mine. No one must know." Whether this fierce determination to let no one know what was in her thoughts was the source or the result of Agatha Christie's famous inability to express herself, it obviously made human relationships peculiarly difficult. As a child, however, Agatha had one ally, one interpreter she could count upon — her mother. The extraordinary grief and depression Agatha Christie was to suffer at the time of her mother's death in 1926 becomes comprehensible when we understand the bond between mother and daughter.

Agatha Christie's early childhood was extremely happy and peaceful, but, as in every life, there was a dark side. Untroubled by the gardener's hanging himself in the stable, little Agatha was inconsolable when Goldie, her canary, was lost for a day, and frightened to the core by the shouts of an angry old man. Most troubling of all was her recurrent nightmare about the Gunman, which she recounts in detail in her autobiography. In its early stages, the dream featured an eighteenth-century soldier, with blue eyes, a three-cornered hat, and a queue, carrying a musket, the kind of soldier a Victorian child might have seen illustrated in a book by Hans Christian Andersen. Christie insists that she was not at all afraid of the gun or of being shot, and this remark is perhaps significant in a simplistic Freudian sense. One of Christie's important characteristics will be her lack of fear or envy with regard to sexuality. It was not the Gunman as male that haunted her, and not anything he did, but the simple fact of his appearing in the place of someone else. Christie's dream developed over time. The initial story-book quality of the Gunman's appearance was lost, with only the steely blue eyes remaining to identify him. Christie's terror centered on the fact that, in her nightmare the Gunman would unexpectedly appear on the most ordinary of occasions — at tea, during a picnic, on a walk — and that he had the power to hide behind the mask of the most beloved and familiar people in her world — her mother, her sister, her brother, a friend.

At the heart of the Gunman nightmare is the idea that people are not what they seem, that the most beloved and familiar person can turn suddenly into a sinister and threatening stranger. Agatha Miller had this nightmare perhaps because she seems to have been unusually aware from early childhood of a split between her body and her observing consciousness and knew that she herself was not what she seemed. In *The Burden*, Christie as Westmacott paints an unforgettable portrait of a little girl who seems placid and withdrawn, almost retarded, yet whose mind seethes with love for her parents and with murderous hatred for the baby sister who has stolen her parents' love. Did Agatha herself have violent thoughts, and did she project them out onto the people in her world and dream of that secret, imperceptible violence being turned back upon herself? It is certain that when her first husband Archie Christie suddenly came to tell her he no longer loved her, the thirty-six-year-old Agatha was overwhelmed not only with anger, grief, and betrayed trust but with childish panic. Archie, the real-life lover, friend, husband, had become the Gunman of her fantasy.

One of the keys to Christie's extraordinary success as

a writer of mystery fiction may also lie in her childhood nightmare of the Gunman. The great strength of an Agatha Christie novel is that anyone, anyone at all, can be the murderer — the elfin child, the sweet young miss, the charming major, the wise doctor, the silly old maid. Agatha Christie's fictional world is one in which mystery, menace, and violence lie just below the surface of everyday life. The Gunman dream indicates that this view of life was not an intellectual conceit or a literary game for Christie, but an elemental structuring fact of her creative unconscious.

By night, dreams might bring fear, but by day little Agatha Miller's world was loving and cozy, filled with books, pets, and delicious sights and sounds and smells. Agatha's happiness as a child rested principally upon two things, her physical well-being and joy at Ashfield, and the love that existed between her parents. Agatha's relation to her parents was loving yet distant, since upper-middle-class children living in large houses with large staffs of servants did not see a great deal of their parents. The Miller parents also traveled frequently for pleasure or in search of health. Perhaps because Agatha was often separated from her mother and father, she perceived or remembered Fred and Clara as living together in effortless harmony. Christie describes her parents' marriage as one of only four "completely successful marriages" she knew in her long life.

Whether the relationship between the Millers was as trouble-free as their daughter believed is impossible to judge, but as usual *Unfinished Portrait* offers a few intriguing hints. In the novel, Miriam/Clara tells her romantic and idealistic adult daughter Celia/Agatha that she had always felt a tension between the demands made by her husband and by her children. Whereas Miriam had preferred to be at home with the children, her husband had been happiest traveling abroad where he had his wife to himself. Celia says several times in the novel that her own "stupid" and unrealistic expectations about romantic love and living happily ever after were founded on her perception of her parents' apparently perfect felicity. Clara Miller consistently advised Agatha in the early years of her first marriage never to neglect her husband or afford him any opportunity to find another female companion. This advice indicates at the very least an experienced wariness about marital relations. Such conversations between Agatha and her mother which reveal a conflict between Victorian cynicism and romantic idealism in regard to heterosexual relationships will form a crucial leitmotif in Agatha Christie's mystery novels.

The love affair between Fred and Clara was perhaps more complicated than a child could understand, but it was real and intense and ended only with Fred's death in 1901, when Agatha was eleven. In Fred's wallet when he died was the little pocketbook which Clara had embroidered for him before their marriage. Clara's passion for her husband was vividly expressed in the days after his death. She sequestered herself in her room in a prostration of grief, and little Agatha was sent in to try and rouse her from an emotional state that Auntie-Grannie found unseemly. Agatha said to her mother, "Father is at peace now. He is happy. You wouldn't want him back, would you?" Clara's response was savage and dramatic. "Yes, I would, I would do anything in the world to have him back — anything, anything at all. I'd force him to come back, if I could. I want him, I want him to be *here*, now, in this world with *me*."

In this scene, a strange contrast emerges between the quaint, Victorian deathbed pieties mouthed by the little girl in imitation of her adoptive grandmother, and the almost Brontëan grief and abandon of the woman. What wonder that Clara Miller cast a lifelong spell over her daughter? Passionate love and admiration, unaffected by the passage of time, until death doth the spouses part, was the pattern of marital love Agatha read in the lives of her parents, and sought to follow in her own life. Passionate love, unfettered by religious faith or moral scruple, was to be one of the most important motives for murder in Agatha Christie's detective novels.

Agatha's father died suddenly and left his family in poor financial condition. The Frederick Millers had never considered themselves rich, but the easy affluence they had enjoyed disappeared after Frederick's death. The fortune made by Nathaniel Miller had been eaten away by poor financial planning and unlucky investment, and Frederick Miller had proved either too indolent or too unskilled to recoup the losses brought about by his American advisers. Monty Miller could be counted upon to dissipate any remnants of the Miller family fortune Frederick's inefficiency had not lost. Madge, although married to the affluent James Watts, could do only so much to help the family out. Clara and Agatha were left with a few hundred pounds a year each, and Auntie-Grannie retained a life annuity guaranteed by one of her husband's partners. It made sense to sell Ashfield but the house was saved from sale by the impassioned plea of Agatha and her brother and sister.

Frederick Miller's early death was devastating for his wife. A widow in greatly reduced circumstances, she could only mourn and miss the man who had been the great love of her life. For Agatha her father's death was an opportunity as well as a sorrow. Madge was married and far away, and Monty could obviously not be counted upon, so there was a slot for Agatha to become her mother's protector and the savior of the family's fortunes. Agatha had always had more pleasure imagining herself as the knight than as the maiden in distress, and here was a real-life opportunity for her to come to her adored mother's rescue. That Agatha harbored this ambition to redeem the family fortunes is indicated by an early remark in her autobiography when Christie proudly discusses her American grandfather. A poor boy from Massachusetts, Nathaniel Miller had risen from office boy to partner, moving up the social scale and making a large fortune that his son and grandson could only fritter away. Tentatively yet significantly, Agatha indicates that she herself was Nathaniel Miller's spiritual heir, using brains and hard work as he had, to make money and take her family back up the social ladder. Personal ambition and the will to succeed are subjects rarely broached in Christie's autobiographical writings, where she portrays herself as a shrinking violet surprised and overwhelmed by her own success. However, Christie's achievements as a writer and as a money-maker make much more sense if we assume that from childhood Agatha dimly felt in herself the energy and the talent that had propelled her grandfather upward in the American social and financial hierarchy.

The death of Celia the heroine's father is one of the many fascinating sections of Christie's Westmacott novel *Unfinished Portrait*. The father's actual death is preceded by a curious scene when he almost suffers a heart attack after discovering the corpse of the family gardener hanging from a beam in the stable. Celia's parents try to keep the gardener's death from her, but she inevitably hears about it from the servants. Celia evinces a cold-blooded interest in the whole grisly business, requesting a piece of the hanging rope as a good-luck charm. This fictional incident, like so many others at least partly a memory from Agatha Christie's own childhood, casts a very interesting light upon the future queen of crime. When Celia's father himself dies in the next chapter, she reacts in a similarly cool and detached way, observing the adults' reactions with grave interest, and is not unhappy to find herself cast in the role of bereaved orphan, with romantic new black clothes. Celia's brother in fact accuses her of being heartless and caring nothing about their father. Did this conversation really occur between Agatha and Monty, and in this instance was it the renegade big brother — their father's favorite child, Agatha Christie tells us — not the good little sister, who spoke the part of virtue? On a deep level, Agatha may not have been too unhappy to have her adored mother entirely to herself and to be able to step into her father's shoes. It is not only young girls of fairy tale and fiction that grow into heroinehood in the wake of their father's death.

From the time of her father's death in 1901 until several years after her marriage in 1914, Agatha and her mother (and later Auntie-Grannie) lived together at Ashfield. Viewed objectively, Agatha's teenaged years must have been ones of relative deprivation, narrowed social horizons, and financial anxieties, but that is not how she remembered them. She remembered living in freedom and happiness in her mother's house where everything was also hers, where she was never forced to retreat into a space set aside for her. She had enough entertainment, enough friendship, and enough society, even though money was always short and Ashfield no longer welcomed famous guests like Henry James and Rudyard Kipling. Gone for the time being from Agatha's life — but held firmly in the memory — were the elaborate dinner parties, consisting, in the Ashfield parlormaid's words, of "two soups, two fish courses, four entrees, a joint — a sorbee, as they call it, two sweets, lobster salad, and an ice pudding." What mattered to Agatha was that she still had her beautiful home, the beech tree in the garden whose beauty sent a thrill down her spine, her piano which she could play for hours on end, the Girls, her band of imaginary friends, and, above all, the uninterrupted company of her adored and adoring mother.

The portrait Agatha Christie paints of Clara as Miriam, the mother of Celia in *Unfinished Portrait,* is one of the most beautiful tributes ever written by a daughter to a mother. Clara Miller's quirky and delightful character emerges from the pages of the novel — her unconventionality, her originality, her resilience, her tolerance, her charm, her shyness. Much of the passionate love, attention, and sensitive intelligence Clara had lavished on her husband seems, after his death, to have been devoted to her youngest child, "my girl," as she liked to refer to her.

For much of her childhood and youth, Agatha's life was dominated by women — her mother and grandmother, her mother's women friends, the female servants, and her sister, though Madge lived far away in Cheshire after her marriage to the wealthy James Watts in 1902. Agatha was partly a romantic, partly a realist, but always deeply faithful to her memory of the women of her childhood. She was

17

sensitive to the romance of her beautiful grandmother, Mary Ann, who at sixteen had run off with a handsome officer; of her mother, Clara, who had fallen in love with the handsome stepcousin eight years her senior, and finally won his lifelong passion and devotion. However, she was also aware of the practical advantages that Margaret West had enjoyed. After an unhappy youthful romance, Margaret had been recruited into hotel work by her aunt, a hotel receptionist. At the age of thirty-six, Margaret married an older wealthy widower. Margaret Miller was to have no children, but she enjoyed not only luxury but also the lasting affection and care of her stepson Fred and of Clara, the niece-daughter whom she had been able to afford to adopt. Margaret's sister Polly, on the other hand, did fancy embroidery to eke out her pension and bring up her three sons. In later life, on a Sunday, Polly would take the bus from lowly Bayswater in central London to lunch at her sister's house in prosperous Ealing and bring the items Margaret had asked her to purchase.

What Agatha learned from her mother and grandmothers was that life could be very pleasant when there was enough money, that marrying for money and living off a husband's income was a reasonable option but if you failed to marry money, you had better be prepared to work hard and earn it. Pussy Richards, whom Agatha says she liked the best of all her mother's friends, exemplified the problem of women and money. Attractive but unmarried, Pussy valiantly engaged in various business ventures, but with limited success. Unlike the married women of her class, she knew what it was to fail and to be hungry. Nonetheless, in young Agatha's eyes Pussy was a rare example of the new woman who competed in the male world of business without losing her feminine appeal. The image of Pussy, sporting bobbed hair and mannish suits and coats during the day and décolleté evening gowns at night, was to have an enormous influence on Agatha Christie's fictional heroines.

Agatha Christie's rather conventional and conservative childhood gave her a lifelong respect for traditional pursuits and crafts and ways of life practiced by women. She frequently expresses her praise for the efficiency and professionalism of female domestic servants such as her family's cook Jane Rowe. She seems sincere when she declares that if the worst had come to the worst, she could have earned a decent living as a parlormaid. Several of Christie's attractive and spunky young women characters will in fact take on jobs as domestic help. Agatha Christie's remark that she began to write detective fiction in the same way that she embroidered pillows has roused the ire of the English feminist and detective writer Jessica Mann. However, embroidery had helped to put food on her widowed grandmother's table, and embroidery was for Christie an art as well as a craft.

Reading, sewing, and playing the piano were the traditional activities of the well-bred young girl, and Agatha was traditional in that she spent a good deal of time in these ways. However, unlike most of her foremothers, Christie was not obliged to spend hours every day ruining her eyes and bending her head as she hemmed brown gingham or darned socks. As child and teenager, Agatha was not confined to the house, but spent hours roaming in the garden, swimming in the sea, and walking in the lanes and on the moors near her home. Swimming was as delightful and as necessary to her as embroidery and music and novels, and this combination of almost masculine freedom of movement with conventional feminine domesticity was to characterize Agatha Christie throughout her life. An important factor in Agatha Christie's success in life was indeed Clara Miller's willingness to allow her daughter to take physical risks. Clara was an unusual mother for her generation because she let little Agatha "run wild as much as possible," as if she were a boy. Six-year-old Agatha was allowed to go out in a sailboat with her unreliable brother Monty, just as she was permitted to go with her sister on the mule trip. At the hotel in Pau, where the Millers repaired when Agatha was six, she made some intrepid new girl friends, joined enthusiastically in their practical jokes and escapades, and did not bat an eyelid about climbing through a tiny fourth-floor window in the hotel and walking out along a foot-wide ledge — to the shocked disbelief of the other guests. Much later, in 1911, Clara paid the handsome sum of 5 pounds to allow Agatha to go up for five minutes in a plane. It was still far from uncommon at this period for planes to fall out of the sky, and Agatha's desire to take to the air was a dangerous as well as an expensive whim. Few mothers would have humored their daughters in such a matter, but Clara Miller said "If you really want to go, Agatha, you shall," paid the money, and gamely watched as her darling daughter buzzed around the sky. Clara and Agatha Miller were shy women, but they were not lacking in nerve.

Agatha says that her mother was convinced that her daughters could do anything they seriously put their minds to, and none of their achievements ever took her by surprise. This kind of blanket confidence is something mothers have traditionally given their sons, but its importance in the development of a woman's self-identity is probably even more crucial. Agatha drew a store of self-esteem from the love and respect she and her mother offered each other. This primary mother-daughter relationship was the rock upon which Agatha built a long, successful, achieving, and happy life, and the confident sense of female identity it gave her is at the heart of the relationships and power structures of Christie's detective fiction.

If Agatha Christie was born a Victorian, educationally she was a throwback to an earlier generation when girls did not go to school, but were given lessons at home by parents, older siblings, and private tutors. This outmoded schooling had advantages and disadvantages. One disadvantage was that until the trip to Pau, Agatha mentions only two regular playmates of her own age — "stolid children with adenoids whom I found dull" — plus another little girl whom she was not permitted to invite home. Agatha seems, in fact, to have been significantly short of peer-group friends until she "came out" at the age of seventeen. Whereas both Madge Miller Watts, Agatha's sister, and her daughter Rosalind Christie Hicks, educated at Roedean and Benenden respectively, were able to refuse the university education which their teachers urged upon them, Agatha, with her home education, did not have the option of Oxford or Cambridge.

In her later life as a notably successful woman, Christie wavered between two apparently contradictory attitudes to higher education. On the one hand, she liked to pooh-pooh the value and excellence of formal education and to dismiss university-educated women as pretentious bluestockings. On the other hand, she sometimes showed a deep sense of inferiority and unfulfilled potential. She liked to refer to herself as a "lowbrow" ("One up for the lowbrows!" she exclaimed in glee on becoming a Companion of the British Empire), and she always deferred to the highbrowness of husband Max, who swam like a fish in the sea of classical studies and became a fellow of All Souls at Oxford, or later of her son-in-law Anthony Hicks, who knew Sanskrit! This sense of inadequacy on Christie's part reflects the educational value system of her generation, class, and nation. At least until after the Second World War, British society honored above all the Lord Peter Wimsey kind of man — learned in ancient languages, familiar with literature, philosophy, antiquities, objets d'art, and fine wines. Agatha Christie's taste for mathematics, music, and logic, her technological, practical bent, did not fit in either with the Edwardians' highbrow ethos or with their ideal of femininity. Had she been born a generation or two later, Agatha might have found a culture more appreciative of her natural strengths and become a first-class natural scientist as well as a writer of detective fiction: the combination might have been especially fruitful. As it was, she strove to find an area where her lack of formal education was no obstacle, where her talents could find expression, and where her deep inner compulsion to excel could be realized.

The field which she first chose as a young girl was not literature, but music. Agatha Christie tells us that she was very nearly good enough to undertake a professional career as a musician, and since she consistently exaggerates her weaknesses and denigrates her talents, this statement has to be given considerable weight. As a fatherless girl whose family fortunes had notably declined during her mother's widowhood, Agatha interestingly resembles George Eliot's Gwendolyn Harleth in *Daniel Deronda*.

Gwendolyn also saw music as one of the few opportunities for middle-class young ladies to achieve fortune and fame. Unlike Gwendolyn, however, Agatha Miller was a real musician, not just a beautiful bourgeois dilettante. During her training in Paris around 1906 she demonstrated the ability and the desire to work for as long as it took to achieve excellence at the piano. She was a star pupil and had excellent teachers.

Agatha's dreams of becoming a professional musician lasted only for a year or so. An expert pianist, asked to listen to Agatha's playing, gave as his opinion that a career as a professional pianist would be impossible for one so excessively shy. Strangely, Christie's acute fear of public performance did not affect her when she sang, but the following year she was again disappointed to learn that her voice was too weak for the operatic roles she aspired to.

In the autobiography written in her sixties and seventies, Christie appears to be so calm and logical about this disappointment, so stoical about "taking it from there" and "putting wishful thinking aside," that it is difficult to take her early musical aspirations seriously. However, as so often, the autobiography is not the best place to find out what Agatha Christie was really thinking and feeling at the time. Proof that at this moment in her life Agatha Miller was not inwardly stoical and resigned, that she did indeed want desperately to play the piano well, that she would have fought to become an opera singer had she had the right voice, that she had invested enormous emotional capital in what she called her "cherished secret fantasy" to be a musician, can be found in her very first Mary Westmacott novel, *Giants' Bread*. Christie's protagonist,

Vernon Deyre, is a musical genius who paradoxically tries for his first twenty years to avoid even hearing music, so intense is his response to it. His childhood nightmare takes the shape of the drawing-room grand piano. Finally providence forces the adult Vernon to attend a concert where he has a visionary dream of a new kind of music and accepts his destiny as a composer. Vernon's ability to capture his musical vision on paper is achieved only after long years of work and at enormous personal expense. In the end, he writes the music he was destined to write, but loses both Nell, his wife, and his beloved ancestral home, Abbots Puissants, to another man. He also allows Jane Harding, the woman he loves and who loves him, to drown. The message of *Giants' Bread* is that music is a ruthless passion and potentially an all-devouring struggle. Through the romantically handsome, aristocratic, and brilliant male character of Vernon Deyre, Agatha Christie was able to express a passionate relation to music that was unseemly and unrealistic in the teenaged girl she once had been. Agatha Christie was never to achieve fame as a Wagnerian soprano, but the dream of fame and the commitment and willingness to work first revealed in her musical ambitions were part of the psychic foundations for her career as a writer.

There is a tendency for talented young women to lose control of their destinies when faced with the biological urges, social expectations, and familial demands that come with sexual maturity. Biological destiny can wreak as much havoc in the lives of sexually attractive women as in those of their plain-Jane Eyre sisters. Such was certainly the case with Agatha Miller. Music had led Agatha to an impasse, but Clara Miller did not let her daughter repine — or follow up on her idea of going to nursing school with a

Paris school friend whom (if *Unfinished Portrait* is to be believed) Clara vaguely suspected of lesbian tendencies. Despite her financial worries and her mother-in-law's opposition, Clara whisked her daughter off to Cairo, where Agatha "came out" in the relaxed, not unfashionable but relatively inexpensive environment of the Anglo-Egyptian community. Agatha was soon caught up in a whirl of balls and dances and excursions, and despite her inability to make polite conversation on the dance floor and her small choice of ball gowns, she was a great success, landing at least one proposal before her return to England.

Back in Torquay, Agatha engaged in the traditional activities whereby English polite society brought its separately educated young men and women together. She was a keen but undistinguished sportswoman, playing tennis, golf, and croquet, as well as riding horseback and roller-skating. She was the star of amateur dramatics and musical events at home and at country-house weekends; she indefatigably sewed costumes, made up tunes, lyrics, and even whole operas, sang the lead soprano roles, and accompanied other people superbly at the piano. Contemporary pictures show Agatha surrounded by other young ladies, and for the first time she had a circle of female acquaintance and some dear girl friends, such as Nan Watts, the sister of Madge's husband James. Above all, Agatha liked men, men liked Agatha, and a rich eligible son-in-law, in the mold of sister Madge's husband James Watts, seemed likely to allay all Clara's fears for the future of her younger daughter. In her old age, Agatha Christie looked back with understandable nostalgia to the period in her late teens and early twenties when she was slim and active, with thick, wavy, waist-long blonde hair and the delicate skin and sloping shoulders that were then all the rage. She never ceased to mourn this youthful self: in later life she was to make constant rueful comments about her weight, and had a horror of being photographed. As she describes her young womanhood, Christie laughingly but proudly details the many suitors she had as a girl, the proposals she received — which seem to have numbered nine — and the two engagements she entered into before meeting Archibald Christie. Agatha had secretly been falling in love with handsome men since she was four years old. She responded with enthusiasm to her new womanly body and was annoyed that her bodice had still to be lined to achieve the fashionable fullness. She artlessly sorted her admirers out into those she would and would not like to kiss and hold hands with, into the practiced and ardent lovers and the inhibited and clumsy ones. As she herself admits, Agatha Miller was "on the prowl" for a man, and at her age and in her generation and class, this meant a husband.

In early-twentieth-century England, marriage was the solution to life pressed upon every young woman by her family, her society, and in many cases her own maturing physical desires. Christie herself seems to be repeating the message of Victorian marriage manuals when she comments in her autobiography that it was exciting being a girl who gambled her life on her choice of a mate and to whom anything, therefore, might happen. "No worry about what you should be or do — Biology would decide. You were waiting for The Man, and when the man came, he would change your entire life!"

Agatha Miller may have been waiting anxiously for The Man who would determine her whole existence to come along, but she did not run off and get married to the first man who proposed. She was a mature twenty-four when she married for the first time, and she had given very serious consideration to marrying at least three very different men before she took the plunge. All three had been educated at the "right" kind of school, possessed charming families, had some kind of private income, were deeply in love, and, furthermore, were acceptable to Agatha's mother. Bolton Fletcher was a rich, older man who wooed Agatha expertly by letter but failed to rouse her desire. Wilfred Pirie offered financial security, lectures on agriculture and spiritualism, and a deeply inhibited public schoolboy love: Agatha was bored and again unaroused, and watched him sail off to South America with relief. Reggie Lucy, a charming, relaxed, but less wealthy childhood friend, whom Agatha loved and who loved her, unselfishly refused to carry her off to India with his regiment, insisting she have the chance to change her mind about marrying him. And change her mind she did when the dashing Archie Christie roared onto the scene on his borrowed motorbike, altering the course of Agatha Christie's life along with the history of British detective fiction.

Coup de foudre, that sudden, unforeseeable, and unreasoning birth of sexual passion that carries all before it, is as strong a motivator in Agatha Christie's fiction as it was in the seventeenth-century French society that invented the term. One explanation for this is, perhaps, that Agatha Christie had experienced a *coup de foudre* in her own life, and had every reason to believe that it could indeed fundamentally change human behavior. Archie Christie went after Agatha Miller with single-minded passion. She in turn responded to Archie's film-star good looks and glamorous service in the newly formed Royal Flying Corps.

They met at a dance, both were excellent dancers, there was an immediate attraction. A few days later, he borrowed a friend's motorbike and called unexpectedly at Ashfield. Agatha was at the house of a friend, but she quickly responded to Clara's anxious summons to come home at once. From the first moment, Clara was not to feel at ease with Archie, never wholly to like him or trust him. Archie was certainly goodlooking, and no doubt brave, but he had absolutely no money of his own and no immediate prospects of earning much. The bluntness, directness, and impetuosity, the sheer machismo of Archie, did nothing to reassure Clara, who feared for the happiness of her shy, introverted, romantic daughter as the wife of such a man.

Clara was clear-sighted about Archie in a way Agatha could not be, and her fears for the couple's future were far from ill-founded. Why did two people who proved later to be so spectacularly incompatible fall in love so passionately? By her own account, Agatha fell in love with Archibald Christie because he was different, other, a stranger whose mind she could not read, whose behavior she could not predict. And, like the valiant younger son in the fairy tales, he loved and desired Agatha with a vehemence that her other suitors had conspicuously lacked, pushing aside every obstacle that threatened to prevent their union. On his part, it was perhaps a case of an attractive but inexperienced young man seeing and falling in love with a woman who incarnated the beautiful, receptive, silent, mysterious female principle that so many men have desired. On Agatha's part, she may have seen in Archie the best personification yet of that dashing, inscrutable Byronic hero so beloved of women in romantic literature. She may also have been "fatally attracted by the energy and freedom that she desire[d] as an escape from the constraints of her own life."

Since Clara Miller realized that her daughter was unworldly, romantic, and deeply susceptible to fairy tales, she refused to allow Agatha to rush into marriage. Clara's quaint and unusual attempt to remedy Agatha's romantic nature was to prescribe a course of French realist novels — the very novels of passion and degradation and death that most well-bred mothers kept their daughters away from at all costs. The attempt to cure love through fiction failed: no doubt Agatha could not see the relevance to her own life of the sad fates of such fictional heroines as Balzac's Eugénie Grandet, deserted by the man she loves and saves, or Flaubert's Emma Bovary, committing suicide after a disastrous series of love affairs with the wrong men. Agatha persisted in seeing the relationship between Archie and herself as a romance. They had no money. They had almost nothing in common. She was already engaged to be married to someone else. He was very likely to be killed in the war then raging. Agatha's beloved mother deeply distrusted Archie. Archie's mother thought that Agatha might be rather fast. Two years of tears, struggle, and separation followed, but at last passion prevailed and Archie and Agatha went out and were married on a day's notice on Christmas Eve, 1914.

CHAPTER
TWO

Mrs. Christie
Styles of Murder

The Christies had a one-day honeymoon in a Torquay hotel, and then Archie had to return to his unit and Agatha went back to live with mother and Auntie-Grannie at Ashfield. She was to continue to live there until September 1918, reunited with her new husband only for rare and brief leaves. Like so many other couples in wartime, the Christies spent only a matter of weeks together over the next three years. While Archie was serving with his Royal Flying Corps unit, Agatha worked, first as a volunteer nurse at the local hospital and then, after August 1915, as a hospital dispensing pharmacist.

Life for the Voluntary Aid Detachment hospital nurse during the First World War was a fairly rugged one, even if one worked only part time and lived at home, as Agatha Christie did. The inexperienced and untrained volunteers were faced immediately with the rigors of ceaselessly cleaning and tidying the wards to the exacting standards of the professional nursing staff, scrubbing countless rubberized undersheets called "mackintoshes" (with chilblained hands in Agatha's own case), keeping on the right side of the prickly sisters, deferring obsequiously to the doctors, and squabbling among themselves to get the regulation three slices of bread and butter at mealtimes. Fainthearted ladies anxious to sooth the fevered brows of "our brave boys" soon dropped out of the program, and only those tough of soul and body stayed the course.

The Torquay hospital dealt with general civilian cases as well as war casualties, and Agatha's prewar training in rolling bandages did nothing to prepare for the realities of life in the ward. As one of a band of volunteers, mostly from less privileged families than her own, Agatha was at the bottom of the medical hierarchy, bullied, snubbed, and condescended to by all the ranks above. Leaving the faded elegance and sheltered freedom of Ashfield behind her, Agatha confronted the suffering of the truly poor and needy, both civilian and military. Nursing was a challenge, but it increased Agatha's self-esteem. It confirmed that she was one of the young ladies who could cope, who could, to use her own examples, steel their nerves to remove the dressings from a badly burned child, who could learn not to faint in the operating room, who could instruct less experienced nurses in cleaning up after amputations and help to dispose of the severed limbs in the furnace. Christie's competence and resilience were rapidly recognized by her superiors, and she got on well with her fellow nurses and with her patients.

The most irksome part of hospital life for Christie was in fact not the hard work and mental anguish, but the unquestioning deference all nurses were required to give to doctors. Accustomed to deal with doctors as social equals or even as inferiors who were invited to dinner only as a favor, Christie found it difficult to be properly obsequious.

Her instincts were meritocratic, and like her famous nursing predecessor Louisa May Alcott during the American Civil War, Agatha was critical of the harshness and inefficiency she noted in many of the doctors. Nonetheless, she learned to serve as a living towel rail for the young interns and to hand a surgeon the tool she observed he needed through the intermediary of the senior operating-room nurse.

Christie was an excellent nurse, and she says several times that given different circumstances, she would have been happy to work as a professional nurse, as she believed her paternal grandmother Martha Messervey Miller had done. Nonetheless, after fifteen months, Christie left nursing to take up work in the hospital dispensary. Christie claims that she dropped nursing because she had been ill in the late summer of 1915, because the hours at the dispensary were more regular, and because two of her personal friends, Eileen Morris and a Mrs. Ellis, were already installed there. On the other hand, Agatha admits that she was soon bored by dispensing, despite the pleasure of working with friends, and that she far preferred the more strenuous but satisfying life of a nurse.

Family pressures probably account for Agatha's sacrifice of the nursing she loved. The pressure came from Agatha's mother and grandmother at Ashfield but also from her husband away at the war. Clara had lost her young women servants to war work, and she was finding it difficult to cope. Managing and maintaining Ashfield was a physically taxing job, and there was also the psychological wear and tear of caring for the increasingly frail, handicapped, and disoriented Auntie-Grannie. As a nurse Agatha had had to work nights and weekends, and she had been unable to do as much as was expected of her at home. In Clara Miller's eyes, nursing may also have seemed an undesirable occupation for a young lady. Agatha's fellow nurses — unlike Mrs. Ellis and Miss Morris — were not on the whole from the debutante class, and Agatha's experiences caring for young wounded men were not the kind of thing young ladies could talk about in polite society.

Agatha might have been able to cope with the material demands of Ashfield, but she was more vulnerable to Archie's emotional blackmail than to her mother's complaints. Archie did not like his wife to work, and he especially did not like his wife nursing. In the novel *Giants' Bread*, where Agatha Christie gives a fictionalized version of her relations with her husband during the early years of the war, she makes it plain that Archie did not want a Florence Nightingale as a wife. Unwilling to discuss his wartime experiences with Agatha or to listen to hers, Archie wanted a wife who was carefree and beautiful, untroubled by the woes of the world. He was irritated by what he perceived to be Agatha's emotionalism and idealism about the war. For her part, Agatha was disturbed with the light, callous way Archie referred to the war and shocked and disheartened by his refusal to sanction the work she herself was doing. He had no wish to hear about her hospital life and begged her to give up her job as a nurse. "It's a filthy job, nursing. I hate to think of your doing it."

For once, Archie and Clara were both working on the same side, and it is not surprising that Agatha submitted to their combined influence and gave up the nursing she loved. What is important for the history of detective fiction is that part-time work in the boring but sociable dispensary left Agatha Christie with time on her hands. It also gave her a working knowledge of poisons. In the anxiety and austerity of wartime Britain, Christie's mind was eager for pleasurable relief and occupation, and she came up with the project of writing a mystery novel, based upon a particularly ingenious way to administer poison.

The idea of writing a novel was not a new one. Agatha's mother had encouraged both her daughters to write for publication, and had put pen and paper into Agatha's hands when she was a bored teenager recovering from an illness. As a girl, Agatha wrote poems, song lyrics, stories, and even a gloomy novel full of incest — the kind of novel she later jokingly attributes to her novelist character Raymond West, Miss Marple's nephew. She had had a few small things published in her late teens and, following her mother's advice, had submitted her work for criticism by a successful local writer, Eden Philpotts. Clara Miller could encourage Agatha to write, but Madge Miller Watts, Agatha's sister, was a role model. Madge, whom Agatha portrays as the brilliant, witty member of the family, enjoyed some early success as a writer, and Agatha was clearly motivated to emulate her.

Madge was not only a writer but a devoted fan of detective fiction, and she certainly influenced Agatha's choice of genre. Conan Doyle, Poe, Wilkie Collins, and Gaston Leroux were as popular as Dickens and Trollope in the Miller household, and Madge is reported to have read Anna Katharine Green's *The Leavenworth Case* aloud to the family when Agatha was only about eight. Thanks to her sister's early indoctrination, when Agatha began to write her own first detective novel, she had a knowledge of the genre that was wide as well as intensive. During one of the friendly discussions of detective fiction that the sisters enjoyed, Agatha declared that she would like to write a mystery of her own, whereupon Madge challenged her to do just that. This challenge exemplifies the friendly rivalry between sisters that spurred Agatha Christie on, but the reasons for Christie's turning to mystery fiction in 1916 go deeper. Fiction writing has since the eighteenth century been one of the rare ways that educated women could earn a living, and by the early twentieth century detective fiction was already a relatively lucrative genre. Despite the upper-middle-class, ultrafeminine persona Agatha Christie projected for herself, she was not uninfluenced by the prospect of earning money. Financial problems had been simmering beneath the surface of her life since the death of her father in 1901. Keeping Ashfield was a priority for Agatha, and by 1916 this was far from easy. Clara had combined her own small income and Agatha's even smaller one with her mother-in-law's annuity, but she was still having great difficulty making ends meet at Ashfield. When Auntie-Grannie died, things would get worse financially. Agatha's marriage to Archie Christie had not improved the Miller family problems. Unlike virtually all the other young men who had courted Agatha, Archie Christie had no money of his own. Even if, as seemed increasingly likely, he survived the war, he would have to remain in the ill-paying service or start a new career in order to earn enough for himself, his wife, and possible children.

Lack of money was a real problem for Agatha Christie, but it was also a challenge. Could the fact that Archie Christie, unlike her other suitors, did not have the means to keep her in the lap of luxury, but needed her active help in making their marital fortunes, have subconsciously been part of his attraction for Agatha Miller? Making a name for herself, achieving a piece of work that the world would recognize, recouping the family fortune, proving herself an active and equal partner with her husband — these ambitions stirred beneath Agatha Christie's surface indolence and conventionality.

So Agatha Christie began in her spare moments to write a murder mystery that she named *The Mysterious Affair at Styles*. When Agatha hit a major roadblock in her narrative, Clara encouraged her to use two weeks of holiday leave to go off alone to a hotel on nearby Dartmoor and work on the manuscript full time. Christie walked the moors alone, talking to herself, and returned to the hotel to type out the material she had developed. She ate heartily, slept long, and finished her novel in a period of intense concentration. It became habitual with Christie to develop the essence of her plot through dramatic scenes that she would rehearse in her head as she walked about or sat in the bath or did some mindless domestic work. Writing seems to have developed out of speech, rather paradoxically in the case of a woman so shy and reserved that she had difficulty expressing her emotions to her closest friends or conducting the simplest conversation with strangers. From the beginning of her writing career, Christie followed a creative pattern of talking her books aloud to herself and playing all the different parts in an imagined scene, just as she had with her Kittens when she was four or with her imaginary school friends the Girls when she was a young teenager.

When Agatha Christie started her first detective novel, she had many goals, avowed and secret, but self-revelation and exploration were not among them. Christie especially hated to "part with information" about herself, and by choosing to work within the fairly rigid conventions of the murder mystery, by seeking to appeal to a reading public with very clear-cut expectations and tastes, she had eschewed overt autobiography and self-expression. She had as it were chosen a fictional mask behind which she could hide. Nonetheless, detective fiction, for all its constraints and conventions, must obey the general rule that all fiction is an exercise in self-revelation, all the more complete because it is largely unconscious. In *Styles* Agatha Christie used little snippets of her real-life experience, and she exploited plots and characters and settings culled from the books she had read. Above all, she explored, on a mainly unconscious or fantasy level, patterns of human interaction that were of particular importance to her. In his or her first book, a writer is often exceptionally self-revealing, and *The Mysterious Affair at Styles* helps us to discover aspects of Agatha Christie that she never tells us about directly.

Rather like a dream, the most superficial level of a fiction incorporates certain elements from the writer's recent experience. Christie's comments on the writing of *Styles* point to two such events — her recent casual acquaintance with a man with an unusual black beard and his elderly wife, and the arrival in England of a large group of Belgian immigrants made homeless by the German invasion. The black-bearded man and his wife become the murderer Alfred Inglethorp and his seventy-year-old wife Emily Cavendish Inglethorp. Seeking a slightly exotic quality for Hercule Poirot, her new detective, Christie makes him a Belgian.

Two other important elements in the novel come straight out of Christie's daily life in 1917. First, the household functions of Evelyn Howard, the novel's co-murderer, parallel those of Agatha at Ashfield. Evelyn competently acts as the Styles Court factotum; she organizes the domestic help, pulls a few weeds, acts as a companion to the owner of the house, and keeps the social atmosphere sweet. When Evelyn quarrels with Emily Cavendish, her employer, and leaves Styles Court, she is immediately able to find a job as a nurse in a local hospital. Like Agatha, Evelyn is exceptionally competent, and her image as the soul of reliability will be one of Evelyn's chief assets as a murderer. Agatha's ability to cast herself, or part of herself, in the role of murderer will prove to be one of her surprising and enduring strengths as a novelist.

Second, the mode of murder in *Styles* comes right out of Agatha Christie's work in the dispensary. By making Evelyn Howard a nurse, Christie makes it reasonable for her to know that potassium bromide precipitates strychnine salts. By making three other characters also potentially knowledgeable about poisons — Emily's younger stepson Lawrence Cavendish trained as a doctor, her young adopted friend and assistant Cynthia Murdoch is a dispensing chemist, family friend Dr. Bauerstein is a toxicologist — Christie makes it possible also that one of them might be the murderer. All have the knowledge and the opportunity to pour some innocuous bromide powder into the big bottle of strychnine tonic Emily Cavendish's doctor had prescribed for her and wait until she takes the last dose with its deadly strychnine residue and poisons herself.

English detective fiction is outstandingly a genre of oedipal struggle in which each new generation of authors exploits and reworks plots, characters, situations, and solutions that have already been developed by the previous generation. As in other highly conventional literary genres such as the medieval love lyric or the classical tragedy, success in mystery writing consists much less in outright originality than in brilliant recombinations of established elements. Christie's own artistic awareness of this point shows up clearly in one of her comments on the conception of *Styles*. "Who was to be murdered? A husband could murder his wife — that seemed to be the most usual kind of murder. I could, of course, have a very *unusual* kind of murder for a very *unusual* motive, but that did not appeal to me artistically. The whole point of a *good* detective story was that it must be somebody obvious but at the same time, for some reason, you would then find out that it was *not* obvious, that he could not possibly have done it. Though really, of course, he *had* done it." As Christie's first attempt at the genre, *The Mysterious Affair at Styles* is particularly revealing of her interaction with mystery-writing predecessors, notably William Wilkie Collins, Edgar Allan Poe, Anna Katharine Green, Arthur Conan Doyle, and Gaston Leroux.

The mysterious affair at Styles is the death of the estate's owner: around dawn on Wednesday, July 18, Emily Cavendish Inglethorp dies in violent convulsions. By chance, Dr. Bauerstein is present at the time of Emily's death, and as a toxicologist he is immediately able to diagnose strychnine poisoning. The novel asks the questions who killed Emily, why, and how was the poison administered? *Styles* reveals its literary origins in having these questions answered not by a policeman investigating the crime in his official capacity, but by an amateur detective. In 1917 as today, real-life criminal investigation was a job for the police. Criminal investigation in books, on the other hand, tended from the very beginning to devolve upon private detectives, the brilliant and dedicated amateurs who, according to fictional tradition, succeed where the police fail. Within this fictional tradition, it appears inevitable that Emily's older stepson John Cavendish, the heir to the Styles estate, should agree to his friend Captain Arthur Hastings' suggestion that a private detective be called in to do some unofficial investigating of his stepmother's death. The man chosen for the job is a Belgian friend of Hastings who happens to be one of the Belgian refugees settled in the neighboring village of Styles Saint Mary. In the first published reference to the great Hercule Poirot, Hastings describes his old friend as "a very famous detective . . . a funny little man, a great dandy, but wonderfully clever." Hastings himself is eager to play detective. Asked earlier by John's wife Mary Cavendish to name the profession he would most like to have followed, Hastings has admitted a "secret hankering to be a detective." "Scotland Yard? Or Sherlock Holmes?" asks Mary, and Hastings plumps for "Sherlock Holmes, by all means."

Hastings's preference for Sherlock Holmes over Scotland Yard comes as no surprise. In 1917, when Agatha Christie started out, as in the time of Wilkie Collins or the young Conan Doyle, gentlemen did not go into the police force and no gentleman (or lady) reader could be expected to have much interest in the adventures of lower-class Scotland Yard types, however brilliant. Poe, Collins, Conan Doyle, Leroux, the great founding fathers, and even Green, the founding mother, agreed that there was no charm in detective novels whose puzzles were solved by policemen. Moreover, what Agatha Christie in 1917 knew of Scotland Yard was limited to her reading of detective fiction plus what she may have gleaned over sherry from the former colonial policemen and Chief Constable types she met socially. In *Murder on the Links*, her third novel, Christie was able to exploit the details of French police procedure provided by French writers such as Gaboriau or Leroux who had written her favorite *Mystery of the Yellow Room*. The English mystery-writing fraternity, by contrast, had not been very forthcoming about the ways and methods of a Scotland Yard it professed to despise.

The policeman's ineligibility to be the Great Detective is a major issue in the formative detective stories of the nineteenth century. In his 1868 best-seller *The Moonstone*, Wilkie Collins introduces the brilliant detective Sergeant Cuff, based on the real-life policeman Jonathan Whicher, who had investigated the famous Constance Kent affair. Cuff is an interesting character, but he is not allowed to solve the whole of the Moonstone case. Cuff's very name places him in the lower servant class, and it is as a servant that he is perceived by the key witnesses to the crime, Lady Verinder and her daughter Rachel. Unaccustomed to opening their hearts to strange men of the servant class, the two ladies refuse to give Cuff the information he needs to discover who stole the Moonstone. Rachel Verinder breaks her silence about the disappearance of the jewel only when Mr. Franklin Blake, a young man of her own class, turns detective. Cuff's professional brilliance is useless without the help of the socially acceptable Blake.

This alliance of policeman with upper-class amateur sleuth appealed as much to the American nineteenth-century reader as to the European. In Anna Katharine Green's *The Leavenworth Case*, 1878, the solution depends on the united efforts of a New York policeman, Ebenezer Gryce, and a young lawyer of the haute bourgeoisie, Everett Raymond. The names once more are fully representative of the different social classes of the two men. In asking for Raymond's assistance, Inspector Gryce explains the social barrier that obstructs a policeman's handling of upper-class crimes. "Mr. Raymond . . . have you any idea of the disadvantages under which a detective labors? For instance, now, you imagine I can insinuate myself into all sorts of society, perhaps; but you are mistaken. Strange as it may appear, I have never by any possibility of means succeeded with one class of persons at all. I cannot pass myself off for a gentleman. Tailors and barbers are no good; I am always found out." This assumption that a person from the lower classes could never pass for a gentleman is indicative of the essentially conservative and bourgeois ideology underlying the detective-novel genre. The corollary was that a gentleman sleuth, such as Sherlock Holmes, had no difficulty, of course, in passing for a tramp or a laborer or a clerk, needing only dirty hands, a shaggy false beard, and some picturesque dialect to fool the lower classes.

Another early detective prototype adapted to the snobbery prevailing among the readers of popular fiction and proved to have far greater immediate fictional potential than the Cuff-Gryce police model. Edgar Allan Poe's amateur sleuth C. Auguste Dupin is a well-bred man of vast intellect, bizarre tastes, and decayed fortunes. Not averse to pocketing large checks for detective services rendered, Dupin nonetheless is not tarred with the professional-police brush, and an actual or aspiring middle-class reader can therefore admire and identify with him. In Sherlock Holmes, Arthur Conan Doyle developed a quintessentially English public school version of the Dupin prototype that was to become a modern myth.

While Agatha Christie was striding over Dartmoor untangling the knots in the *Styles* plot, Conan Doyle was still, reluctantly, supplying his fans with new Holmes adventures, and other avatars of the eccentric upper-middle-class sleuth, such as E. C. Bentley's Philip Trent, dominated the detective-fiction landscape. It was inevitable, then, that the aspiring young writer Agatha Christie should be influenced by the Sherlock Holmes tradition. Hercule Poirot, like Holmes, is a bachelor eccentric, capable of brilliant deductions and uninfluenced by the prejudices and passions of ordinary men. Moreover, for her first book, Christie borrowed from Poe, Conan Doyle, Gaston Leroux, and others a first-person narrative structure wherein an admiring associate writes down the adventures of his friend the Great Detective. As Holmes had his Watson, so Poirot at the beginning has Captain Arthur Hastings to recount the facts, describe the clues, transcribe the conversations, and come to all the wrong conclusions. Separated from the mind of the detective by the screen of the narrator's intractable thickheadedness, the reader is supposed to share the narrator's awe and admiration of the Great Detective's superior powers.

Even more basic to the detective genre than the amateur-detective convention and the Holmes-Watson narrative framework is the construction of the fictional plot around a sequence of clues which the Great Detective must "read" in order to solve the mystery. Clues are the elemental units in the crime story, and the detective and the Actively Detecting Reader engage in the search for "a hidden story inscribed in everyday reality [which] has the effect of transforming the world of the novel into a conglomeration of potential signs." Agatha Christie's achievement as a detective novelist depends in large part on the extraordinarily brilliant way she uses clues to build up her stories. *The Mysterious Affair at Styles* already reveals this brilliance to an astonishing degree.

Two major clue traditions, which can be labeled "material" and "logical," existed in friendly rivalry in the literature at the time that Christie began to write *Styles*, and she seems to have had an intuitive understanding of the strengths and weaknesses of both. Material clues are probably the most obvious and famous kind, and they were prominent in the work of Poe and Conan Doyle. For example, in "The Murders in the Rue Morgue," Dupin observes his friend the narrator so minutely that he reads his mind and is able to supply the very words his companion is about to pronounce. In "The Adventure of the Blue Carbuncle," Sherlock Holmes is able to deduce a man's IQ, social rank, financial status, drinking habits, and personal hygiene down to the flavor of his hair cream merely by inspecting a lost hat. The ability to develop complex, consistent, and probable scenarios on the basis of small material signs is at the heart of the Great Detective's magical appeal.

Logical clues exist alongside material clues in most detective fiction and appeal to different, perhaps less scientific or technologically minded, detectives and readers. Gaston Leroux is an early writer who spurns the Conan Doylean tradition and invents a detective with a doubting Thomas attitude toward material clues. In *The Mystery of the Yellow Room*, Leroux's most famous detective novel, his detective Joseph Rouletabille remarks several times to chronicler Sainclair that it is not his habit "to attach a great deal of importance to the exterior signs left behind by a crime." Rouletabille exclaims in lofty derision, "O you literary detectives, building mountains of stupidity on the basis of one footstep in the sand, or of one handprint on the wall." Agatha Christie was impressed by Leroux's work, and she seems to have accepted his doctrine on material clues. Like Rouletabille, Hercule Poirot will be much less concerned with material clues than with understanding the overall logic of the crime, with untangling Leroux's famous "short end of reasons" from a mass of contradictory data.

In her first novel, Christie tries out a range of different clue possibilities. *Styles* contains clues of every type, and the inexperienced author multiplies subplots with reckless abandon. Throwing down a challenge to all detective novelists who have gone before, Agatha Christie puts her brand-new sleuth Hercule Poirot through his paces by laying out a set of clues so diverse and complicated as to tax the brain of the greatest of detectives, as well as of the most dedicated detective fan. *Styles* was not without structural problems, but this first novel has a complexity of plot that absorbs the reader's attention. If, like Ariadne, we follow the clue of thread leading through the textual maze of *The Mysterious Affair at Styles*, we are offered a great opportunity to appreciate the subtle and intricate logic of Christie's mind.

Almost immediately after Emily Inglethorp's death, Captain Arthur Hastings gives his old friend an eyewitness account of the events at Styles Court. Poirot then proceeds to Styles and, in classic detective style, examines the scene of the crime. Emily's bedroom contains six things which we Actively Detecting Readers easily identify as "clues." We are almost sorry when Poirot obligingly lists five of them for his more obtuse sidekick, Hastings: a coffee cup ground into powder, a despatch-case with its key, a stain on the floor, a fragment of green fabric, a splash of candle wax. The sixth clue, we discover some time later, is an empty packet of bromide powders with no pharmacy label on it. A seventh clue is the fresh dirt Poirot points out to Hastings on the floor near the desk in Emily's downstairs boudoir.

Lists of important clues, of questions to be answered and points to be considered, will be a standard feature in Agatha Christie's novels, and should be taken with a handful of salt. Dear Mrs. Christie is so helpful, or so it seems, and when Poirot recites his list of clues, the reader relaxes, having entered familiar territory. Each item on the list belongs in the Holmesian repertoire of material clues, things like cigarette ends, matches, bloodstains, and footprints. Each item on Poirot's list is, moreover, an honest clue in that it throws some light upon the complicated sequence of events preceding Emily Inglethorp's death. Nonetheless, the Actively Detecting Reader is advised to beware of Agatha Christie's helpful lists. More often than not, obvious, classic, material clues in Christie's novels are red herrings. Nowhere is this generalization more apt than in *The Mysterious Affair at Styles*, where it is revealed at the end that Emily Inglethorp's bedroom did indeed contain two pieces of evidence incriminating the murderers, but neither of them figured on Poirot's little list of clues. The proof of the crime committed by Evelyn Howard and Alfred Inglethorp must be deduced out of the items on the list.

The logical sequence of clues in *Styles* is highly complex even when unjumbled from the story and set out in the proper order. However, in order to appreciate Agatha Christie's craft as a crime writer, it is important at least once to set our minds to do the kind of work that she performed in the prewriting stages of novel creation. First, the question of the coffee cup.

On the evening before Emily's death, the family party at Styles composed of Emily and Alfred Inglethorp, John, Lawrence, and Mary Cavendish, Cynthia Murdoch, and Arthur Hastings, dined at 7:30 as usual, and coffee was served after the meal. Emily elected to take upstairs the coffee which her young friend and assistant Cynthia Murdoch had poured out for her. Seeing the coffee cup ground into Emily's bedroom carpet just after the murder, Hastings (and probably the reader) leaps to the reasonable conclusion that the strychnine was administered in Emily's coffee. Poirot's minute inquiries about the coffee result in the following discoveries: (a) Anyone present at Styles Court at dinnertime had the opportunity to tamper with Emily's coffee, which was left for several minutes unguarded in the hall. (b) Alfred Inglethorp never takes coffee. (c) Cynthia Murdoch never takes sugar in coffee. (d) Six coffee cups are left uncleared in the library overnight, and all had contained sugared coffee. (e) Dr. Bauerstein, who had been involved in a minor accident, arrived at Styles after dinner and was offered and took coffee. One of the six cups left in the library is, therefore, his; and Cynthia's cup remains unaccounted for.

Poirot puts the question of Cynthia's missing coffee cup together with a small and seemingly irrelevant observation reported to him (and to the reader) by Hastings. Just after the men have battered down the locked communicating door between Emily's bedroom and that of Alfred Inglethorp, Hastings notes Lawrence Cavendish staring over his,

Hastings's, shoulder in unaccountable horror. Poirot deduces that Lawrence had seen that the communicating door between Emily's room and Cynthia's room was unlocked and therefore jumped to the conclusion that Cynthia was somehow involved in Emily's death.

Lawrence's reaction is reasonable. As a dispensing chemist at a hospital, Cynthia has access to poisons, and she could easily have put poison in Emily's cup when she poured out the coffee after dinner. To protect Cynthia, the woman he loves, Lawrence manages to grind Emily's coffee cup underfoot to prevent it from being analyzed, and at the inquest he falsely asserts that the door between Emily's and Cynthia's rooms was bolted. Poirot sends Lawrence a message via Hastings, telling him that all his fears will prove groundless if he can only find another coffee cup. Lawrence eventually does find a cup hidden in a deep brass vase, and Poirot is able to prove that it was Cynthia's (since its contents were unsugared) and that it contained traces of a bromide. Cynthia is thus proved innocent. On the night of Emily's death, she had been drugged to prevent her awaking as someone, presumably the murderer, crept into Emily's bedroom.

The stain on Emily's bedroom carpet also turns out to be a coffee stain. Poirot observes how easy it is to tip over the small incidental table in Emily's bedroom and hypothesizes that Emily never drank her coffee at all, but accidentally spilled it. Having eliminated coffee as the poison vehicle, Poirot next sees a small spirit stove and saucepan in the bedroom, and a cup containing the dregs of a cocoa and rum mixture. It seems that Emily was accustomed during the night to heat up cocoa which the maid Annie earlier left in her bedroom. When questioned further on the subject of cocoa, Annie testifies that she had noticed a sprinkling of powder on the tray just before she took it upstairs on the night of the murder but had assumed the powder was coarse salt. The police test the cocoa dregs for strychnine and find none. Poirot, however, has taken his own sample, and he establishes that the cocoa contained bromide. Someone had tried to ensure that both Cynthia Murdoch and Emily Inglethorp slept very soundly on the night of Tuesday, July 17. Do we assume that that someone was the murderer?

The presence of a mysterious someone in Emily Inglethorp's room shortly before her death is attested directly by the candle wax on the carpet, item five on Poirot's list. The maids at Styles are far too efficient to tolerate wax on the rug for more than a few hours. Furthermore, Poirot discovers that item four, the fragment of green fabric, which was caught on a hinge of the door from Cynthia's room, came from the green armband of the landgirl uniform that Mary Cavendish wears on the farm. It was therefore Mary Cavendish who drugged her mother-in-law's cocoa and Cynthia's coffee, in order to get unnoticed into Emily's room during the night by way of Cynthia's.

Why does Mary Cavendish secretly enter her mother-in-law's bedroom at the crack of dawn? The answer to this question lies in a quarrel in Emily's boudoir on Tuesday afternoon (i.e., some twelve hours before Emily's death) between John Cavendish and Emily Cavendish Inglethorp that is overheard by both the maid Dorcas and Mary Cavendish. From the words she hears Emily speak loudly in anger, Dorcas assumes, and asserts to the investigators, that Emily is talking with Alfred Inglethorp and accusing him of carrying on an affair with a local farmer's wife, Mrs. Raikes.

At the inquest, Alfred truthfully denies having quarreled with his wife, and Mary Cavendish does not divulge that she knows full well that Emily was talking not to Alfred, but to John. It is because she has heard Emily's words to John and has been filled with jealous passion about Mrs. Raikes that Mary creeps into Emily's room at dawn. Mary expects to find a letter Emily had received which Mary believes to contain proof of John's infidelity. When Emily wakes suddenly in agony from the effects of strychnine, Mary is disturbed in her search, spills wax from her candle, and returns to the hall through Cynthia's room. There she joins the men who have come to answer Emily's agonized cries for assistance. Once back in Emily's room, Mary manages to slip the bolt on Cynthia's connecting door but not before Lawrence has spotted that it was drawn. Mary claims that she was alerted by the sound of furniture overturned in Emily's room, but Poirot proves that she could not have heard such a sound from her room in the next wing.

Thus far, elucidation of Poirot's clues has established only that Cynthia and Mary had no part in Emily's murder and that, where you expect to find strychnine, you mysteriously tend to find bromide instead. Poirot's sixth item, the empty bromide packet, also appears to be a red herring. At the inquest, the coroner discovers that Emily Inglethorp had a regular bromide prescription, and Poirot discovers that the prescription was usually filled by Cynthia Murdoch, hence the lack of an identifying pharmacy label on the empty packet. Also at the inquest, Mr. Albert Mace, a chemist's assistant from the neighboring village of Styles Saint Mary, comes forward with the apparently damning testimony that on Monday, July 16, he had sold Alfred Inglethorp some strychnine to poison a sick dog. However,

Hercule Poirot can soon provide the police officers with incontrovertible evidence that, at the time of the strychnine purchase, Alfred was far away from Styles Saint Mary and in full view of several disinterested eyewitnesses. Subsequently, a bottle of strychnine and spectacles similar to those of Alfred are discovered in John Cavendish's room, and a false black beard turns up in the attic. The Alfred Inglethorp signature written in the village chemist's poison book looks much more like John Cavendish's handwriting than Alfred Inglethorp's. John Cavendish, unlike Alfred Inglethorp, has no alibi for 6 p.m. on Monday evening; his claim that a letter in handwriting oddly similar to his own had decoyed him away to a lonely place cannot be substantiated.

John Cavendish is therefore sent to trial for the murder of his stepmother. The case against him rests essentially on the material evidence of the signature in the poison book at the Styles Saint Mary pharmacy and the incriminating items found in his room, on top of his wardrobe, which suggest he had impersonated Alfred Inglethorp. John also has the best motive for wishing his stepmother dead. He and Emily had quarreled violently on the afternoon of the murder, and she was threatening to turn him out of the house over which she had life control, and out of the will by which she was to dispose of her own large fortune.

Emily Cavendish Inglethorp's last will and testament — with emphasis on the word "last" — appears to lie at the heart of the mysterious affair at Styles. As Poirot scrupulously indicates for the benefit of Hastings and the reader, a crucial question that must be resolved is why, on a very hot July day, Emily ordered a fire to be lit in her bedroom. This aberrant fact is the kind of logical clue that excites the interest of ratiocinating detectives such as Leroux's Joseph Rouletabille and Christie's Hercule Poirot. Furthermore, among the ashes in Emily's bedroom fireplace, Poirot finds a tiny piece of charred paper with the partial inscription "ll and" on it, and soon after that he comes upon an old envelope in Emily's boudoir showing various trial spellings of the words "I am possessed." These two pieces of textual evidence lead Poirot to deduce that in the course of her last afternoon Emily had written up a new will.

As every reader of British mystery novels knows, where there is a will, there must have been witnesses. By gazing in admiration at the newly planted begonias outside the boudoir, Poirot leaps to the correct deduction that the logical persons for Emily to call upon to witness her will would be the two gardeners busy planting begonias outside her window. When the gardeners were in the boudoir, they left traces of mud from their boots on the carpet, which Hercule Poirot duly notices the following morning.

In the novel's penultimate chapter, Poirot explains that Emily Ingelthorp had ingested the fatal dose of strychnine not from her coffee or her cocoa but from the tonic her doctor had prescribed for her. The tiny quantity of strychnine in the large bottle of tonic had been deliberately precipitated by the addition of bromide powder, causing a deadly sediment to fall to the bottom. When, following doctor's orders, Emily finished the last dose of her tonic, she administered to herself the fatal dose of strychnine that was now left in the bottle. This revelation takes us back to the scene of the crime and to Poirot's first listing of clues. Number six on the list, we recall, was an unmarked empty package that had contained bromide powder. The bromide issue raised implicitly by the empty package has, as we have seen, led in the direction of Mary Cavendish, who doctored Emily and Cynthia's drinks, and to Cynthia, who measured out the powder at her dispensary. Both leads are red herrings. Nonetheless, Christie is being fair to her reader in the insistent way she points to the bromide powders. Less fair is the fact that Christie eliminates all mention of the tonic bottle. Had the bottle been present in Emily's room, Poirot would logically have submitted it also for chemical analysis, as he did the coffee and cocoa. The strychnine-laden sediment at the bottom of the bottle would have been found without difficulty, and the means of poisoning would have become immediately apparent.

If the affair at Styles is to remain mysterious for some twenty chapters, not only must Emily's empty bottle of tonic not be found, but the textual clue incontrovertibly establishing the identity of the murderers must also be lost. This clue is a letter that Alfred Inglethorp writes to his absent accomplice Evelyn Howard to reassure her that Emily's death has not failed to occur, but has simply been deferred by one day. Emily finds the letter in Alfred's desk when she goes to look for stamps. Shocked and horrified, Emily has a fire lit in her bedroom specially so that she can burn her new will, and she then locks the proof of her husband's treachery for safe keeping overnight in her purple despatch-case. The letter is still in the case when Poirot and Hastings examine the room and its contents for clues. The careful and portentous listing of five clues and Poirot's teasing refusal to name item six, the empty packet of bromide, serve to take the reader's attention away from the contents of the despatch-case. Poirot lists the despatch-case and its key as item two on the list, but he declares that professional ethics forbid him to examine Emily's private papers without the presence of her lawyer or next of kin. These scruples are essential to the course of the plot, since Poirot's delay in looking at the contents of the despatch-case gives co-murderer Alfred an opportunity to slip into Emily's bedroom unseen, break into the locked case, for which Poirot has retained the key, find the incriminating letter, and hide it.

Just as there would be no mystery at Styles if Poirot had immediately found the letter during his initial search, so no shred of evidence would point to Alfred and Evelyn if only Alfred had destroyed the letter rather than hidden it at the scene of the crime where Poirot could eventually find it. If, for example, Alfred had chewed up his letter and swallowed it, the murder would have been a perfect crime and he and Evelyn could have retired to the south of France on the proceeds. But murder, in Golden Age detective fiction at least, is not allowed to pay, and Alfred Inglethorp hides his damning letter where every lover of detective fiction might expect to look for it, even if he or she did not have Poirot's obsession with symmetry. The meticulous Poirot straightens the objects on Emily Inglethorp's mantelpiece both at the time he first searches the room and an hour or so later, when he returns to the room to examine the contents of the despatch-case with John Cavendish and lawyer Wells. Late in John Cavendish's trial, Hastings recalls that Poirot nervously twiddled the things on the mantelpiece a second time. Poirot realized that someone, presumably the murderer, had intervened to disturb the symmetry of the mantelpiece ornaments.

The mantelpiece features a "spill jar," that is, a jar containing long strips of paper used to light cigarettes, cigars, or pipes from the fire. This spill jar is a prop Christie has borrowed from one of her favorite books. In *The Leavenworth Case*, Anna Katharine Green's sleuth Ebenezer Gryce finds an incriminating letter torn up and thrust in the spill jar on the mantelpiece. Green herself is in turn relying on the classic principle set out by Edgar Allan Poe in "The Purloined Letter" that the best way to hide a document is to change its appearance and then place it in full view. Thus, Agatha Christie is following in an illustrious tradition when she has Hercule Poirot rush back to Styles and discover the vital clue in the shape of a letter, torn into ribbons and placed in the spill jar.

The Actively Detecting Reader who wants to discover the solution to an Agatha Christie mystery can learn three valuable lessons from studying the solution to *The Mysterious Affair at Styles*. First, give careful consideration to every mention of a written document, and analyze any text included in the novel with special care. Second, be suspicious of material clues, especially if they appear in the textual equivalent of neon lights. Third, place more reliance on your knowledge of novels, particularly detective novels, than of science. It is true that Agatha Christie is renowned for her unusual, and chemically accurate, use of poisons in her murder plots and a comparable expertise might help a reader to solve her mysteries. However, an overall knowledge of English fiction and a devotee's expertise in the detective novel will be far more likely to lead us to the solution of a novel like *The Mysterious Affair at Styles* than, say, a career as a dispensing chemist. This last lesson is particularly important if we look at the difficulty of guessing who killed Emily Inglethorp. A person highly likely to discover the murderer's identity is, strangely enough, a devotee of

Henry James. In *The Wings of the Dove*, James constructs an ingenious plot whereby two poor people in love, Kate Croy and Morton Densher, arrange that Densher shall marry the rich but doomed Milly Theale, thereby inheriting a fortune that will enable Croy and Densher to marry and prosper after Theale's death.

The profusion of clues — ground-up coffee cup and upset table, wax on the carpet and cloth in the hinge, fresh dirt on the boudoir carpet and a spill jar on the bedroom mantel — testify to Christie's expert knowledge of detective fiction and her debt to earlier writers. However, in her very first attempt at a detective novel Agatha Christie is already setting tradition as well as following it, and *The Mysterious Affair at Styles* exemplifies aspects of Christie's narrative art that will make her the acknowledged queen of crime. Two elements in *Styles* already marked Christie off from her competitors — the complexity of her plot and the extreme simplicity of means by which that complexity was achieved.

Christie's ability to reason logically, compress the evidence, and extract the most from the simplest element is well illustrated by her development of the apparently trivial detail of Alfred Inglethorp's beard. In *An Autobiography*, Christie tells us how important the idea of a bearded murderer was to her initial idea for the novel. A man Christie had recently met struck her as a suitable figure for the murderer, since he had a black beard — an unusual and sinister feature in Christie's class at this period — and was married to a rich woman considerably older than himself. From a real-life observation, Christie devises a plot in which the beard works on several different levels. First, the beard works as a social marker for a man not quite of the best society. Alfred Inglethorp always strikes Hastings and the Cavendish brothers as a "bounder." Second, it works as a cultural marker for someone sinister. Alfred Inglethorp murders his trusting older wife. Third, and more complicatedly, Christie uses the beard to establish a red-herring double for her murderer. One of Christie's most common devices for confusing the reader is to lay a clue which appears to be crucial to the solution of the mystery — such as a black beard — and then to associate the clue equally with two or more characters. So, in *Styles*, the sinister bearded Inglethorp is doubled by the equally sinister Dr. Bauerstein (who turns out to be a John Buchanesque German spy), and Emily's passion for the bearded bounder Alfred is doubled by Mary Cavendish's apparent absorption in the bearded bounder Bauerstein.

The doubling of Inglethorp and Bauerstein gets even more diabolically complicated. Murderer Alfred explains his wife's last words ("Alfred, Alfred . . .") by insisting that Emily was not accusing him of her murder, but rather calling out for assistance to Dr. Bauerstein, the bearded man she saw standing in front of her bed, whom in her delirium she mistook for her husband! Fourth, the beard is used as an important material clue. It is not Alfred who enters the Styles Saint Mary chemist shop, but Evelyn, his cousin, dressed as Alfred and signing the register in John's handwriting. Evelyn's impersonation of Alfred in the chemist shop depends on the instant recognizability of his beard. When a false beard is later found, the assumption is that John had impersonated Alfred, having acquired the beard from a theatrical supplier.

Christie's art as a detective-fiction writer lies not only in maximizing the use of apparently simple and everyday items, like a black beard, but also in telescoping an extremely intricate set of events into a time frame that is only barely possible. Just such a telescoped time frame occurs in *The Mysterious Affair at Styles* during the late afternoon of Tuesday, July 17. On that afternoon, the habitually leisured pace of life at Styles accelerates dramatically. Between 4 and 5 p.m. a string of letters including two very important ones are written — as well as a will — one emotional scene after another unfolds in Emily Inglethorp's boudoir, and a gardener speeds to and from Styles Saint Mary on his bicycle. And once again we come to admire the complexity of Agatha Christie's mind if we reconstruct the events of the Tuesday afternoon in detail.

After lunch with the aristocratic Mrs. Rolleston, Emily Inglethorp drops her companions Lawrence and Hastings off at the Tadminster Hospital some 15 miles away and returns to Styles to write some letters. Between three and five o'clock, Lawrence and Hastings have an enjoyable tea party with Cynthia at the hospital, and on their way home through Styles Saint Mary in the Cavendish family dogcart, the three unexpectedly encounter Hercule Poirot. Meanwhile, back at Styles Court, Emily Inglethorp is heard at four o'clock having a heated quarrel about marital infidelity. Dorcas, in the hall, believes the quarrel is with Alfred Inglethorp. Mary Cavendish, seated reading outside the boudoir window, knows the quarrel is with her husband John. A little after four, Emily dispatches one of the gardeners on his bicycle to purchase a will form in the village. The gardener comes back, Emily writes out a new will on the form, and gets both gardeners to witness it. As the blotter in Emily's checkbook proves, the new will disinherits John and leaves her whole personal estate to Alfred Inglethorp.

Having resolved the vexed question of John Cavendish, Emily returns to her letters and finds that she has no stamps. She goes to Alfred's desk to borrow some stamps and discovers an unfinished letter from Alfred to "Dearest Evelyn." Emily learns that Alfred and Evelyn are lovers and had planned to murder her the previous night. Not unnaturally upset, Emily summons Dorcas to ask — for what else, in an English murder mystery! — a cup of tea. Emily also asks Dorcas to light a fire in her bedroom in the evening. Since every scrap of paper is conserved at Styles for reasons of wartime economy, Emily intends to burn the will in Alfred's favor that she has drawn up less than half an hour earlier. Emily also writes to her lawyer and to Evelyn Howard. As Emily is drinking her tea and warning Dorcas never to trust a man, Mary Cavendish enters the boudoir demanding information about John's misconduct with Mrs. Raikes. Emily is too upset to discuss John, but she still holds Alfred's letter in her hand, and Mary Cavendish is mistakenly convinced that the letter refers to John. Mary determines that she must get hold of that letter at all costs.

The half-finished letter from Alfred Inglethorp to Evelyn Howard is a striking example of what I like to call "textual" clues. Other textual clues found in *Styles* are the poison-book signature; the scrap of charred will; the envelope with practice spellings of "I am possessed"; the letter, apparently dated July 17, from Emily to Evelyn Howard; the letter in a counterfeit of John's own handwriting used to decoy him to a lonely place at the time the strychnine was being purchased. Whereas material clues tend very often to be red herrings in Agatha Christie's work, the textual clues are almost always important. Wills, letters, checks, maps, plans, signatures, etc., are essential elements in many of Christie's greatest mysteries, and they are one of the keys to her success in the genre.

When we are presented with some important material clue in a book, we have to rely on someone like the narrator to point it out to us, describe it, and evaluate it in some way. Such descriptions are very tricky for both writer and reader, since the reliability of eyewitness accounts is one of the things which modern fiction in general and detective fiction in particular have trained us to suspect. When it comes to material clues, the reader is necessarily in a position of dependence, since he or she is unable actually to see things like the various expressions on the face of Dupin's friend in "The Murders in the Rue Morgue" or the hat which Sherlock Holmes holds in his hand in "The Adventure of the Blue Carbuncle." As a result, the reader can rarely make deductions from material clues and is placed in the position of admiring onlooker as the Great Detective does his stuff. What is more, the reader rarely has the precise esoteric expertise which allows the Great Detective to identify such famous material clues as watermarks, cigar butts, fingerprints, bloodstains, fragments of cloth, and pinches of dust.

Textual clues, on the other hand, written words on paper, invoke the Great Detective's skill not as an orientalist or organic chemist or bibliophile, but *as a reader*, and the very nature of the genre allows the novel reader to compete. Documents, whether handwritten, typed, printed, or sketched, can be reproduced on the page of the novel for the reader to pore over at leisure. Faced with a piece of paper reading "ll and" and an envelope scribbled with "I am possessed," we too can deduce with or even before Poirot that Emily Inglethorp had been writing a will. Textual clues in the novel play the same role as visual clues in the motion picture, allowing the reader to pit his skills against those of the Great Detective and, if not prevail, at the very least offer informed appreciation. By the preference Christie displays for textual clues over material ones, she plays fairer with the reader than almost any other mystery writer. This is no doubt one of the reasons we still like her books.

Perhaps the most salient example of Agatha Christie's ability to both synthesize elements from the existing tradition of detective fiction and forge something new and original is her creation of Hercule Poirot, the second most famous fictional detective, after Sherlock Holmes. Poirot appears in Christie's first novel and goes on to star in almost every one of her most celebrated and admired novels. Christie's achievement as a detective novelist is closely intertwined with this one character.

The Great Detective is described thus: "Poirot was an extraordinary looking little man. He was hardly more than five feet, four inches, but carried himself with great dignity. His head was exactly the shape of an egg, and he always perched it a little on one side. His moustache was very stiff and military. The neatness of his attire was almost incredible. I believe a speck of dust would have caused him more pain than a bullet wound."

As we look back at this first description of Christie's famous sleuth, it is surprising how little more we know of Poirot at the end of his long fictional life than at the beginning. Physically, Poirot will remain astonishingly the same. By the time of *The ABC Murders* in 1935, Poirot is admitting to dying his hair and whiskers. In more tropic climes, he exchanges his black clothing for white garments just as impeccable and unsuitable. In 1963's *The Clocks*, Poirot is a shade more reluctant to leave his apartment than in earlier days and no longer runs wildly around when inspired as he once did in the gardens of Styles Court. In *Curtain*, written during the Second World War and published in 1975, Hastings finds Poirot confined to a wheelchair and contemplating death, but Christie has trained her readers to suspect any character whose movements appear to be restricted. In essence the Poirot of the novels written in the late sixties is extraordinarily the same man as the Poirot of 1917. To the moustaches, the shining green eyes, the egg-shaped head, the tight black patent-leather shoes, the meticulous neatness and love of symmetry will be added a fondness for hot chocolate and fruit syrups, and remarkably little else.

It is not only Poirot's physical persona that Christie establishes definitively in *Styles*. Virtually everything we know about his past is included here. That isn't much and Poirot's biography will to the end remain essentially unexplored. Following what Hastings describes, in true detective-novel hyperbole, as "the world-wide notoriety" of the mysterious affair at Styles, Poirot is to become famous as a private detective operating not only in England and France but in the Middle East and the Balkans. Through his professional involvement, Poirot will become friendly with policemen like Japp, Battle, and Race, in various novels and with young Colin Lamb in *The Clocks*. He will become rich enough to employ a valet, the invaluable Georges, and a secretary, the repressively efficient Miss Lemon, and to subcontract out to the expensive detective agency of Mr. Goby. His fame will earn interesting social engagements from the likes of millionaire Mr. Shaitana, famous actor Charles Cartwright, and retired diplomat Sir Henry Angkatell. But in all his long life, Poirot has only two people who could be labeled friends — Hastings between 1920 and 1937, plus the final adventure in *Curtain*, and Ariadne Oliver, between 1936 and 1973. Poirot is to remain forever an exile without compatriots, a retired man without a past, a single man without relatives, a man without lovers, a man without childhood friends, yet a man profoundly content with his life and destiny.

In her autobiography, Christie comments on the "mistake" she made in creating a sleuth who was already retired and elderly at the time of his fictional birth, and who has to be about 120 years old in his last adventure. The implication of her remarks is that Poirot was a kind of youthful error, an unlikely product of inexperience which the oddness of public taste forced her to continue with for the rest of her life, just as Conan Doyle had been forced to live with, and even resurrect, Sherlock Holmes. However, Christie is misleading here, as on many other occasions, and her comments mask two vital points.

First, Poirot is not an aberration, since Christie's later sleuths — Miss Marple, Mr. Parker Pyne, and Mr. Satterthwaite — are just as elderly and unmarried as Poirot. Only detectives Tommy and Tuppence Beresford start young in 1922, end up almost correctly old in the 1970s, and enjoy "normal" lives with marriage, children, friends, houses, careers, etc. Second, Christie's success as a writer of detective fiction correlates very strongly with elderly sleuths in general and with one elderly sleuth, Hercule Poirot, in particular. Most readers agree that

Tommy and Tuppence star in some of Christie's worst novels, even though these married sleuths seem to have been the novelist's personal favorites.

The strangeness of Christie's invention of Hercule Poirot needs to be put in context to be appreciated. Detective-story writers, particularly men, have tended to have a strong psychological investment in their Great Detectives. Some, like Dashiell Hammett and Ross MacDonald, capitalize on their youthful experiences as private eye, journalist, or navy man by creating a private eye who is partly a real self of the past. More commonly, writers fashion a Great Detective who relates not to the lived experience, but to the writer's dreams and fantasies and self-projection. Unfettered by reality, the seedy young American Edgar Allan Poe invents an aristocratic European genius of decadent allure who can read minds and compel a respect that the writer himself would never enjoy. Arthur Conan Doyle, a struggling young provincial doctor, invents a man of razor-sharp intellect, able to diagnose complex cases on sight, untouched by the familial cares and social pressures weighing upon his creator.

The popular novelist fixes his conscious mind firmly on pleasing the public and making money, but thereby his unconscious is allowed to wander at will and to invent heroic detectives whose hyperrationality appeals, paradoxically, to deep emotional needs in both writer and reader. Edgar Allan Poe, Conan Doyle, Gaston Leroux, E. C. Bentley, G. K. Chesterton, R. Austin Freeman, Leslie Charteris, Raymond Chandler, Mickey Spillane, Rex Stout, Dashiell Hammett — all endow their master sleuths with enlarged, simplified, highlighted facets of their own nature. Meanwhile, ambitious women detective-story writers of the same generation, such as Dorothy L. Sayers or Margery Allingham, with no professional experience in the world of crime and criminals to draw upon but as intent as the men on success, create male detectives who start out as able copies of the male models and end up as romantic heroes.

In striking contrast to her contemporaries, both male and female, Agatha Christie at the very outset created a Great Detective who was a reverse image of herself and who had no romantic-hero potential. A tall, attractive, reticent, married, rather untidy young Englishwoman created a short, plain, talkative, old Belgian bachelor of meticulous neatness. Poirot is not an idealized version of Mrs. Agatha Miller Christie, nor does he bear much resemblance to anyone Christie knew. It is notable that from the very first, Christie established a relationship between herself and her Great Detective which is unusual in that it is not autobiographical, not idealized, and not romantic.

Poirot is in fact best seen as an efficient narrative unit rather than as a person. That he arose armed and ready from Christie's brain in her first novel, like Athena from the head of Zeus, is a measure of Christie's genius for detective fiction. Immediately, instinctively, Christie established some of the essential elements for a successful series detective. Poirot's curriculum vitae may be skeletal, but each bone is essential and well articulated. Christie carefully exploits the narrative potential of the basic facts, invented at the outset of her career, that Poirot is (a) an outstanding intellect, (b) a physical oddity, (c) a social anomaly, (d) a foreigner, (f) a gentleman, and (g) an ex-policeman.

Physically, Poirot is instantly recognizable in the way a cartoon character is. The egg head, the moustache, the gallicisms function like the hat and chin for Dick Tracy, or the curls and round blank eyes for Little Orphan Annie. As we have seen, extreme economy of effect is at the heart of Christie's success as a crime novelist, and a few lines of text are all she will ever need to present her detective and get the plot moving.

In appearance, Poirot is alien not only to his creator but to every fictional colleague, client, suspect, and murderer he encounters. "Comical," "ridiculous-looking," "the sort of little man one could never take seriously," "a funny little man with enormous moustaches" — those are the kind of responses Poirot meets with routinely. Physically unimpressive, Poirot is also a social oddity. He will have a lifelong preference for black patent-leather shoes, even in the country, and for this will always be in danger of being labeled a "dago" or even a "bounder" by some people. In the eyes of women, Poirot is clearly a failure; no woman will ever sigh after his square chin, bulging muscles, and immaculate sports clothes.

As a character, however, Poirot works very well. Murderers tend to underestimate Poirot, with fatal consequences. Moreover, the discrepancy between Poirot's ridiculous appearance and his formidable intellect makes a certain elementary appeal to the public's sympathy. The reader too may feel that he or she hides brilliant abilities beneath an unprepossessing exterior and may therefore tend to root for the little Belgian outsider. What is more, by making her Great Detective a small, funny little foreigner, Christie sets him outside the upper-middle-class British milieu she chooses for her murder scenarios and makes him fully aware of its failings and foibles. As Christie's target readership moves further away in space and time from the postimperial English middle classes, Poirot's ironic detachment from class values becomes increasingly important.

A key to Poirot's popularity is his identification in the public mind with the Holmes tradition of the amateur sleuth. That Poirot is a gentleman, even if a Belgian gentleman, is attested to implicitly by his friendship with the impeccably conventional and pukka Englishman Hastings. Through his relationship with Hastings, and later with Ariadne Oliver when Hastings has been packed off to a farm in South America, Poirot gains entrées into the upper-crust world closed to the likes of Wilkie Collins's Sergeant Cuff. Captain Hastings' correct social affiliations are implicit in his very name and rank (Christie's captains are always good guys), and Ariadne Oliver, for all her shyness, knows the right people. Through these two friends, Poirot will gain access to the drawing rooms and upstairs corridors of places like Styles Court and thus be in a situation to get the upper-class suspects to betray themselves in conversation.

Poirot was once a policeman, and a highly successful one. This is virtually all we know about his past life, but it is of crucial importance. A rudimentary realism requires even the detective-story writer to acknowledge that the police hold most of the cards in the game of criminal investigation. Simply because of his police past, Poirot wins the cooperation of Scotland Yard, gains access to police files, enjoys the collegial friendship of Japp and Battle and also the useful rivalry of Giraud of the Sûreté, in *Murder on the Links*, or of Inspector Crome, in *The ABC Murders*. To succeed, the private sleuth must somehow persuade the police to tell him what they know and to respond to his suggestions and requests. So, when two men from the Yard come down to the Stylites Arms for Emily Inglethorp's inquest, there is a structurally essential scene of mutual recognition between them and Poirot. From now on, Poirot will be able to add all the facts known to the police to those he has gleaned himself through his contacts with the Cavendish family. The detective's famous "little grey cells" will always prove a match for the police, but they are put to work on an exclusive combination of information from internal and external sources.

Poirot's peculiar social alienation — his lack of family, class, and nation — makes of him that interested yet disinterested observer, that friendly yet impartial analyst, that just but relentless pursuer after truth that Christie sought for the intellectual puzzles lying at the heart of her novels. Stripped of a few mannerisms, Poirot is nothing but the detached and sagacious principle of detection in the novel which the reader seeks to emulate. He is also the personification of the logical, unemotional, detached side of the novelist. Thus, in a strange way, Agatha Christie might after all have said, in imitation of Flaubert, "Hercule Poirot, c'est moi."

Agatha Christie wrote *The Mysterious Affair at Styles* at a time of extreme international turmoil. Even though Christie had withdrawn from the hardships and sufferings of the nursing wards into the calm order of the dispensary, even though neither her husband nor her brother were to die in the war, nonetheless for Agatha Christie the First World War was a period of trauma. What is more, the revolution in Agatha's settled existence represented by her marriage with Archie Christie was far from complete. Since the outbreak of war, Archie and Agatha had lived apart, seeing each other only for a matter of days during the first three years of their marriage. The precious hours spent together were always hectic and strained. Deeply in love, fascinated by each other's difference, husband and wife had no established patterns to fall back on, and the uncertainty of their relationship was both compelling and alarming. Though Agatha insisted that she found it thrilling to be a woman and wager her whole life on a relationship with The Man, living with the reality of that wager was not entirely comfortable, especially with The Man so far away. The question of how men and women can know and relate to one another was much on Christie's mind, and her first novel reveals that preoccupation. Christie structures the relationships between male and female characters in highly idiosyncratic ways, and *The Mysterious Affair at Styles* offers fascinating evidence of how, deep down, she viewed female and male roles and familial and marital interactions.

Passionate embrace, pulsating climax, steamy nakedness are consistently and famously absent from the Christiean universe. Never does a Christie heroine so much as gaze with passionate intensity at a man's sun-blushed throat, as Harriet Vane does in Dorothy L. Sayers's *Gaudy Night*. Tommy and Tuppence Beresford may exchange a companionable kiss, but that is about as far into carnal knowledge as Christie is prepared to go. In the autobiographical writings Christie is similarly reticent. We know that physical attraction and shared activities were far more important in drawing Agatha Miller and Archie Christie together than were psychological affinities, but when the two retire to bed after the dancing and tennis and walking and swimming and golf, we are not told how they get on. Silence can be interpreted in a thousand ways, but the evidence from Christie's fiction makes it clear that just as sexual desire, that of both female and male, was for Christie one of the foremost motivators in human existence, so the expression of sexual desire in lovemaking was essentially unproblematic. "Passion can be taken for granted," Christie remarks offhandedly in her autobiography. A thought lent to Miss Marple may illustrate Christie's attitude. " 'Sex' as a word had not been much mentioned in Miss Marple's young days, but there had been plenty of it — not talked about so much — but enjoyed far more than nowadays, or so it seemed to her. Though usually labelled Sin, she couldn't help feeling that that was preferable to what it seemed to be nowadays — a kind of Duty."

From her very first novel, Christie makes sexual attraction important both to the physical identity of her characters and to the dynamics of her plot. Both Archie and Agatha Christie were attractive young people, and it is not therefore surprising that a high proportion of Christie's characters are also outstandingly goodlooking. In *The Mysterious Affair at Styles*, John Cavendish is clearly a ladies' man, Lawrence has a dark and melancholy charm, and Cynthia Murdoch, with her thick, wavy auburn hair and small white hands, captivates not only Lawrence but also the susceptible Hastings. It is Mary Cavendish, however, who is the beauty of the piece, tall and slender with tawny eyes. Mary Cavendish is the first in a long line of Christie beauties that will include such goddesses as Marthe Daubreuil in *Murder on the Links*, Jane Finn in *The Secret Adversary*, Jane Wilkinson in *Thirteen at Dinner/Lord Edgware Dies*, and Elsie Holland in *The Moving Finger*. Herself tall, slender, fair-skinned, and golden-haired as a young woman, Christie delighted in recreating variations and idealizations of that young self and in inventing mates of equal beauty and charm. The extraordinarily handsome male is as common in Christie's fiction as the stunning female. Captain Ralph Paton in *The Murder of Roger Ackroyd*, for example, is described by Poirot as "what your lady novelists would call a Greek god."

The theme of sexual passion and physical attractiveness is announced loud and clear in Christie's novels: men and women, young and old will murder or risk murder in order to secure the sexual partner they desire or to exact sexual revenge. Yet although Christie stresses the importance of sex relations in the motivation of her murders, she also manages to prevent the reader from perceiving where precisely such motivation might be operative. At Styles, for example, love is everywhere. John and Mary Cavendish, in collaboration with Mrs. Raikes and Dr. Bauerstein, are engaged in some complicated campaign of feigning indifference to each other and flaunting the attraction they feel for other sexual partners. Lawrence loves Cynthia but won't admit it, and Hastings nourishes hopes of winning the fair redhead for himself. All this romantic nonsense, so familiar to the reader from other popular novels, combined with the heavy emphasis on the straightforward financial motives the Cavendish brothers have for murder, distracts our attention from the really crucial love relation, that between Alfred Inglethorp and Evelyn Howard.

One of the mystery writer's most basic goals is to keep the reader guessing until the last pages of the novel. One of the keys to Agatha Christie's success in the genre is her ability to do just this, over and over again. If we are to reach the end of the book totally unprepared for the revelation that Emily Cavendish Inglethorp was murdered by her husband Alfred and her friend Evelyn, then the psychology of the murderers and the relationship between them must be carefully hidden. The obfuscating role of the narrator Hastings turns out to be crucial here. Hastings sees John, Lawrence, Cynthia, Mary, and of course himself as attractive, sexually active people. Alfred, on the other hand, he perceives as a stiff, peculiar Uriah Heep type, and Evelyn as a gruff, square, vaguely dyky woman in her forties who inspires trust, not passion. Neither the Cavendish brothers nor their good friend Hastings can account for Emily's marriage to Alfred. The fellow is so obviously an outsider. Good Lord, he has a bushy black beard and insists on wearing patent black boots in the country, if you can imagine it! "Pukka sahibs," men like John and Lawrence and Hastings who went to the right schools, are conspicuously clean-shaven and keep their black patents for evenings or, in a pinch, the City. Bearded bounders like Inglethorp or that other foreign chap Bauerstein have a fascination for English gentlewomen that English gentlemen cannot plumb. The reverse situation will occur in Christie's novels when the gentlemen themselves fall victim to the charms of hustling lower-class blondes like Brenda Leonides in *Crooked House* or Rosaleen Cloade in *There Is a Tide/Taken at the Flood*.

To return to the relationship that motivates the murder of Emily Inglethorp, there are only three indications that Evelyn and Alfred are related as lovers. First, Hastings and Poirot are allowed to remark that Evelyn's proclamations of virulent hatred for Alfred strike them as excessive and forced. As Hercule Poirot will note on a similar occasion in *Death on the Nile*, hate and love can look very alike.

Second, there is the essential background fact, to which Agatha Christie cunningly gives no prominence, that it was Evelyn Howard who introduced to Styles the man whom she now professes to abominate. Third, we have the essential and astounding fact that the fifty-year-old Alfred Inglethorp has persuaded his seventy-year-old boss to marry him. Such a marriage would raise a good many eyebrows even today, and Christie makes it clear that Emily has risked social disapprobation and even ridicule when she agreed to marry her secretary. Can Alfred be quite the unattractive stick that Hastings presents to us? What qualities attract Emily to Alfred, and could those qualities also account for Evelyn's "hatred" of Alfred?

Characteristically, Agatha Christie does not probe the inner world of her characters, and we know nothing of Alfred's or Evelyn's or Emily's thoughts and desires. Several points emerge, nonetheless, from the few short scenes between Alfred and the Cavendishes. Despite the beard and the boots, Alfred is a relatively young man, barely older than John and Lawrence, and, although Christie never draws our attention to the point, Alfred's youth presumably had something to do with Emily's decision to marry him. Furthermore, Emily is described as a woman "who had not the gift for commanding love," and we see that she goes to her grave, after a tortured death, unmourned by anyone in her household. Judging by John's treatment of his wife and Lawrence's avoidance of Cynthia, overt affectionate solicitude toward women is not characteristic of the upper-middle-class English male. Thus, when Alfred is shown treating Emily with "tenderest care," John Cavendish is sickened and Hastings is filled with "a firm and rooted dislike," but presumably this kind of attention is not irrelevant to Alfred's success with women. The simple fact is that Alfred Inglethorp can and does do more to please Emily Cavendish than John, Lawrence, Cynthia, and Evelyn do, and the last wills she writes, both in Alfred's favor, are eloquent testimony to her pleasure. Asked what a rich, powerful, elderly person, whether man or woman, might want, Agatha Christie from her very first novel implicitly gives a rather striking answer: an attentive and much younger spouse. Christie herself, of course, will follow up on her own analysis by turning to the affectionate care and respect of a man fourteen years her junior after the savage debacle of her first marriage.

The marriage whereby Alfred Inglethorp can expect to gain control over Emily Cavendish's fortune is unconventional, but similarly unconventional is the whole social structure at Styles. Until the advent of Alfred Inglethorp, Styles Court was a matriarchy, a small hive with drone males and female workers, ruled over by Queen Bee Emily Cavendish. Until Emily extended her female prerogatives by marrying an attractive younger male and thus confusing the whole question of the succession, Styles was also a stable matriarchy.

Matriarchies are rare and atavistic structures, threatened, according to Western tradition, by "progress" in the shape of revolt by the sons. In *The Mysterious Affair at Styles*, Agatha Christie allows the Cavendish sons to triumph at last and thus appears to bow to tradition: John and Lawrence end the book with both the money and the women they have desired. Ironically, however, their success is not the result of their own efforts. They remain more or less passive and uncomprehending players throughout the game of murder and mayhem. John and Lawrence win only because Hercule

Poirot intervenes, deus ex machina, to prevent a brilliantly planned and executed female coup. For Alfred is not a lone sexual marauder: he has been introduced into Styles as an instrument in the sexual and financial designs of Evelyn Howard. Evelyn the pawn has ambitions to be queen, but this can only happen when the existing queen has been removed from the board. It is this struggle to the death between two active and energetic women that powers the mystery of Styles, though not its denouement.

A real estate agent might refer to Styles as a "gentleman's residence," but it is in fact the home of a lady, Emily Cavendish Inglethorp, and of her extended family. A distinguished woman in her seventies with a strong energetic personality, Emily enjoys complete dominance in family affairs. Emily is wealthy in her own right and also has life control over the greater part of her late husband's estate. On Emily's death, the entailed estate of Styles will revert to her oldest stepson, John Cavendish, but Emily has the testamentary right to dispose of her own large fortune, and Emily has no children. Emily Cavendish Inglethorp is considered an eager overachiever by her entourage. She is constantly busy, organizing bazaars, lunching with the sister of Lady Tadminster — "one of our oldest families," as she happily tells Hastings in classic eighteenth-century style and providentially superintending the welcome of Belgian refugees to the village.

Her stepsons John and Lawrence, meanwhile, are refining the English public school version of that pleasant relaxation in indolence called dolce far niente. An amiable man in his late forties whose drawing-room conversation apparently makes even Hastings sound like Oscar Wilde, John has read for the bar and practiced briefly as a barrister but has long since preferred the duties of "country squire." We never discover what these duties entail, but they clearly leave John plenty of opportunity to exercise a bit of droit du seigneur with the women on the estate. Married for only two years to the ravishing Mary, John is nonetheless conducting a scandalous affair with the gypsyish wife of farmer Raikes. Meanwhile John's younger brother Lawrence, forty-five, has shown as little interest in medicine as John showed in the law. Delicate in youth, Lawrence also lives with his stepmother at Styles and devotes himself to writing poetry. Bachelorhood seems even more congenial to Lawrence than to his older brother, since Lawrence has not even proposed to the woman he admires, much less married her. John and Lawrence Cavendish are the first in a long series of pathetically dependent and passive upper-middle-class men in Christie's novels. If the young men Agatha had met in her man-hunting phase were like the Cavendish brothers, one can see why Archie Christie, for all his faults, made such an impression on her.

The dependence of John and Lawrence is financial as well as psychological. Both brothers are in dire economic straits. Before the advent of Alfred, both had anticipated inheriting some part of Emily's fortune. They have spent the money left them by their father and are now wholly dependent on the generous allowance given them by Emily, which they regard as their due. Lawrence's money has gone on expensive private printings. John's may have been dissipated in pursuit of the Mrs. Raikeses of the world, but this is speculation. Certainly, while both brothers grumble about their dependence on "the mater" and resent the terms of their father's will, neither has thought to leave Emily's table and go out and earn a living. Could old Mr. Cavendish have been shrewd in his decision to keep the family money in Emily's hands for as long as possible?

Emily Cavendish's activities as Lady Bountiful require a surprisingly large support staff that includes a male secretary. If Agatha Christie is to be trusted, secretaries to prominent persons tended to be male at this period, and because of this fact the mechanism of murder at Styles is set in motion when Emily Cavendish marries her secretary, Alfred Inglethorp. In Christie's fiction it is, as it was, unusual for a younger male employee to marry his older female employer, but the reversal of social and gender dominance so striking in the case of Emily and Alfred is not unique to them. Both men and women in Christie's fiction can be classed as conservatives, but the women are more often dynamically conservative and the men passively conservative. The traditional equation of women with passivity and inferior status cannot be applied across the board in the world of Agatha Christie's novels. Christie's female characters tend to be energetic and efficient, and seem more often than their menfolk to be striving purposefully to gain or manage money — perhaps because the women are usually a lot poorer.

Certainly, in *The Mysterious Affair at Styles*, it is the women who work while the men remain idle. John and Lawrence, as we have seen, are neither breadwinners nor family men, but simply cast themselves in the passive role of heirs. The two brothers fill in the time as agreeably as possible while waiting for Emily to die. Where John refers vaguely to the life of country squire, his wife Mary gets up at 5 a.m. and works until lunchtime on the farm or in the dairy. Working until 1 or 1:30 may not sound too stressful, but well into the 1930s Christie's male characters habitually eat breakfast between 9:30 and 10:30. Sometimes they drift downstairs even later, though by that time the servants are cross and the deviled kidneys lack charm. While Lawrence Cavendish is occupied writing unpublishable verse, Cynthia Murdoch is holding down a responsible part-time job as a dispenser at the local hospital, and is required to be useful writing letters and the like for her benefactress Emily after work. Most saliently of all, Evelyn Howard, Emily's housekeeper, companion, and Jill-of-all-trades, keeps the whole household running. Evelyn presides over Dorcas, Annie, other unnamed house servants, and three gardeners, a wartime staff which Christie quaintly refers to as skeletal. The world of the Cavendishes is emphatically not a working world. It rests upon the labors of Dorcas, Annie, and the other servants still there, who can still be relied upon and whose work therefore goes unreported and unnoticed. In her autobiography, Agatha Christie reports rereading her early novels and feeling amazed at how little the characters do but drink tea on the lawn. Nonetheless, we see the women in the Cavendish household equipped for work — Evelyn in her stout shoes with her gardening gloves, Mary in her landgirl uniform with its telltale green armband, Cynthia in her white overall, Emily with her locked purple despatch-case. While the women go purposefully about their duties, John and Lawrence stand around looking decorative.

The attribution of work and the distribution of active and passive roles that we find in *The Mysterious Affair at Styles* are strange and unexpected, but they reveal crucial aspects of Agatha Christie's views on female identity. The same kind of domestic structure occurs again and again in Christie's fiction, with only superficial changes. In 1946's *There Is a Tide/Taken at the Flood*, for example, the Cloade men appear to fill conventional male social roles, since they actually practice the professions for which John and Lawrence Cavendish had merely trained. Jeremy Cloade is a partner in a prominent law firm, and Lionel is the local GP. Their nephew Rowley has bought and manages a small farm. Only their widowed sister Adela Marchmont seems a throwback to prewar times in her joblessness and precarious dependence on a diminishing private income. Nonetheless, as the novel progresses, Agatha Christie is at pains to show us that the financial independence of Lionel, Jeremy, and Rowley is illusory. Like Adela, they have relied on the periodic generosity of rich businessman brother Gordon Cloade to keep their heads above water. When Gordon is killed in the Blitz without making a new will, his whole estate passes automatically to Rosaleen, his recently wed young wife. Jeremy, Lionel, Rowley, and Adela get none of the large inheritance they had confidently looked forward to, and it becomes apparent that the superficially active male Cloades have been as defined by their status as heirs apparent as had been the idle Cavendish brothers. Lionel cannot bear the idea of continuing to practice medicine and is desperate to retire early to a life of independent research. Rowley's farm has no future without the large injection of capital promised by uncle Gordon. Jeremy Cloade, apparently the most successful of the quartet with his elegant house and aristocratic wife, turns out to be in the worst situation, since he has embezzled a very large sum of money from his legal clients. Adela's dependence differs from her brothers' only by being at once obvious and modest. Adela needs only a few hundred pounds to buy new tiles for the roof and fuel for her furnace, and even this need makes Adela's proud and independent daughter, Lynn, both angry and mortified. Moreover, Adela at least asks for the money she needs directly. Jeremy, on the other hand, forced to borrow thousands of pounds if he is to avoid bankruptcy and prison, allows his wife Frances to touch Rosaleen for the money — and to plan more dubious tactics when the touch fails. When Rosaleen Cloade dies suddenly, all the members of the Cloade family come under suspicion because, in the Christiean scheme of things, murder, usually of one of one's nearest and dearest, is a more natural and logical option than a life of bourgeois industriousness.

Crooked House, 1946, one of Christie's favorites among her own novels, offers us another variation on the Cavendish family theme and perhaps the best example of the strong Christiean woman. Sophia Leonides is part of an extended family on the Styles model. Her parents Philip and Magda, her uncle Roger Leonides and aunt Clemency, her siblings Eustace and Josephine, their tutor Laurence Brown, and maternal great-aunt Edith de Haviland all live at Three Gables, the home of grandfather Aristide Leonides. Murder enters the world of Three Gables after eighty-year-old Aristide exercises his patriarchal privileges and marries Brenda, a very young woman. Brenda Leonides is a dumb-blonde version of Alfred Inglethorp, the "bounder" who marries the elderly Emily Cavendish in *Styles*. Still following the Styles pattern, Aristide is duly poisoned, and the motive for murder appears to hinge upon the terms of Aristide's last will. Shrewdly surveying his family, Aristide has decided that neither his two sons nor his grandson have the qualities necessary to guide the family business. In his elder granddaughter Sophia, Aristide has seen a younger version of himself, a chip off the old block, and he has made Sophia his heir, much to the despair, despite, and rage of her male relatives. Only Sophia's teenage sister Josephine poses any real threat to Sophia's inheritance, and Josephine has to be dealt with in a very special way.

In Sophia Leonides, Agatha Christie portrays an unusual woman who will carry the family fortune into the postwar era. It is remarkable that all the female characters in *Crooked House* except Brenda are exceptionally able and talented. Magda, a successful actress, and Clemency, an equally successful scientist, both take dominant roles in their marriages. Edith de Haviland is respected in the family as having the same kind of character and determination as her tycoon brother-in-law Aristide. In fact, the careful reader soon realizes that talent, energy, and character are what count in the Christiean world, not gender. If Christie's female characters like to look nostalgically back to the past rather than forward to a new feminist future, they are conservatives who refuse to rely on feminine wiles and intuition. Energetic, decisive, and logical, Christie's women do whatever is necessary to return to the Golden Age.

On the surface, the world of Styles Court that Christie portrays in her first novel is a patriarchal world in which Hercule Poirot can intervene to maintain the status quo and prop up the failing potency of the sons. It is also a world where women have a great deal of power, where they feel free to work to earn money, act in their interests, using trickery and violence if necessary, and occupy any of the traditional male roles without fearing for their femininity. Ambition, energy, desire are not the traits habitually associated with Agatha Christie; they are certainly not the traits she cares to apply to herself in her autobiographical writings. Yet Christie's consistent creation of exceptionally active, successful, and sexy fictional heroines and villains must have some reference to her own self-conception and to the way she tried to direct her own life. After all, Agatha Christie herself was to redeem the fortune of the Millers, lost by her father and brother, and make millionaires of her daughter, grandson, and great-grandchildren.

CHAPTER
THREE

Agatha Christie
Kings and Commoners

Had Archie Christie not had the soul of a stockbroker in the body of a romantic hero, had he not become addicted to golf and the City, had he been a more responsive and understanding partner, had he not been given the opportunity to fall in love with another woman, had he and Agatha had more children, or at least one other child more in Agatha's own image — had any or some of these possibilities been realized, Agatha might perhaps have devoted herself to husband and family, repeating the family career of her mother. As it was for Agatha's happily married sister, Madge Watts, writing for Agatha might have been an interesting and occasionally fruitful hobby, not a lifetime professional commitment. However, fate — or Agatha's unconscious choices — decreed that romance, in the shape of the dynamic but alien Archie, should not fulfill Agatha's emotional, intellectual, cultural, and financial needs.

Prosperity, not adversity, sounded the death knell of the Christie marriage. The early married years of the Christies were not easy, but Agatha and Archie had the energy and good humor to survive both the separation during the war and the financial difficulties of the immediate postwar years. Rosalind's birth in 1919 strengthened their marriage. Archie had initially been very unenthusiastic about the prospect of a child, particularly of a son, who he felt would necessarily compete for his wife's love and attention. He felt guilty for causing Agatha not only constant physical discomfort (she vomited throughout the nine months) but also the eventual suffering of labor. He was also anxious about what pregnancy would do to his wife's looks. As it turned out, the birth of Rosalind, the Christies' baby, was a profoundly moving and — as far as the contemporary obstetrical practice would allow — shared experience for both husband and wife. It reaffirmed their commitment as lovers and companions, and was one of the moments of greatest intimacy Archie and Agatha ever experienced.

Even more important, Archie's fears about a child rival were quite unrealized, since the baby turned out to be a girl and a small replica of her father in both good looks and temperament. Agatha's reaction to having a daughter was somewhat more ambiguous. Whereas both Archie and Clara were delighted with the birth of a girl child, Agatha herself had wanted a son. The experience of giving birth seems also to have revived that uneasy sense of observing herself playing a part in her own life which Christie reports feeling from early childhood. In the autobiographical account of her daughter's birth that she gives in *Unfinished Portrait*, Christie confesses that she felt quite unreal in her new role of young mother.

Agatha was delighted with the beauty and responsiveness of her child, but she followed Clara's advice and was careful never to put her baby before her husband. A month after Rosalind's birth at Ashfield, Agatha left the baby with her mother and a nurse and went up to London to find a new flat and hire staff. *The Unfinished Portrait* account of this early return to Archie/Dermot is interesting. "The reunion with Dermot was particularly joyous. It was like a second honeymoon. Part of Dermot's satisfaction arose from the fact (Celia discovered) that she had left Judy (i.e., their baby daughter) to come up to him." The triangle of relationships between the three Christies was always to be a complicated one. Here Archie and Agatha drew closer to each other and excluded the infant Rosalind. Later, when Rosalind was a small child, she and Archie were to strike up a friendship, based on community of interests and temperament, that Agatha would feel excluded her. When Clara — who adored Agatha and had never been wholly reassured about Archie — took her place in the group, the relational configuration became even more difficult.

The portrait Christie paints of herself as a young housewife just after the war tells us a lot about her as an individual and about the way of life and social expectations of her social class. Even when the Christies first set up house in London in the last months of the war and money was very tight, they relied on domestic servants. First Archie's batman, Bartlett — a real-life version of Peter Wimsey's Bunter — did the housework while regaling Agatha with admiring tales of "the Colonel's" wartime exploits. Then the building's caretaker, Mrs. Woods, agreed to "do" for them, as well as handle the basic cooking. Archie, who had not left the RFC, was out all day at his new job at the Air Ministry, and once Agatha had moved in with him, there seems to have been no question of her working. Agatha was lonely in the tiny flat with its lumpy beds. She missed her family, friends, and hospital colleagues, her work, her spacious home, her piano, and Torquay itself. Christie does not seem to have written anything for about two years after composing *Styles*, which did not find a publishing contract until 1919. Deprived of all her familiar activities and relations, Agatha was reduced to talking about rationing and the finer points of shopping with Mrs. Woods, whom she adored, and to taking a course in shorthand and bookkeeping. Sometimes Agatha got to prepare a meal for herself and Archie, but her increasing expertise as a gourmet cook went largely unappreciated. Archie's nervous stomach cried out for treacle pudding, not his wife's rich experimental soufflés.

Even though Agatha was lonely and unoccupied, even though she was acknowledged to be an exceptionally competent woman, it was clearly impossible for the Christies to imagine Agatha herself "doing" for them. When Rosalind was born and Archie, who had resigned his commission, was earning a modest City salary, the Christies used their extra income to rent a larger apartment and to hire a nurse for the baby and a maid of all work. Christie herself remarks that it seems odd that a young couple, living on 700 pounds a year in rented accommodations, unable to afford a motor car, buy new clothes, entertain their more affluent friends, or take a taxi on a rare evening out, should find it essential to hire two full-time servants. The Christies' spending priorities seem to have been dictated by class prejudice rather than by financial logic. All the same, Agatha and Archie's unquestioning assumption that she had the right to employ domestic labor and to devote hours of the day to her own pursuits was a not inconsiderable factor in her career as a writer. Leisure was in Agatha Christie's view the most precious commodity in life, and she defined leisure as that time in which the mind is calm and relaxed enough to be creative.

A certain restlessness and dissatisfaction with the postwar grind, as well as a hands-off attitude to child rearing, can be diagnosed in the Christies' decision in 1921 to leave Rosalind in the care of Madge and Clara and set off around the world with Major Belcher's British Empire Exhibition Mission. Major Belcher was an ex-schoolmaster and civil servant whom Archie had known as a schoolboy at Clifton College. An excellent public relations man, Belcher had convinced the British government to send him on a colonial mission to drum up support for a new international fair on the model of the famous 1854 Great Exhibition at the Crystal Palace. He persuaded Archie to go along as financial adviser and right-hand man. All expenses for Archie were paid, as well as all Agatha's travel. The Christies reckoned, overoptimistically as it turned out, that Archie's fee of 1,000 pounds would cover Agatha's hotel expenses and pay for a month's holiday for the two of them in Hawaii. As Agatha emphasizes in her autobiography, taking off to see the world was a big risk. Apart from the strain of leaving their young child in the care of relatives, the Christies knew that Archie's job was not being held for him and that jobs were very difficult to come by. However, Archie and Agatha were united in their decision to take the risk and seize a unique opportunity to do the traveling that they both loved. The importance of being able to take risks is one of the themes Christie sounds loud and clear in all her work.

It is not clear that Agatha Christie saw any risk in leaving her daughter behind for such a long period or imagined she might possibly cause her lasting psychological pain. Christie's own parents had often traveled together without children, and Agatha and Archie were following the pattern of the Millers and many other middle-class parents in leaving their child in the care of servants or close relatives. Agatha poignantly records the deep sadness and loss she herself felt when left with her grandmother in Ealing for a prolonged period when she was about nine. Perhaps she felt that Rosalind was simply too young to miss her parents, and would be perfectly happy in the devoted care of her nanny and her aunt and grandmother. Perhaps Archie was quite decided to go on the tour and Agatha simply could not bear to let him go off alone, whatever the cost to her as a mother. It does not seem to have occurred to Christie that from birth she had been teaching her daughter not to rely on her constant presence, but rather to accept mothering from other female caretakers — from her various nannies, her grandmother, her aunt "Punkie," her governess "Carlo" Fisher.

The ten months of their world tour were probably the high spot of the Christie marriage. Agatha certainly was in high spirits. She and Archie were alike in their energy and curiosity, in their love of travel, adventure, and vigorous exercise. For example, they spent most of their Hawaiian vacation in the sea, learning how to surf and in the process suffering second-degree sunburn, coral-slashed feet, and exhaustion. While she was away on her trip, Agatha's second book, *The Secret Adversary*, was published to considerable acclaim, and she carried a reputation as a coming author with her to Africa, Australia, New Zealand, and North America.

For most of the trip, Archie and Agatha formed part of a hard-working official visiting party. In Australia, however, Agatha seized an opportunity to go off alone to join a lively houseparty at Coochin, a farming station near Brisbane, with some new friends, the Bells. Agatha reacted with enormous enthusiasm to the energetic, athletic, and talented Bell family, and she records in a letter that she had great success singing and doing comedy skits in an amateur show the Coochin party put on one night. Here, Agatha was clearly a social success, an outgoing, independent woman, taking center stage with confidence and charming all those she met. Furthermore, on one occasion Agatha was called upon to give an extemporaneous speech to the Canterbury Women's Club in New Zealand and acquitted herself honorably. Such a speech is remarkable only when one considers Christie's later refusal ever to make a speech, even when she became the president of the Detection Club of Great Britain.

Agatha Christie's ten-month trip round the world would have daunted a less resilient soul. Major Belcher proved to have an execrable temper. Agatha was sick every time the sea turned rough, and she suffered agonizing neuralgia in her shoulder for two months after her surfing exploits in Hawaii. Archie's sinus problems flared up again, and he fell very seriously ill from multiple allergic reactions to pollen after visiting Canadian grain silos. When the Christies ran out of money a month before their scheduled return, Agatha was reduced to a diet of hotel breakfasts, odd official dinners, and bouillon in her hotel room. This was a notable trial for an exceptionally hearty eater who records wolfing down twenty-three oranges fresh from the tree on one Australian afternoon! Yet through all adversities Agatha displayed vivacity, good humor, efficiency, and endurance.

The Christies returned to England from their international adventure in December 1922, and Agatha came home a happier, more confident, and outgoing woman than she had left.

Financially the years 1923 to 1926 were a boom period for the Christies, after a slightly rocky start. Immediately after his return from abroad, the thirty-four-year-old Archie, as expected, found it hard to get a good job in the City. For a time he suffered from the inevitable anxiety and nervous irritability of the man who cannot support his family. Agatha dismissed the servants, took over the housework herself, and refused Archie's suggestions that she take Rosalind and go and live with Clara or Madge. Life took a turn for the better when Archie landed a new job with a reliable old friend, Clive Baillieu, and from this point on he began his steady ascent in the business world. By early 1924, the Christies had moved thirty miles out of London to Sunningdale in the stockbroker belt, settling first in a large flat and then in their own large house. Sunningdale was chosen because it offered excellent train service into the City, a greener environment for a growing child, and a first-class golf course. Archie had been introduced to golf by Agatha, a poor but originally not unenthusiastic player, and he rapidly passed his wife in skill and enthusiasm.

While Archie devoted his weekdays to business and his weekends to golf, Agatha managed the household. She had already shown real talent for hunting down good rental properties, and had proved a cool aggressive negotiator in real estate transactions. She had also learned to interview, hire, and supervise the activities of her domestic staff. By 1925 this staff had grown to include three full-time servants and a governess-secretary, the invaluable

Scotswoman Charlotte Fisher. Miss Fisher, known as Carlo, supervised Rosalind's education and helped Agatha to deal with her increasingly large correspondance and organize her personal and professional commitments. Apart from managing her own household, Agatha joined with Madge in caring for Clara and for brother Monty, who was an invalid now and becoming increasingly difficult in other ways. Clara divided her time between Ashfield, Abney, and Sunningdale, where she at one time had her own apartment.

Agatha also continued to write, publishing a book a year with increasing success though little financial reward. Book royalties from Agatha's contract with The Bodley Head were small, and served mainly to pay special expenses — for example to pay half the wages of the various people employed to look after Monty and to contribute to the upkeep of Ashfield. Archie insisted that an unexpected check for 500 pounds from the *Evening News* for the serialization rights on *The Man in the Brown Suit* should not be saved, but spent on a new luxury for Agatha — a car. It was Archie who gave Agatha driving lessons and forced her rapidly to become competent at the wheel. The car was a revelation to Agatha. She writes movingly of "the sheer joy of driving," of how she reveled in the freedom to go anywhere she liked and to visit places hitherto out of reach. Best of all, she could take her mother along for the ride, and Clara loved motoring as passionately as she did. "I don't think anything has given me more pleasure, more joy of achievement," Christie writes, "than my dear bottle-nosed Morris Cowley."

The new prosperous way of life of the Christies was symbolized by the house they purchased in 1924. The

Sunningdale purchase gave Agatha her first opportunity to mold a whole house to her taste, but whereas Archie and Rosalind liked the new house, Agatha did not. The Sunningdale house was pretentious, "a sort of millionaire-style Savoy suite transferred to the country," with lots of bathrooms but no real elegance. Agatha looked forward to the time when she could totally redecorate the interior and comforted herself with the beauty of the long, narrow, stream-bordered garden. At Archie's suggestion, the house was renamed Styles, and the painting commissioned by The Bodley Head for the cover of *The Mysterious Affair at Styles* hung on one wall. The sinister implications of the name Styles evoked by the painting were prophetic. The house had a reputation of being unlucky when the Christies moved in, and it was to witness the crumbling of the Christie marriage.

Styles failed to replace Ashfield in Agatha's affections, and its architecture, interior decor, and location were only partially to blame. Agatha and Archie were failing to reproduce that atmosphere of love and conjugal harmony that Agatha remembered in her parents' home. Unlike the idle and sociable Fred Miller, Archie spent most of the weekday hours in London earning his family's livelihood, and he often brought work home. On weekends he liked to relax, and relaxation increasingly came to mean playing golf and hanging around the clubhouse with his golfing friends. Tired from work or sport, Archie hated to give or attend the dinner parties which his wife enjoyed. He sulked if she invited nongolfing friends to stay for the weekend, and played the martyr if she insisted on his accompanying her on one of the country jaunts they had once enjoyed so much. Agatha, for her part, missed the theaters and dance halls of London, as well as the parties and amateur dramatics and music-making she still found with her old friends in Torquay. She did not especially enjoy the members of the golfing fraternity or their wives.

Absorbed in his own activities, happy with his own set of friends, Archie was anxious that his wife should be independently happy also. He vetoed his wife's suggestion that they now have another child, but by encouraging Agatha to splurge on a car and to learn to drive, Archie was seeking in his own way to promote her happiness. He saw the potential profit to be made from Agatha's writing and urged her to continue as a novelist. When, in 1920, Agatha was afraid that Ashfield might have to be sold, it was Archie who made the practical suggestion that Agatha write another novel, as this was her best hope of earning money to give to Clara. As Agatha's novels started to sell and the royalties began to be meaningful, Archie appreciated the extra income, which made it easier for the pair to travel first class on trips abroad, buy a large, expensive house, and later buy a second, luxury car. Agatha's writing occupied her time and gave her pleasure in ways that suited Archie. Nonetheless, Archie was probably more of a hindrance than a help to his wife's career as a novelist. He was always discouraging or indifferent when Agatha tried to discuss her ideas for a book with him, and he did not enjoy the London literary world to which she was being introduced. The two Christies were in fact drifting apart, spending less and less time together. Such mild marital estrangement was considered normal by the society of their day, and whereas Agatha missed the passionate companionship they had once shared, Archie seemed to find parallel living both acceptable and usual.

*

While Archie Christie was making an increasingly good living in the City and bringing his golf game up to par on the Sunningdale courses, Agatha was earning a reputation as a detective novelist. A feature article on her appeared in the tabloid newspaper *The Sketch* in 1923, with several informal photographs of the novelist at home with her notably photogenic daughter and her collection of wooden African animals. Hercule Poirot had gone down well with the British public and as book began to follow book in a nice regular flow, Christie's publishers began to show some appreciation of her talent and professionalism.

Writing a good detective novel is much harder than it looks, and that apparently simple product, a great plot, is something very few people can actually put together. The effortless ease of the reader's progress through the pages is a consequence of much laborious slogging on the writer's part. Two of Christie's early books in particular, *The Mysterious Affair at Styles* and *Murder on the Links*, proved that Agatha Christie had the elusive narrative gift. In sixty-thousand-odd deceptively simple words, she could construct a plot with enough complexity to satisfy the demands of a crossword-puzzle or bridge fanatic and with enough pace to meet the commuter's definition of a good yarn. Weaving a narrative web as involved as *Styles*, however, took up a great deal of intellectual energy. As Mrs. Ariadne Oliver, Christie's detective story-writing alter ego, would have cause to remark, "Idea? I've got any amount of ideas. In fact, that's just the difficulty. I can never think of even one plot at a time. I always think of at least five, and it's agony to decide between them. . . . One actually has to *think*, you know. And thinking is always a bore."

From the outset of her long career Agatha Christie evolved the system of interspersing complicated detective novels like *Styles* with lighthearted adventure stories or thrillers. These rolled off the pen without too much effort and yet served to keep her name before the public. The first of these thrillers, *The Secret Adversary*, the second novel Christie published, introduced Tommy and Tuppence Beresford, the sleuthing couple whose early lives had much in common with her own and Archie's just after the war. Unlike Christie's other, more famous detectives, who are eternally old, Tommy and Tuppence start off young in the twenties, and in their five novels they aged along with their creator. They made their final appearance as grizzled, rheumatic grandparents in *Postern of Fate*, 1973, the very last novel Christie wrote. Christie regarded the Beresfords almost as fictional friends, so they stand in a very different relationship to her than Poirot, or even Miss Marple.

Why was Christie so fond of Tommy and Tuppence, given that the novels featuring them were not among her personal favorites and have won little critical acclaim? The answer lies more in the relationship Christie created between her two sleuths than in their detective exploits. Superficially, Tommy and Tuppence have highly conventional middle-class lives, with conventionally segregated sex roles. In the 1929 *Partners in Crime*, for example, Tommy masquerades as head of a detective agency, while Tuppence is merely his secretary. Once Tuppence is pregnant, Tommy pursues a successful bureaucratic career while his wife devotes herself to the children and the house. The Beresfords, however, lead conventional lives only in the spaces in between novels. The novels' action, as opposed to the biographical link passages, show the Beresfords as a team of equals, not as boss and female sidekick. As the plot carries them into one death-defying situation after another, each relies on the other's competence and admires the other's special talents. Tommy provides the common sense, the brawn, and the professional contacts, while Tuppence provides the brainpower, the flair, and the audacity.

These two charming, intelligent, and energetic people figure in a fantasy world, and a rather dated one at that. Nonetheless, their panache — the combination each has of being hot and cool, humorous and sexy, needful and independent — offers an unusual and vital form of male-female professional and private cooperation. The central male-female relationship in the Tommy and Tuppence novels is notably different, for example, from the one we commonly find in novels of the American hardboiled school of detective fiction. The heroes of Chandler or Spillane or Hammett fall for mysterious blondes who do them wrong, and they employ intelligent, snappy, hard-working, reliable, loyal brunettes as secretaries. Tommy Beresford, as it were, falls in love with one of the secretary types, persuades her to marry him, and never regrets it. The Tommy and Tuppence variety of successful heterosexual bonding recurs with variations in all of Christie's early thrillers as well as in the subplots of her classic detective novels. An even more humorous and sparkling form of Christie's basic romantic duo is found in 1924's *The Secret of Chimneys*, a novel that tells us a good deal, without really meaning to, about Christie's attitudes toward men and sex.

Chimneys was Agatha Christie's sixth book, and the last she published with editor John Lane at The Bodley Head. Dissatisfied since 1922 with the attention Lane was giving her, aware that the contract she had signed in 1919 was notably disadvantageous to her (she had earned a mere 25 pounds in royalties from *Styles*), Agatha had found herself an agent, Edmund Cork. Under Cork's guidance, Christie signed an excellent new contract with an enthusiastic publishing house, Collins. *Chimneys* served to fulfill Christie's contractual agreement with The Bodley Head, but it did not engage its author's full mental energies as the next novel, *The Murder of Roger Ackroyd*, would do. *Chimneys* is a relaxation, a romp, a holding action, and a collage of some of Christie's favorite literary bits. Of all Christie's adventure novels, *The Secret of Chimneys* is the craziest and the most amusing, a mixture of Ruritania and Blandings Castle that shows the author's talent for light comedy as well as deft detection.

The secret to be uncovered at the great country house of Chimneys centers on the recent history of Herzoslovakia, a small, entirely mythical Central European kingdom. Christie's Herzoslovakia has much in common with the worlds of Sigmund Romberg's *Student Prince* and the Marx Brothers' *Duck Soup*, but its direct literary ancestor is the Ruritania created by Anthony Hope in *The Prisoner of Zenda* and its sequel, *Return to Zenda*. Cast in the same mold of aristocratic machismo as Robin Hood, d'Artagnan, Sir Percy Blakeney, and Zorro, Hope's hero, Rudolf Rassendyll, seems custom-made for Douglas Fairbanks Jr. or Errol Flynn to play on the screen.

The Prisoner of Zenda is not a favorite with today's youth, but for more than fifty years it was a kind of middlebrow classic in England. Upon the imaginations of romantic English girls around the turn of the twentieth century *The Prisoner of Zenda* laid an enduring spell. Agatha Christie, Dorothy L. Sayers, and Josephine Tey, for example, would all in different ways write under the charm of Hope's hero, the royal imposter Rudolf Rassendyll. In *The Secret of Chimneys*, Agatha Christie fuses Hope's English Rudolf Rassendyll and Ruritanian King Rudolf into a single, mysterious, ambiguous, but unequivocally sexy hero king.

The story of *The Prisoner of Zenda* hinges on the unlikely yet entrancingly romantic premise that two persons, born into widely different backgrounds, are yet physically indistinguishable. As a result of some royal dalliance in a previous generation of his family, Rudolf Rassendyll, the handsome, cultured, and daring younger son of the Earl of Burlesdon, is the double of Rudolf of Elphberg, King of Ruritania. When the wicked Prince Michael of Ruritania kidnaps his half brother the king, those loyal to the Ruritanian monarchy persuade the English Rudolf to impersonate the king and foil Prince Michael's plot to usurp the throne. Rassendyll is, naturally, not only King Rudolf's Doppelganger but also a speaker of impeccable royal German.

Whereas the real Ruritanian Rudolf had been a first-class drinker but a second-class king, the English Rudolf is a perfect monarch in all but blood line. Identical to Elphberg in body though Rassendyll may be, the Englishman's superior nature somehow shines through, and he wins the deep devotion of the king's male entourage. What is more, one look at Rassendyll in his kingly disguise turns the coldness of Princess Flavia, the king's fianceé, into burning passion. Provoking such *coups de foudre*, we may deduce, is one of the advantages enjoyed by English aristocrats educated at the right public (i.e., private) schools. Nonetheless, the romance of Flavia and Rudolf Rassendyll is doomed, by the implicit old-Etonian ethic. Rassendyll's pursuit of self-perfection is stronger than his passion for Flavia, and his noblesse obliges him to rescue the real king from his dungeon and set him once more on the throne — and therefore in Princess Flavia's bed. Sir Anthony Hope Hawkins was clearly more interested in sublimated homosexual bonding than in heterosexual love, however refined. Yet, to many a female reader, at least, it has seemed too bad that the glamorous Rassendyll must bid Flavia a tearful farewell and return to England alone to nurse his memories over sherry at the club.

Fortunately, this is the precise flaw that Agatha Christie sets out to remedy. In her own Ruritanian romance, *The Secret of Chimneys*, the fantasy love affair between royalty and commoner will be a full-blooded heterosexual affair, with a happy ending. Christie's hero, Anthony Cade, alias Nicholas of Herzoslovakia, has Rassendyll's charm of Eton and Oxford as well as Elphberg's Central European blue blood, and he is showered with rewards by his appreciative creator. He will return to his kingdom accompanied by his passionately loved and loving Queen Virginia, as well as flush with petrochemical company financing.

Anthony Cade is first encountered in a very un-Ruritanian milieu — he is guiding a group of slightly truculent tourists around the sights of Bulawayo, a town the Christies had visited on their world tour in 1921. Prince Nicholas has rebeled against the family heritage as a student at Oxford, taken up red ties and radical politics, and, after being sent down (that is, kicked out) by his college, has disappeared into the wilds of the British Empire. He seeks out "rows" and revolutions wherever he can find them and is not at all averse to "potting" a few cannibals to rescue a chum. How much this amazing cannibal story is Christie's tongue-in-cheek parody of a typical Bulldog Drummond incident is not clear.

It is plain from his employment as a tourist guide that Prince Nicholas, alias Anthony Cade, alias also Gentleman Joe, has made no great fortune in the colonies. As his friend Jimmy McGrath notes, Cade is "never a hog for regular work." But he survives in that world of manly men that the colonies were assumed to be in British popular legend. Lean, tanned, fit, ready for a scrap, loyal friend to rough diamonds like Jimmy, Cade is a black sheep who yet can sweep rich, beautiful, and sophisticated women off their feet and make conventionally successful men pale in comparison.

This invincible charm is much in evidence in Cade's first meeting in London with Virginia Revel, which has all the illogical inevitability of a dream narrative. Virginia Revel has just discovered a dead man in her living room and has realized that she has been framed for murder. Convinced that what she chiefly needs is "a man . . . an ordinary level-headed, unemotional man," she realizes that her old friend and admirer George Lomax is not at all this kind of man. George, politician, diplomat, member of the establishment, would not want to be mixed up in murder. George would think not of her, but of his own position. So Virginia goes to her front door and finds there "a beggar," the shabbily dressed man, apparently a World War I veteran down on his luck, who had just solicited a contribution. "Virginia noted his bronzed face and long lean body with approval." Here, self-evidently, is "a man," and one, moreover, who proclaims himself to be "Eton and Oxford. . . . Come down in the world entirely from my own incapacity to stick to regular work." This, it seems, is all Virginia needs to know before inviting the man in and displaying the corpse. Virginia's instincts are not at fault. The man entirely understands Virginia's position, and the reasons why she had not swiftly turned the man in her living room over to the police when he tried to blackmail her some days earlier. He obligingly offers to get rid of the body for her. Getting rid of bodies and incriminating weapons is clearly not regular work, but it is the kind of odd job men like Cade excel at and that women like the Hon. Virginia Revel appreciate them for.

Agatha Christie's own life provided two obvious models for Anthony Cade — Archie Christie, before he metamorphosed into a pillar of the City establishment, and her brother, Louis Montant "Monty" Miller. Archie, when Agatha fell in love with him, was young, slim, film-star handsome, and no doubt tanned from his vigorous life as a Royal Air Corps pilot and a motorcyclist. The colonial-black-sheep part of Cade's character came from Christie's older brother, who left Harrow without being able to pass his examinations, fought in the Boer War, joined the King's African Rifles during the First World War, and remained in Africa to make good, with conspicuous lack of success.

As an older brother, Monty Miller left virtually everything to be desired. When a teenager and a young man, Monty had little time for the "scrawny chicken" sister ten years his junior, whose adoration he treated with indifference at best. As Monty grew older, things got worse. Not content with running through the last remnants of the Miller family fortune, Monty lived out the last years of his life at his sisters' expense and was a consistent source of worry and embarrassment. For example, while living at Ashfield with his mother and a native servant, Monty relieved his boredom by taking potshots out of his bedroom window at animals and even at any visiting neighbor who came in range. When complaints were made to the police about this behavior, Monty was indignant that a marksman of his caliber could not be trusted to take a few shots without killing anyone.

Agatha's attitude toward her brother was complicated. A meeting in 1929 after Monty's death, with a Colonel Dwyer of the King's African Rifles who had known Monty (as "Puffing Billy" Miller) during the world war, helped her to work out her feelings. Colonel Dwyer testified that Monty had been "one of the bravest chaps I have ever known," as well as a resolute nonconformist, one of those who are "eccentric, pigheaded, almost geniuses, but not quite, so they are usually failures . . . the best conversationalists in the world — but only when they feel like it." Christie welcomed this testimony from a comrade in arms and agreed that there was much in her eccentric brother to admire. Monty had certainly been brave and ready to stand up for his beliefs, and physical bravery and moral stalwartness in Christie's world were never an irrelevance. Monty also had charm. Even when sick, dying, and broke, Monty infallibly found someone to pay his bills and a woman only too delighted to take care of him.

Christie muses thus on the apparently disastrous way her dead brother had lived his life and on the nature of success and failure: Monty "had not succeeded at anything he had attempted. But was that perhaps only from the financial point of view? Had one not to admit that, despite financial failure, he had for the greater part of his life enjoyed himself?" Christie herself lived by a very different code from her brother, and was far from indifferent to conventional financial definitions of success and failure. At the same time, physical beauty, courage, and zest for living were extremely important to her, and the rebellious Monty, as the incarnation of those qualities, deeply influenced her outlook on life and the narrative patterns she wove in her novels. As heroes or as villains, lean, bronzed men of action recur throughout her fiction, ill-adapted to civilized living in the stockbroker belt, often weak and unscrupulous, but earning the undying love and admiration of strong, successful women.

The revelation that the shabby, louche, slightly caddish Cade is in fact the long-lost Prince of Herzoslovakia is the secret unveiled at the very end of *Chimneys*, but Christie takes great delight in hinting at Cade's real identity throughout the book. Each time Anthony is introduced or refers to himself, Christie underlines the point that names are slippery and unreliable forms of social currency. When one of the Bulawayo tourists, Miss Taylor, asks if his name is indeed Joe, he replies ambiguously, "I thought you knew it was Anthony." At the end of her first meeting with Cade, Virginia is made to ask not *who* her manly rescuer is, but *what is his name*, and he in turn carefully — replies, "My name? My name's Anthony Cade." When interviewed by Superintendant Battle in relation to the murder of Prince Michael of Herzoslovakia, Cade insists jokingly, "Whatever I am, I am not the agent of the Red Hand." Throughout Christie's fiction, names will be crucial clues, and here she is playing with the technique of appearing to say, but not in fact saying, who a character is.

Cade's "real" identity remains a puzzle until the final pages because the biography provided for Cade apparently fits him as well to be the underworld mastermind King Victor as the long-lost heir of Herzoslovakia. This choice between two identities for Anthony is not just a trick ending for the novel but also encodes the novel's political values. The issue of what values should be attached to royal blood is, in fact, an issue introduced in the first pages of the novel when Anthony remarks "vaguely" to Miss Taylor that "kind hearts are more than coronets." Anthony Cade might not perhaps *be* King Victor, but he has had to actively fight the potential of being *like* King Victor. The master criminal and his accomplice-mistress, Queen Varaga, viewed Herzoslovakia and the monarchy simply as a source of loot. Prince Michael, Anthony's cousin and the heir to Herzoslovakia before his untimely death at Chimneys, was similarly motivated by lust and greed, though his designs upon Herzoslovakian assets, unlike King Victor's, were strictly legal.

Prince Nicholas takes on the identity of Anthony Cade because he is sickened by the stupidity, cupidity, and sexual dilettantism of his royal uncle and cousins. Nicholas's years as an ordinary Joe in the rough-and-tumble real world not only readied him psychologically but qualified him morally to accept his responsibilities. As one who after this experience has the kind heart to go with his coronet, he is fit to take on the family business of reigning. This "message" of *Chimneys* illuminates both Christie's politics and her theology. Politically, she seems to feel that monarchies are bad but not as bad as corrupt democracies or violent revolutions. Theologically, Christie rejects the conventional Protestant ethic of demonstrating salvation through good works, and espouses the idea that sowing wild oats in youth can lead to a wiser maturity and even to redemption.

As Christie free-associates on the theme of kings and queens and romance, she is led to the story of King Cophetua and the beggarmaid. Two of Christie's favorite authors, Shakespeare and Tennyson, both use this story, and it structures several aspects of the plot of *Chimneys*. First, a revolution in Herzoslovakia that has overthrown the Obolovitch dynasty was occasioned by the infatuation by King Nicholas IV (Anthony Cade's uncle) with a modern-day beggarmaid — a music-hall artiste who persuades him not only to marry her but to proclaim her Queen Varaga. Christie makes plain that Varaga is a scheming adventuress who continues her liaison with her lover King Victor and who uses Nicholas strictly for what she can get out of him — most notably the Koh-i-Noor diamond.

This first straightforward if unromantic version of the Cophetua story is doubled in the next generation of Obolovitches, with an apparent reversal of sex roles. The highly aristocratic Virginia Revel falls in love with the young man begging at her door, and honors the implications of her name by rebeling against convention and common sense and relying on her instincts. When Virginia finds that, in fact, the beggarman is a king in disguise, choosing to be chosen entirely for himself as a man, not as a monarch, the story moves back into conventional channels.

The Anthony-Virginia relationship is an idealized version of the relationship Christie remembered or fantasized between herself and Archie, and that she feared was slipping away. The intense romanticism of the love interest in *The Secret of Chimneys* is a factor of the role that it was playing in its author's fantasy life. Nonetheless, Christie makes the love affair between Anthony and Virginia work reasonably well for the reader also by setting it against a background of adventure, detection, and comedy. Anthony's lovemaking has to be fitted into the chinks in his other activities — stashing dead bodies in trunks at railway stations, climbing high trees to hide lethal weapons, turning up at the wrong moment for a murder, trailing master criminals to gloomy suburbs, and cracking cryptic clues. Who killed Prince Michael of Herzoslovakia? is the question the various detectives at Chimneys must answer, and the answer turns out to be pure Christie. In the final pages, Christie divulges that Anthony Cade is a king in disguise; that King Victor, for all his evil ways, never takes a life; that the murderer is, in fact, a woman, the ex-music-hall artiste and seductive queen, Varaga, disguised impenetrably as the mousy French governess Mademoiselle Brun. She, in turn, is killed by Boris, the fanatically faithful old retainer to the Obolovitch family, the only person to sniff out a royal prince of Herzoslovakia in Anthony Cade! The End.

Broad comedy of a Marx Brothers kind is the mark of all the Herzoslovakian characters in *The Secret of Chimneys*, from the ineffectual terrorists of the left, the Comrades of the Red Hand, to the stuffed-shirt noblemen of the right, led by the unpronounceable Count Lolopretjzyl. However, Christie gains her best comic effects from those members of English high aristocratic society whom she presents gathered in traditional style at the weekend houseparty at Chimneys, the ancestral home of the Marquises of Caterham.

As Agatha Christie moved out of the straight detective novel toward what she called a "thriller," she also moved her characters far up the social hierarchy. The great mansion of Chimneys is several notches higher than the gentleman's residence of Styles Court or the comfortable French villa setting used in Christie's third novel, *Murder on the Links*. With Chimneys, we are in fact entering not the scene of small country houses that Christie knew from personal experience, but a composite of aristocratic literary landscapes. Not only is Hope's romantic Ruritanian castle of Hentzau evoked, but Wodehouse's comic Blandings Castle, and even the solidly realistic world of Anthony Trollope's Palliser novels.

Christie never describes Chimneys, and in the matter of descriptions she consistently falls short when compared with her Golden Age contemporaries. For example, in 1937's *Hamlet, Revenge!* Michael Innes sets out on another journey into Trollope country, and presents his own great fictional palace, Scamnum Court, home of the Dukes of Horton. Innes dedicates three prefatory pages to an evocation of the house, its architecture and precious art, its history, and the rolling countryside that surrounds it, using the full resources of his magnificent literary and historical culture to introduce us to the setting for his magnificent murder. In stark contrast, Agatha Christie, ever the lowbrow, drives us in through the gates of Chimneys in the banal company of Dr. Cartwright, and Inspector Badgeworthy and Constable Johnson of the Market Basing police. "The car passed through the park gates of Chimneys. Descriptions of that historic place can be found in any guidebook. It is also No 3 in *Historic Homes of England* price 21s. On Thursday, coaches come over from Middlingham and view those portions of it which are open to the public. In view of all these facilities, to describe Chimneys would be superfluous." For those of us who, like Christie herself, enjoy actually looking at great country houses rather than reading about them (and any way prefer to get on with the plot), Christie's funny, tongue-in-cheek reference to guidebooks and coach tours works well.

Agatha Christie was far from unsusceptible to the romance of princes and palaces — she was notably tickled in later life by the attention given her by the British royal family. Nonetheless, she somehow stops short of that curiously naive and breathless snobbery common to so many other aspiring middle-class authors. Unlike Innes, Sayers, and indeed Trollope, she does not create fantasmical alter egos who feel thoroughly at home in lordly palaces their creators could know in real life only as day trippers.

Christie characteristically refuses to invest much emotional energy in the ultra-high-society world she presents in *The Secret of Chimneys* and chooses to adopt the tone of comedy rather than of reverence or romance. In fact, the whole presentation of Chimneys and its inhabitants is infused with the spirit of Christie's contemporary P. G. Wodehouse, whose short stories and novels had already in 1925 achieved enormous popularity with the English upper-middle-class. When *Chimneys* was being written, Wodehouse's definitive creations — Blandings Castle, Lord Emsworth, the Hon. Freddy Threepwood, Bertie Wooster, and Jeeves — lay still in the future, but already in the early twenties Wodehouse had become associated with a certain comic treatment of the English aristocracy that Agatha Christie obviously found congenial. Four of the *Chimneys* characters in particular have strong Wodehousean resonance — Lord Caterham, his daughter Bundle, their friend Bill Eversleigh, and their neighbor George Lomax.

Clement Edward Alistair Brent, ninth Marquis of Caterham, is a prototypical comic nobleman, with his shabby, inconspicuous appearance, meek, dithery manner, and taste for old books, a quiet life, and pretty women. When, in Chapter 9 of *The Secret of Chimneys*, Lord Caterham avoids the police by sneaking off for a whole morning's tour of the estate, we wonder if some mighty porcine creature like Wodehouse's Empress of Blandings will delight his eye. Comic lords seem inevitably to come equipped with impeccably deferential butlers and stolidly truculent head gardeners. Hence we are not surprised to learn from *The Seven Dials Mystery*, the sequel novel Christie wrote about the Brents, that Lord Caterham also commands the services of Macdonald, a stony Scot. Macdonald delights in denying his masters the fruits and flowers from their estates and speaks "as head gardeners should speak — mournfully, but with dignity, like an emperor at a funeral." Christie's Macdonald is one in a line of such head gardeners that will include the Murdo MacDonald of Michael Innes's *Hamlet, Revenge!*.

All the grandeur of the house of Brent, so signally lacking in the weedy and tweedy current marquis, is found transposed in the imposing figure of Tredwell, the white-haired butler. Whereas Tredwell's majestic self-assurance is unassailable, corpses, doctors, and policemen sadly break Lord Caterham's routine, and we see him over breakfast behaving with Tredwell very much as he might once have behaved as a spoiled and anxious child with a compliant nursery maid. "'Omelet,' said Lord Caterham, lifting each lid in turn. "Eggs and bacon, kidneys, devilled bird, haddock, cold ham, cold pheasant. I don't like any of these things, Tredwell. Ask the cook to poach me an egg, will you?" With an impassive "Very good, my lord," Tredwell retires in search of the humble eggs he knows full well his employer, once placated, will reject in favor of the habitual menu.

Like many Wodehousean fathers, Lord Caterham has both affection and admiration for Lady Eileen, his vivacious and determined eldest daughter, but he expects to exert little or no control over her life. If Lord Caterham is a grown-up child, his daughter is very much the confident adult, and the days of the heavy Victorian father and the submissive Young Person seem long gone. Lady Eileen, commonly known as Bundle, is a charming and capable hostess, who keeps an eye on her younger sisters, Dulcie and Daisy (created to justify the existence of governess-murderess Mademoiselle Brun!) and shepherds her father on his prescribed route around the country, from Chimneys up to the London house, to Cowes and Deauville in the summer, and then to Scotland in the autumn.

Agatha Christie will give more details of such aristocratic peregrinations in her 1930 book *The Mysterious Mr. Quinn*. In mid-January every year, regular as clockwork, Mr. Satterthwaite left England for two or three months in the more clement climate of the French Riviera. May and June were spent in London, and Satterthwaite's activities always included Ascot and the Eton-Harrow cricket match. In the summer, he paid a few country-house visits before repairing across the Channel once again, this time to one of the northern seaside resorts — Deauville or Le Touquet. September and October were devoted to shooting parties, and the rest of the year was spent "in town," that is to say, in London.

Such was the stereotypic life of the English upper classes, and Christie, like many other writers of her time, both mocked and aspired to it. Christie's own family, at least in part because of her extraordinary earning power as a writer, was in fact to realize the British middle-class author's dream and move sharply up the British social scale. At the end of her life, Agatha Christie and her family were moving in the set of the country squires and Old Etonians, and had done the British equivalent of rejoining the Social Register set to which Agatha's American father, Frederick Alvah Miller, belonged as a young man.

This progress up the social ladder can be measured in several ways. Agatha herself had to "come out" in Cairo because it was cheaper, but her daughter Rosalind was to be presented at court and have a proper London debutante season. Agatha was not, however, able to accompany her daughter to the palace, because she was a divorcee. The schools Christie's male family members attended also serve as subtle social markers, as the public schools have long been a major support of English class distinctions. Agatha's brother Monty was enrolled at England's second most famous school, Harrow, though he was hardly a model pupil. Archie Christie attended the rather humdrum Clifton College, where his stepfather was a housemaster. The Clifton connection was probably one of the signs of Archie Christie's unsuitability as a husband in the eyes of Mrs. Clara Miller. Max Mallowan proclaimed his status as the intellectual son of successful immigrant parents by attending the middle rank public school of Lancing, as did Evelyn Waugh, and hating every minute of it. By the time Mathew Prichard, Rosalind's only son, was ready for school, the doors of Eton were open. Both Mathew's dead father, Hubert Prichard, and his stepfather, Anthony Hicks, had the right social connections for Eton, and his grandmother's wealth no doubt helped. One of the proudest moments of Agatha Christie's later life was watching Mathew play in the Eton-Harrow cricket match, the same event that her fictional Mr. Satterthwaite had attended so assiduously thirty years before.

The Hon. Eileen Brent's preference for the absurd name of Bundle seems all of a piece with her status as a high aristocratic Bright Young Thing. Such preppy nicknames were all the rage. As noted earlier, Christie's own sister Margaret, "Madge" Miller Watts, was known as Punkie in later life, and Christie was to coin the even more egregious nickname of Egg for a later young-lady aristocrat, Hermione Lytton Gore of *Murder in Three Acts/Three Act Tragedy*. Another, slightly odd sign of Bundle's rich and emancipated lifestyle was her dabbling in "red-hot Socialist" political opinions and her taste for very fast cars. Anthony Cade/Prince Nicholas, we may remember, had similarly expressed his youthful rebelliousness by becoming a radical, and Christie seems to imply that socialism is some kind of phase that trendy young upper-crust people go through. Speeding is taken no more seriously by Christie than socialism, but given a lot more space, and here she seems definitely to reflect the literary conventions of her period. Driving recklessly through the English countryside in an open Daimler, Hispano, or Panhard is an important activity for upmarket mystery-story protagonists at this period. Lord Peter Wimsey indulges in the sport regularly, as does his beautiful nephew, and in two of her between-war novels Christie's characters stage road accidents as a kind of lark that will secure them entrance to the home of a suspicious person. We shall have to wait until 1939 and *Ten Little Indians* for Christie to recognize the reality of modern traffic conditions and actually murder a dashing young blade who has run over a small child with impunity.

Bundle Brent's delight in automobiles is matched by her appreciation of men. When introduced to the delectable Anthony Cade, Bundle does not beat about the bush. She gazes earnestly at Anthony, sizing him up like an object without addressing a word to him. She then begs her friend Virginia to explain how she manages to pick up such goodlooking men. When Virginia walks away with Lord Caterham, Bundle says challengingly to Anthony, "Do you talk . . . or are you just strong and silent?"

Bundle Brent, like Tuppence Beresford in *The Secret Adversary*, and Anne Bedingfeld of *The Man in the Brown Suit*, is a good example of Christie's version of the New Woman. Always few in number but great in publicity, such women, with their short skirts, rouged faces, and liberated lifestyles, were a target of protest and abuse in the 1920s, for example from social satirists like the Catholic novelist Evelyn Waugh. Such abuse was not new, and came from men and women alike. For example, the Victorian journalist Eliza Lynn Linton achieved fame with her 1868 essay "The Girl of the Period" — a girl who is known for her "slang, bold talk, and fastness," is "a creature who dyes her hair and paints her face, as the first articles of her personal religion; whose sole idea of life is plenty of fun and luxury; and whose dress is the object of such thought and intellect as she possesses."

Christie is habitually seen as politically conservative and socially conventional, but her attitude toward the New Woman is radically different from Mrs. Lynn Linton's or from Waugh's. What could be called the Lynn Linton line on socially emancipated women is echoed in the 1923 *Murder on the Links* when Christie has Poirot's friend Captain Hastings react in distaste at the fashionable young lady he meets in a railway carriage. Hastings tells the reader outright that he is an old-fashioned man who likes women to be womanly. He cannot abide modern neurotic girls like Dulcie Duveen, who swear like troopers, smoke like chimneys, and "jazz from morning to night." Hastings's disapproval of modern young misses like Dulcie is emphatically not an expression of Christie's own views — on the contrary, Hastings's reaction to Dulcie is just one example of what a complete ass the man is. Christie will turn the tables by making Hastings fall head over heels in love with Dulcie and finally carry her off to marital bliss in Argentina.

In general, Christie looks upon her bright young women with indulgence, enjoying their chic, admiring their spunk, understanding their boredom and pique, even, as in the case of Freddie Rice in *Peril at End House*, their dependence on drugs and alcohol. In Christie's novels, smart, attractive, intelligent women like Tuppence and Bundle will continue to star right into the seventies but by this time they will have, significantly, moved down the social scale from debutante to hairdresser, and no longer seem exceptional.

Those of them who have money, even temporarily, enjoy it to the full. When the chronically broke Tuppence Cowley earns an unexpected 50 pounds, she immediately blows 10 on lunch at the Ritz for herself and Tommy Beresford, followed by a dinner dance in the evening. Hairdresser Jane Grey of *Death in the Air/Death in the Clouds* wins 100 pounds on the Irish sweepstakes and uses the cash for a two-week luxury vacation. Those women with no money, as we have already seen in *The Mysterious Affair at Styles*, work hard to get it. They do this not so much in the professions — where Christie's women, like herself, seem to find no niche — but in business and the arts. Thus, Carlotta Adams of *Thirteen at Dinner/Lord Edgware Dies*, is a hard working young American actress helping to support a beloved younger sister. Carlotta's good friend Jenny Driver owns her own hat shop and earns a good living, as does that extremely practical and down-to-earth fashion model Emily Trefusis of *Murder at Hazelmoor/The Sittaford Mystery*.

Some of Christie's young women characters will be murder victims, some will be detectives, some will be murderers. Christie is a strict sexual egalitarian in that she is able to imagine a cold heart beating under a soft young feminine breast, a calculating mind working behind the brown curls and dancing blue eyes. However, whatever the narrative slot she chooses for a young woman character, Agatha Christie will never condemn her just because she is attractive, dressed in the height of fashion, anxious to make a great deal of money, meet a fabulous man, see the world, and generally turn upside down the life her parents laid out for her. Francesca Annis, the actress who has portrayed Tuppence Beresford in the successful British television series based on the Tommy and Tuppence stories, superbly personifies the intelligent, energetic, and chic charm of the typical Christiean young woman.

Unlike the smart-as-paint Bundle, Bill Eversleigh is a silly young ass, straight out of P. G. Wodehouse by Oscar Wilde. Agatha Christie takes pleasure in lampooning his incomprehensible public school accent, his partiality for exotic actresses, and his boyish (at age twenty-five) incompetence. She tells us that Bill's skills are as a golfer and cricketer, rather than as a diplomat, and that he owes his Foreign Office position not to his brains, but to his social connections. She goes on, with characteristic antiestablishment irony: "For the work he had to do he was quite suitable. He was more or less George's [his boss George Lomax's] dog." In *The Seven Dials Mystery*, her (much inferior) 1929 sequel to *The Secret of Chimneys*, Christie introduces a whole gaggle of silly young asses, equipped with nicknames like Pongo and girl friends with names like Socks. Jimmy Thesiger, who appears to be the richest and least motivated of the set, ambles down to breakfast at 10:30 in the morning — late even by the relaxed Brent standards — and has a determined disinclination ever to meet his aunt Jemima before four in the afternoon. As we readers follow the activities of Jimmy and Gerry and Ronnie and Bill and Pongo, we feel ourselves transported into the world of Oscar Wilde, and expect the redoubtable duo of Gwendolyn and Lady Bracknell to arrive for cucumber sandwiches at any moment. All the same, Actively Detecting Readers, sensitive to Christie's use of the throwaway line, should prick up their ears when Thesiger remarks languidly, "I've sometimes thought — well, that it isn't possible for anyone to be quite the ass old Gerry makes himself out to be."

The Hon. George Lomax, whose goggly eyes have earned him the nickname of Codders from his assistants, is little more than a caricature civil servant. No one at Chimneys likes George Lomax, though they put up with him because he is "one of them," a member of the ruling caste to which the Brents and their friends belong, and a man who has also achieved political power. Lomax is interesting because he is a character Christie tosses off without much reflection, thereby, paradoxically, revealing important parts of her outlook on life that she habitually keeps under wraps. By seeing more exactly why Christie finds George Lomax so objectionable, we get a better picture of what she finds interesting and admirable. Throughout her work, Agatha Christie reveals a profound disregard for politicians of all stripes. She distrusts politics as indifferent or even hostile to the truly important spheres of life, religion and interpersonal relationships. George Lomax is Permanent Undersecretary to the Foreign Office, and immediately suspect on that count alone. What is worse, George Lomax offends because he is unattractive, excessively busy and self-important, and given to long-winded, boring speeches. All of these are critical faults in the Christiean fictional universe, where charm, good looks, and a sense of humor are often more important traits in a man than power, competence, or earning power.

We first meet George when he has, literally, buttonholed Lord Caterham in the street outside his club, and is wounding that gentleman's sensitive ears with a lecture on the Herzoslovakian situation. Agatha Christie herself was extremely sensitive to loud voices, and the author's point of view on Lomax merges indistinguishably with that of her fictional peer, who is deeply bored by politics and politicians in general and with the self-important George Lomax in particular. Whenever Lomax appears, Christie makes fun of his pompous ineffectuality, his reliance on the labors of his secretary, and his inability to make an impromptu comment because, like all British civil servants, he has been accustomed to having advance notice of any question he might be required to answer. In *The Seven Dials Mystery* Lomax will become even more ridiculous and unpleasant when, emulating Jane Austen's Mr. Collins in *Pride and*

Prejudice, he makes a ridiculous, unexpected, and wholly undesired proposal of marriage to Bundle Brent.

Christie's prejudice against politicians and diplomats is largely personal and idiosyncratic, and was one of the fortunate results of an exceptionally sheltered childhood. She shows a signal lack of that structured indoctrination into the ideology of the upper-middle-classes that is so poignantly exposed by Christie's great contemporary E. M. Forster. By refusing as far as possible to take sides with the political right or left, by limiting her cast of characters to people from her own social caste whom she knew about, by seeing people as individual creatures of God who are good or evil, rather than right or wrong, oppressor or oppressed, Christie keeps herself and her fictional world out of the political arena. Her novels are relatively — though far from absolutely — free of the narrow conventional pieties about the wickedness of the Labor Party and its "Bolshy" allies, the attractiveness of the Fascists, the inferiority of "niggers" and "chinks," etc., which occur so often in the works of British prewar popular novelists.

Thus, Lord Caterham, who seems in large measure to represent Christie's own political position, is a loyal Tory who can nonetheless relish the idea of the government's being embarrassed by the publication of the Stylptitch memoirs, an insider's exposé of the Herzoslovakian revolution and the overthrow of the Obolovitch dynasty. Caterham — or Agatha Christie — is as familiar with the slogans of the left as of the right. He relishes the idea of uncomfortable questions being raised in the House of Commons about the threat to the "broadminded and democratic" regime in Herzoslovakia posed by "bloodsucking capitalists" eager to reinstate a puppet member of the "tyrannous and corrupt" Obolovitch dynasty. It is in some measure because of her antipoliticism and refusal to subscribe to the tribal loyalties of her nation and class that Christie's novels of the twenties and thirties remain readable and eminently adaptable to the television and film screen.

There is, however, one kind of popular prejudice to which Christie did unfortunately subscribe. A kind of jingoistic, knee-jerk anti-Semitism colors the presentation of Jewish characters in many of her early novels, and Christie reveals herself to be as unreflective and conventional as the majority of her compatriots. We can laugh with her as she pokes mild fun at silly Bill and stuffy George, but the portrayal of the Jewish financier Herman Isaacstein in *The Secret of Chimneys* is hard to forgive.

Isaacstein comes into the story because he is the representative of a syndicate that is seeking to negotiate rights to exploit the oil fields recently discovered in Herzoslovakia. The negotiations are being conducted by George Lomax, on behalf of Her Majesty's government, by Isaacstein's British syndicate, and by the current senior member of the deposed Obolovitch dynasty, Prince Michael. The assumption made in the story that the very highest financial power in Great Britain should lie in Jewish hands is in itself, of course, stereotypic. The financial power in England of families like the Rothschilds was far from mythical, but only cultural mythology can take a Lord Rothschild as typical or representative of English Jewry. What is more damaging, Lord Caterham — who, as we have seen, speaks very much for the author in matters political in this novel — is exaggeratedly unable to recall the financier's name, refers to him unpleasantly as "Mr Ikey Hermanstein" and "Noseystein," and makes an offhand crack to the effect that no one with a name like Isaacstein can be British. The view of Jewish people as being essentially and irremediably foreign to the culture and nation in which they live is, of course, basic to anti-Semitic persecution.

This same stereotyping of Jews as obviously different from their compatriots continues in Christie's physical presentation of Isaacstein. Many Englishmen have large noses and sallow complexions, and few are famed for effortless elegance, yet Christie's opening description of Isaacstein will stress these features as marking his unmistakable, alien Jewishness. "He was dressed in very correct English shooting clothes which nevertheless sat strangely upon him. He had a fat yellow face, and black eyes, as impenetrable as those of a cobra. There was a generous curve to the big nose and power in the square lines of the vast jaw." That we are probably dealing here with a literary stereotype of how a Jew looks, rather than with a description of a real person known to the author, is confirmed by a comparison with Dorothy L. Sayers' almost contemporary description of a Jewish financier in *Whose Body?*: "The body which lay in the bath was that of a tall, stout man of about fifty. The hair, which was thick and black and naturally curly, had been cut and parted by a master hand, and exuded a faint violet perfume. . . . The features were thick, fleshy and strongly marked, with prominent dark eyes, and a long nose curving down to a heavy chin." Christie repeats essentially the same denotations in the opening description of Sebastian Levinne as a mature man in Chapter 1 of *Giants' Bread*. "He was a big man, rather too well covered with flesh. His face was yellow and impassive, his eyes beady and black, two enormous ears stood out from his face and were the joy of caricaturists."

Christie's insensitivity in racial matters did not of course go unnoticed, particularly in the huge American middle-class market, where there was probably a significantly larger representation of Jews than in England. Particularly in the postwar period, Christie's publishers responded to criticisms directly and edited out racist remarks from Christie's books. How extensive such editing was is not clear, but at least on the basis of the texts as published, it seems that Agatha Christie, like many of her compatriots, began in the late thirties to realize that prejudicial remarks about Jews could not simply be laughed off. The origin of this change in attitude may have been an experience Christie records in her autobiography.

In 1932 or 1933, she and Max found themselves at the home of Dr. Jordan, a German who was Director of Antiquities in Baghdad, a charming, cultured, considerate, gentle man, of splendid good looks, who had played for the Mallowans the Beethoven Agatha loved so much. However, when some casual mention was made of Jews, Dr. Jordan's face took on an extraordinary and unforgettable expression. The Jews must be exterminated, he said, and Christie was astonished to realize that he meant exactly what he said. "It was the first time," she comments, "that I had come across any hint of what was to come later from Germany."

Christie's anti-Semitism had always been of the stupidly unthinking rather than the deliberately vicious kind. As her circle of acquaintance widened and as she grew to understand what Nazism really meant for Jewish people, Christie abandoned her knee-jerk anti-Semitism. What is more, even at her most thoughtless and prejudiced, Christie saw Jews as different, alien, and un-English, rather than as depraved or dangerous — people one does not know rather than people one fears. In those of her novels such as *The Big Four* and *The Secret Adversary* that center on the constantly popular story of a master spy plot to destroy the civilized world, she conspicuously refuses to buy into the obsession with a secret world Jewish-Communist-Freemason conspiracy that still haunts so many otherwise sane Europeans of her generation and the next.

Thus, even though Christie's conception of Isaacstein in *The Secret of Chimneys* is a mass of silly English anti-Semitic prejudices, she does not cast him as the villain. In fact, in all her many novels, Christie will tend to use Jewish characters as red herrings who tempt the reader to indulge in prejudice instead of following the trail of evidence. In *Murder in Three Acts*, for example, the darkly handsome young Oliver Manders is the prime suspect because he not only is Jewish and illegitimate but also professes wild communist views and drives a motorcycle. Those readers who seize upon Manders as the murderer are destined for a fall, as in fact Manders is cast in the role of romantic lead and will end the novel as the fiancé of the aristocratic lady sleuth, "Egg" Lytton Gore.

The best key to Agatha Christie's attitude toward Jews is, as so often, provided by her writing as Mary Westmacott. In *Giants' Bread*, published in 1930, Christie chooses to make one of her five protagonists a Jew, and she addresses head-on the anti-Semitic prejudice of the English upper-middle-class she belonged to. In some ways, Sebastian Levinne can be seen as Christie's way of working through her own ideas on the Jewish question and raising the issue for her readers.

Sebastian Levinne is the only child of an extremely rich Jewish family of recent Russian origin. Sebastian enters the life of Christie's antihero, Vernon Deyre, when the Levinne parents purchase Deerfield, the country estate of the impoverished Sir Charles Arlington. Deerfield adjoins Vernon's ancestral home, Abbots Puissants. Christie's conception of the Levinnes is rooted in popular prejudice and fictional stereotype, and as these have rarely been positive, the presentation of the Levinne family has many of the unpleasant features we have seen in Christie's earlier character Herman Isaacstein. Heavy-bodied, sallow of complexion, lisping of tongue, and inclined to rich clothing with an oriental flavor, Christie's Jewish characters in this period are both physically unattractive and vaguely out of place on the English social scene. Their alien Jewishness is largely unaffected by their conversion to the Church of England or by their established position in the English social order. This is how Christie describes the Levinnes' first public appearance in the country area they have just moved to. "The Levinnes proved to be a very Christian brand of Jew. They appeared in church on Sunday, having taken a whole pew. The interest of the congregation was breathless. First came Mr. Levinne — very round and stout, tightly frock-coated — an enormous nose and a shining face. Then Mrs. — an amazing sight! Colossal sleeves! Hour-glass figure! Chains of diamonds! An immense hat decorated with feathers and black tightly curling ringlets underneath it! With them was a boy with a long yellow face and protruding ears."

What might be called the Rothschild syndrome dominates Christie's Jewish characters, who, throughout her fiction, are overwhelmingly endowed with financial acumen and vast wealth. The Levinnes are apparently only one generation removed from the world of the pogrom, yet they already have the money to purchase properties like Deerfield from impoverished but ancient English families such as Vernon's own. However, being rich is emphatically not a sin in Agatha Christie's book, especially if one has been clever and innovative about getting rich. This point emerges clearly from Christie's presentation of the Deyres, on the one hand, and the Levinnes, on the other.

Vernon's mother, a gloriously beautiful woman, seems obviously superior to the overweight, overdressed figure of Sebastian's mother, but in fact Christie makes it plain that this physical beauty masks an insensitive, conventional, and ignorant mind. Mrs. Deyre and other members of her wealthy north-of-England industrial family represent the worst in English cultural philistinism. As for Vernon's father, Captain Deyre, Christie is gentle and sympathetic toward the man's crippling reserve and sexual peccadillos. She is also uncompromising in her revelations of the tragic consequences of Deyre's chronic incapacity to secure for his descendants the family estate that he loves. Able to spend money but not make it, hopelessly dependent for the realization of his dreams and ambitions on the money and good will of others, notably his wife, Captain Deyre ultimately responds to the financial and marital mess he has made of his life by going off to the Boer War to find a quick death. The child Vernon is left to cope with the death duties and the grieving widow. One may recall here that Christie's own delightful but financially incompetent father died when Agatha was ten, leaving behind a financial mess that dramatically reduced the circumstances and expectations of his family and threatened to force the sale of Ashfield, the home Agatha loved.

In contrast to the elegant but doomed Deyres, the Levinnes have life skills as well as financial skills. They understand the workings of English county society as well as they do the stock market, and by judicious investment in local charities, lavish domestic improvement, and much unruffled kindness, they overcome the raw anti-Semitic reaction that greeted their move into the neighborhood. Lady Coomberleigh condescends, after all, to call upon Mrs. Levinne, who abandons diamond chains and feathers in favor of the tweediest tweeds, at least when down in the country.

Endowing some of her characters with fabulous wealth obviously gives Agatha Christie great pleasure and reflects her own ambitions to make money, join the world of the arts, and rise in the social hierarchy. She stresses not the narrowness of the nouveau riche, but the ethical and aesthetic opportunities which money opens up for talented and creative people such as the Levinnes. Unlike his friends Vernon and Vernon's cousin, Josephine Deyre, who have a lifetime problem of reconciling their great personal ambitions and refined tastes with limited financial means, Sebastian has the money to finance his wildest dreams.

"Oh you . . . Jew!" is Vernon's way of reacting to his old friend's ambition, but at this point in the story Christie is clearly on Sebastian's side, not Vernon's. Although Christie does not give Sebastian the physical beauty that the other four protagonists in her novel enjoy, in every other way Sebastian represents an ideal for Christie and is used to express her own views and values. Sebastian is rich and pragmatic, gifted with a talent for putting his dreams into action. He is exceptionally attuned to the creative and artistic movement of his generation and is dedicated to using his vast wealth to promote new art and new ideas of every kind. But perhaps more important, underlying these financial and aesthetic gifts is what Christie describes as "an unemotional and unerring sense of values." What Christie means by this can best be understood if we compare Sebastian's life more closely with the lives of two of the other main characters in *Giants' Bread*, Vernon Deyre and Nell Vereker.

The gloriously beautiful Nell equates happiness with material luxury, and she sacrifices love and personal integrity to get it. At the end of the novel, Nell owes her life to Vernon, the first husband she has rejected and betrayed, and must live with the guilty knowledge that Vernon is still very much alive and that her life of wealth and consequence as a married woman and the mistress of Abbots Puissants rests on his contemptuous acceptance of her deceit. For his part, Vernon has from youth wanted three things in life — to retain his beloved family home, to marry Nell Vereker, and to write the great music he hears in his head. Vernon regards his love affair with Jane Harding and her devotion to him and to his music as incidental to the essential goals of his life. However, Vernon, like his father, is unable to face reality squarely. He does not listen when Sebastian warns him that his three goals are irreconcilable and that he must choose. It is only after Jane has died, without his putting out a hand to save her, that Vernon realizes that it was Jane whom he really loved and needed, that his passion for Nell was a delusion of the senses, and that love of Jane and love of music always were wholly compatible. At the end of the novel, Vernon lives an anonymous and exiled life of loneliness and self-reproach, his flesh and bones ground to make the giants' bread of music.

Unlike Vernon, Nell, and Jane, Sebastian is allowed at least a chance of happiness, and this is related to his "unerring set of values." In Christie's terms this is seen in the fact that, from childhood, Sebastian dreams not only of becoming one of the great art entrepreneurs of the world but also of winning the love of his friend Joe Deyre. Christie presents Joe as a woman of many faults who makes serious mistakes in her life and who yet is worth wooing and winning. When Vernon, Sebastian, Joe, and Nell are children, it is the orphaned and sadly worldly-wise Joe who challenges the explicit anti-Semitism of English society and seeks out the lonely Sebastian as a friend. When Sebastian greets the Deyres' first friendly overtures with hostility, it is Joe who understands that he is acting to forestall the aggression he has come to expect, who sees that this immensely rich and privileged boy is deeply lonely and longing for friendship. It is Joe's uncompromising directness, her refusal ever to echo conventional pieties, her championing of the less fortunate, as well as her great beauty, that lead Sebastian to fall deeply in love.

When, at the end of the novel, Sebastian convinces Joe, who is dying from tuberculosis, that she has always loved him in her heart, and that together there can still be a future for them, we appear to be in a silly women's novelette world where love can conquer even the tubercular bacillus. Undoubtedly, Christie was a romantic, and she loved to reward love and devotion and to bring together, by some melodramatic fictional device, people like Joe and Sebastian whom life's complexities drive apart. At the same time, it must be noted that sallow, jug-eared, prosperous, Jewish Sebastian is as unusual a romantic hero as Joe is an unconventional romance heroine. The plot that Joe acts out in her life is far removed from the patterns of romance novelists like Christie's contemporaries Georgette Heyer and Barbara Cartland. Christie in *Giants' Bread* is as sparing as ever in her love scenes, but there is no attempt to conceal the fact that Joe — like the equally attractive female protagonist opera singer Jane Harding — acted upon her ideological commitment to free love and has had more than one passionate and disastrous love affair with a less than savory man. Remaining a virgin is not the key to personal virtue or even to eternal redemption for either male or female in Christie's books. Those women who feel and even act upon sexual passion, and then face squarely up to the consequences of their actions, earn the authorial accolade and can even be seen to represent the author's female ideal in a less than ideal world.

The whole novel *Giants' Bread* assumes an absorbing interest in contemporary music. Vernon Deyre devotes much of his adult life to composing music that breaks unequivocally with the past, Jane Harding is a soprano who devotes her career to post-Wagnerian roles, the very roles Agatha Miller had wanted in vain to sing. Sebastian consistently seeks out, sponsors, and imposes upon the public a challenging and avant garde art form that the musically provincial English would distrust and ignore if left to themselves.

It is perhaps unexpected that Christie should so firmly champion the aesthetic avant garde, opening her novel with a description of a new opera-pageant by a supposedly Russian composer that mingles elements of Wagner, Schoenberg, and Debussy. Christie humbly accepted the lowbrow label, yet a careful reading of her works shows that she had an instinctive appreciation of modern music and art. Apart from the complex character of Vernon Deyre, Christie gives us two other sensitive portraits of artists. The painter Amyas Crale in *Murder in Retrospect/Five Little Pigs* and the sculptor Henrietta Savenake in *Murder After Hours/The Hollow* are artists whose work is representational but yet untraditional, following a personal style that is far from the taste of the hoi polloi. Michael Rogers, the first-person narrator of *Endless Night*, a young man from a poor and culturally impoverished background, first gets the imperative urge to be rich when he walks into a London gallery to gaze hungrily at a painting that speaks to him like nothing he has ever seen in museums. After his marriage to the rich heiress Ellie, Michael will take immense pleasure in working with a revolutionary young architect on the plans for his new home at Gipsy's Acre.

By late 1926, Agatha Christie had published six novels and her name was well known in England. Her first novel with Collins, *The Murder of Roger Ackroyd*, was her first masterpiece, showing all the ingenuity and complexity of Styles and yet breaking out of the shadow of her great male predecessors. The brilliant but unorthodox ending to the book was a minor cause celebre, yet even the indignant howls let out by certain readers and critics did not hurt the book's success. Agatha Christie had moved into the forefront of British detective-story writers. Ironically, her very fame and success were to make the next, and most dramatic episode in her life, even more traumatic.

CHAPTER
FOUR

Teresa Neele
Disappearance and Divorce

The years 1926 to 1929 were the most painful and arduous in Agatha Christie's life. Her hitherto successful combination of domestic happiness and public fame crumbled, and she suddenly found herself fighting for her sanity. Some of the psychic wounds inflicted at this time never totally healed, and the lessons Christie learned from the events of 1926 were not all salutary. Nonetheless, in the end she gained far more than she lost by being forced to leave "the land of lost content" and enter a new world of far greater emotional, social, and cultural richness.

The crisis in Christie's life occurred in December 1926, when she abandoned her car and her overnight belongings by the side of the road at Newlands Corner in Surrey and disappeared. Eleven days later she was found, apparently the victim of amnesia, in the Hydropathic Hotel in Harrogate. This was the one dramatic act in her life, the stuff of many sensationalist front-page articles, of a novel, of a major motion picture, of endless speculation. Yet despite all the pages that have been devoted to the subject of Agatha Christie's disappearance, surprisingly little hard information is available.

In the remaining forty-nine years of her life, Agatha Christie never wrote about her disappearance or allowed it to be referred to in her presence or in any biographical material she sanctioned. Amnesia was the medical explanation given for her behavior at the time of her disappearance, and Agatha acted as if she was still afflicted by total lack of memory of the eleven days. Her authorized biographer has told us that, with the help of a psychiatrist, Christie did in fact regain some memory of her journey to Harrogate and stay in the Hydropathic Hotel, but she never owned to this. That she was permanently traumatized by what happened in 1926 is attested not by Christie's words, but by her lifelong silence. Even when, in calm and happy old age, Christie came to write an autobiography for publication only after her death, she included no account at all of her flight to London from Newlands Corner or her stay in the Harrogate Hydro, or indeed of the whole period from August 1926 to February of 1927. On the dictaphone recordings from which the first drafts of Christie's autobiography were composed, Christie's voice, we are told, is almost inaudible when she deals with the events of 1926. Christie never filled in the eleven missing days in her life.

Other people who were close to Christie before and after her disappearance presumably had stories they could have told, but these people did not talk for the record. During the search to find the missing novelist, some of the protagonists in the drama —

Archie Christie, his brother Campbell, his mother Mrs. William Hemsley, Agatha's friend and secretary Carlo Fisher — were interviewed by the press. Once Agatha was found, however, all those close to her maintained a strict and lifelong silence about what they had done and seen and what Agatha had said to them. The most notable silence is that of Max Mallowan, who in 1930 was to become Agatha's second husband. He had no first-hand knowledge of what had happened in 1926, but it seems safe to assume that Agatha would have confided in him if in anyone. Mallowan published his memoirs soon after Agatha's death and shortly before his own, but in the two chapters devoted to his famous wife, the familiar textual hole opens up and Mallowan says nothing about Agatha's disappearance.

The Christie family broke its silence only in the early eighties. Rosalind Christie Hicks decided that there was a need for an official biography of her mother, and commissioned Janet Morgan to write one. Morgan says that she was given unlimited access to the many papers, photographs, and other memorabilia which Agatha Christie had left and which no one else outside the immediate family had looked at. Mrs. Hicks also discussed her own memories with Janet Morgan and related what Agatha had told her about the missing eleven days — memories that Christie had not included in her own autobiographical writings.

Despite the warm cooperation of the Christie family and her own zealous research efforts, Janet Morgan clearly suffered insuperable disadvantages when she attempted to fill in the famous eleven-day hole in her subject's life. She found that the Surrey police files relating to the case had been destroyed, presumably during the Second World War. The press accounts from December 1926 are contradictory, even about such simple matters as whether the lights on Christie's abandoned car were still burning when it was discovered. The press reported that Christie addressed three, and possibly four, letters at the time of her disappearance, but none has been published. Most importantly, in the almost sixty years that had passed since the events, all but one of the protagonists — Archie Christie, his brother Campbell and second wife Nancy Neele Christie, Carlo Eisher, the Wattses, their son Jack, and of course Agatha herself — were dead. None of these persons is known to have left an account of the events of December 1926, except for Carlo Fisher, who gave a long letter to Rosalind Hicks setting down all she knew. This letter is summarized but not reproduced by Janet Morgan, and forms one of the most important documents in the case. Only one of the main characters in the drama was alive and willing to talk to Janet Morgan in 1980 — Rosalind Christie Hicks, who was seven years old when her mother disappeared. The kind of investigation in retrospect that Hercule Poirot and Miss Marple engage in with such success in such famous Christie novels as *Murder in Retrospect/Five Little Pigs* and *Sleeping Murder* was impossible in reality.

When considering the case of the disappearing detective novelist, it turns out to be useful to learn the lessons Christie herself has taught us in her detective fiction and set down a list of questions and puzzling facts, just as Hercule Poirot might do. Why did Christie drive away from her home in Sunningdale late at night? What did she do in the next five or six hours? Why did she abandon her car and other possessions by the road at Newlands Corner, just beyond Guildford in Surrey, at most an hour's drive from her home? Is there some significance to the fact that Newlands Corner, where Agatha ditched her car, is only a few miles from Godalming, where Agatha's husband and Miss Nancy Neele were staying for the weekend with friends? Having abandoned her rather randomly packed traveling case and coat in the car, how did she manage to make the journey to London and then to Harrogate? How did she afford a new wardrobe and a room in an expensive hotel? In the period just prior to her departure from Styles and during her stay in Harrogate, whom did Christie write to and what did she say? If Christie was suffering from amnesia during the eleven days she was missing, what caused such an uncommon condition? How does Janet Morgan's *post hoc* diagnosis that Christie was enacting an "hysterical fugue" advance our understanding of Christie's behavior?

One fact accepted by all those who have written and speculated about Agatha Christie's disappearance is that she had been deeply depressed throughout much of 1926, so depressed that she had been unable to complete a commissioned novel, *The Mystery of the Blue Train*. Her depression was caused by two events: the unexpected death of Agatha's mother and the even less expected request by Archie Christie that Agatha give him a divorce so that he could marry a mutual friend, Nancy Neele. Clara Miller died in the spring at Abney, Madge Watts's home in Cheshire. Agatha was not with Clara when she died. Archie dropped his bomb when visiting his family at Ashfield to celebrate Rosalind's August birthday. For insight into this crucial period in Agatha Christie's life, we must, as usual, turn to the Westmacott novels. In *Unfinished Portrait*, Agatha Christie gives a barely fictionalized account of her first marriage, and the heroine Celia is a kind of exorcism of the woman that Agatha became in the last months of her marriage to Archie Christie.

The Christies seem to have been having marital problems well before Colonel Christie took up with Miss Neele. In *Unfinished Portrait* the onset of middle age and middle-age spread seems to have been one important issue. From the beginning of their marriage, Dermot, the heroine's husband in the novel, passionately worships his wife's beauty and insists that she not lose it. This emphasis on her physical appearance makes Celia deeply uneasy. When she asks for assurance that he will still love her even if she does lose her looks, Dermot is evasive. He is obviously far from sure that he will. If Archie Christie also minded very much indeed how his wife looked, it is significant that by 1923 Agatha was no longer the beautiful woman of earlier years.

Companionship, or the lack of it, was another thorny issue between the Christies, and it is addressed directly in a conversation in *Unfinished Portrait*. Some years after her marriage, Celia wonders aloud about the truth of the belief "that men only wanted women as bedfellows and housekeepers? Was that the whole tragedy of marriage — that women wanted to be companions, and that men were bored by it?" Far from contradicting her, Celia's husband agrees matter-of-factly that "women always want to do things with men — and a man would always rather have another man."

Communication was also a major problem. It is not clear how much the Christies' relationship had ever been based on words, how much they ever confided in each other, expressed their hopes and fears out loud, discussed their feelings for each other and other people. If Dermot is indeed Agatha's portrait of her husband, then Archie considered it a great waste of time to talk of thoughts and feelings or to imagine "things that weren't so." Furthermore, Dermot is said to dislike "being touched, or leaned upon for comfort, or asked to enter into other people's emotions." Agatha was temperamentally reluctant to let other people into her private world, but for Archie she made an exception. He was one of the two or three people in the world with whom she was anxious to share her thoughts. When he rebuffed her confidence, the depth of her hurt was equal to the rareness of that confidence.

Two matching scenes in *Unfinished Portrait* indicate this difficulty of communication between the Christies and also the differences in their interests and social patterns. One evening, during a dinner party, Celia emerges for once from her shell and converses with great animation and wit. Flushed with a new sense of confidence and social adequacy, Celia returns home in a happy daze, only to be reduced to silent tears and desperate confusion by her husband. Dermot flatly contradicts Celia's interpretation of what happened at the dinner party. He informs her that she has been exceptionally silly all evening, and that he hates silly women.

Was Archie Christie as crushing as the fictional Dermot if his habitually shy wife showed signs of becoming the life and soul of the party? The scene certainly reads with all the painful intensity of actual experience, and it contrasts vividly with another scene of a dinner party to which Celia goes alone. Seated between a publisher and a world traveler,

Celia enjoys herself thoroughly. She flirts with both men, confessing to one neighbor that she longs to see more of the world, particularly the East, and to the other that she keeps a novel manuscript stuffed away in a drawer. After the dinner, Celia agrees to sing a solo, the publisher asks to see her manuscript, and the traveler makes a pass at her. Celia resists — but only because she thinks Dermot would expect her to. Christie probably did not attend a dinner party exactly like this, but the things that excite Celia's interest and conquer her reserve — a cultured man, writing, music, the names of Ispahan and Baghdad — are precisely what will make for Agatha Christie's real-life happiness once she has been forced to slough Archie.

During the Sunningdale years when the Christie marriage was quietly crumbling, Rosalind may also have been a subtle disappointment to Agatha. On this point, there is a difference in testimony by the author herself, between *Unfinished Portrait*, written in 1933, and *An Autobiography*, drafted around 1960. Agatha in her autobiography gives a lively character sketch of Rosalind as a child, describing her as handsome, energetic, outgoing, forthright, and determined. Christie says that it was fascinating to watch so promising a child grow up. Agatha also makes it clear that she respected her adult daughter's abilities, encouraged her independence, appreciated the originality of her mind, and relied upon her support, especially after Rosalind's second marriage to Anthony Hicks. Mother-daughter conflict is conspicuously absent from all accounts of Agatha Christie's life; yet at the same time, there is never any claim that Agatha Christie enjoyed with her daughter the easy and joyful communication she had known with Clara.

That Agatha and Rosalind may have had some fairly

serious problems to work out between them is indicated clearly in *Unfinished Portrait*. This Westmacott novel deals with the Rosalind character (named Judy in the novel) only up to the age of about five, but for this very reason, the hostility between mother and daughter is surprising. Christie presents little Judy as a stranger and rival, a child who looked down upon her mother, Celia, and loved above all to be with and imitate her father, Dermot, whom she so immensely resembled. Christie also refers to this resemblance in her autobiography, but in the novel she allows us to understand the importance that resemblance held for a woman who was already deeply anxious about her relationship with her child's father.

While Judy is still a baby, Celia looks forward happily to repeating with her daughter the relationship of mutual adoration she had with her own mother. She wants to open the doors to the world of fantasy to Judy, reading the old beloved fairy stories and telling the new stories of princesses and dragons that teem in her own brain. Unfortunately, this scenario is never enacted. Judy proves to be not at all like her mother. She likes the active, almost violent organized games that her father plays with her and has no use for make-believe. What is worse, Judy at age four already seems to despise her mother's vein of fantasy and considers it silly to pretend that the lawn is a sea and the hoop she bowls there is a river horse. In Judy, Celia finds a miniature version of her husband's cool, judgmental common sense and resistance to intimacy. United by temperament and interests, Dermot and Judy are "puzzles" to Celia, who feels an outsider in her own home.

In constructing this fictional account of her relationship with her daughter, Agatha captures her own emotions with her habitual clarity and pathos. Omitted from the fiction, but scrupulously included in the later autobiography, are the facts that Rosalind Christie had in some part been given over from birth to the care of a sequence of more or less adequate nannies, that she had always been accustomed to her parents' going away without her on more or less lengthy vacations, and that for much of the time Agatha was preoccupied and unavailable to Rosalind as a result of her increasingly engrossing work as a writer. Agatha and Rosalind may have been born with very different natures, but they were also brought up in very different circumstances, and it was both natural and unrealistic of Agatha to imagine that she could simply reproduce her childhood, with herself playing Clara's role.

Later in the novel, Celia sums up her relation to a daughter who is now married and an adult. "I don't know whether I've failed with Judy or succeeded. I don't know whether she loves me or doesn't love me. I've given her material things. I haven't been able to give her the other things — the things that matter to me — because she doesn't want them. I've done the only other thing I could. Because I love her, I've let her alone. I haven't tried to force my views and my beliefs upon her. I've tried to make her feel I'm there if she wants me. But you see she didn't want me." These words were probably written in 1933, when the real-life Rosalind was about fourteen. They cannot be taken as a considered assessment of the relation between Agatha and Rosalind as adults. Nonetheless, they seem prophetic of the coolness and distance that were to exist between these two loving women at least until the birth of Rosalind's only child, Mathew Prichard, in 1942. Perhaps it was primarily the combined influence of two easygoing, agreeable, and like-minded men, Max Mallowan, Anthony Hicks, and finally of Mathew Prichard as he grew up, that allowed Agatha and Rosalind to deal with the unfinished business between them and acknowledge their shared love and need.

If we are to believe the testimony of *Unfinished Portrait*, neither Archie nor Rosalind gave Agatha the love and trust she enjoyed with her mother — or perhaps neither of them was allowed to. Even in the period of greatest married happiness for the Christies, it was Ashfield that was "home" for Agatha, not the various London apartments she rented with Archie in their early married years and certainly not Styles. When she went to Ashfield, she relaxed, feeling free to be herself, able to gossip and chat and tell her mother all the feelings and impressions that her husband and daughter found boring and silly. Agatha openly adored her mother, and — unlike Archie and Rosalind, who never seemed to miss anyone — Clara withered when Agatha was gone and opened up like a watered flower when "her girl" came back to her. Given the increasing difficulties that Agatha and Archie were having in their married life, given the crucial slot that Clara occupied in her younger daughter's life, it is not surprising that the unexpected death of Clara Miller in the spring of 1926 precipitated a crisis in the Christie family.

The death of her mother is almost always a critical point in a woman's life, but the depth of Agatha's sense of loss when Clara Miller died was unusual. It seems to have approached the neurotic state that Freud describes in his famous paper "Mourning and Melancholia." Over the next seven or eight months, Agatha was to experience a nervous breakdown all the more devastating because she liked to think of herself and present herself to the world as a happy, rational, matter-of-fact woman who could always be relied upon to cope. Both *Unfinished Portrait* and *An Autobiography* make it clear that Archie Christie was absolutely no help to his wife at this time of trauma: quite the contrary. Archie believed that one simply grew out of people one had once loved, and he could not see why a thirty-six-year-old woman should go to pieces when she lost her mother. Archie may even have been glad that Clara was dead and would no longer come between him and his wife.

Probably for the first time in her married life, Agatha forgot her mother's advice to put her husband first. She neglected Archie, withdrew into herself, and mourned. Agatha had been successful — perhaps too successful — in convincing Archie that she would never allow love for her child to come before love for him, but she was unable to put aside her filial grief, as he requested, and be again the joyous partner of old. In later life she referred to this as a fatal mistake, but it is far from clear whether it was in her power to remedy the situation. Increasingly Agatha had been asking for emotional intimacy, for the kind of rapport she had known with her mother, and this need was now paramount. She had ceased to be at all content with "passion and comradeship" and simply "having him in her bed at night." Archie, for his part, was unable to enter into his wife's emotions and now could not support Agatha in her mourning for Clara. Worse, he began actively to dislike a wife who in her distress had become the antithesis of the attractive, vivacious, game young woman he had courted. In *Unfinished Portrait*, Dermot tells Celia outright that he cannot bear people who are ill or unhappy, and he soon makes it crystal clear that he cannot bear Celia. The icy look Celia sees on Dermot's face reminds her uneasily of the Gunman of her childhood.

Things came to a crisis in August 1926. The Christies saved money by renting Styles for the summer, and Agatha, accompanied by Rosalind, spent the summer in Torquay clearing up the Miller family's accumulated belongings and preparing Ashfield for possible rental. Archie remained in London, staying at his club, and made practical excuses for not coming down to Torquay. Madge Watts was attending to things at home in Cheshire, and had left her sister to cope with Ashfield. Carlo Fisher had been called to Scotland to attend her father, who was feared to be dying. Given what we know of Agatha's mourning for her mother and her intense love of her family home, it is not difficult to understand why Agatha fell into even greater distress during the weeks spent sorting through the possessions of forty years. That she felt the need to present a front of normalcy to Rosalind increased Agatha's difficulty, as did the fact that Rosalind played merrily and appeared, at least, to be quite unconscious of what her mother was feeling.

Physically weary, emotionally unsupported, Agatha began to lose her identity, even forgetting her name when she came to write checks. However, both Archie and Madge had promised to come to Torquay on August 5 for Rosalind's birthday. This date had special significance for Agatha, as she retained an intense and romantic memory of how close she and Archie had been on the night of Rosalind's birth. Archie had agreed that after the birthday celebration he and Agatha would leave for a two-week holiday together in Italy, and Agatha was clinging to the thought of that vacation as to a lifeline.

Yet when Archie now at last came, it was to admit to Agatha that he had fallen in love with Nancy Neele and wanted a divorce as soon as possible. As Agatha saw it, he had turned, apparently overnight, from her most intimate companion to a hostile stranger, intent on separation, willing to hurt or even destroy his wife if that was the price of his freedom to marry another woman. She was prostrated by his insensitivity to her needs, by his apparent unawareness that the anniversary of Rosalind's birth also commemorated a special moment in their relationship. The nightmare of Agatha's childhood had become a reality. Archie was the Gunman.

After Archie Christie fell in love with Nancy Neele, he seems to have demonstrated the same determination to have his way as when he sought the hand of Agatha Miller in 1913-1914. The startling otherness which had aroused Agatha's romantic and passionate devotion revealed itself to her now in 1926 as a man's petty absorption in his own desires. Agatha's portrait of Archie at this period is devastating. It is also necessarily one-sided and shaped by the writer's disillusion and resentment. One of the twentieth century's most expert writers of dramatic dialogue is at work here, crucifying her husband with words that seem to have come from his own mouth — and perhaps did! We do not have his side of the story, and he was not the kind of man who went in for self-analysis or self-exoneration. No doubt Archie Christie was in most of his dealings a decent, jolly, efficient, active, honorable man: he seems to have made his second wife very happy, and she him. Nonetheless, as we read Agatha's portraits of Archie/Dermot and her apparently word-for-word transcriptions of crucial conversations, we are convinced by this portrait of stark egocentricity. "I did tell you once, long ago, that I hate it when people are ill or unhappy — it spoils everything for me." "I can't stand not having what I want, and I can't stand not being happy." And then a fast turn: "Everybody can't be happy — somebody has got to be unhappy."

Archie was prepared for his wife to be unhappy, he expected tears and protestations, but he did not expect opposition. He was taken aback when Agatha fiercely resisted his request for a divorce. She could accept that he no longer loved her, though this was terribly hurtful, but she could not at first believe that he actually planned to abandon Rosalind and herself to marry another woman. Agatha was opposed to divorce on religious grounds, and she also felt it her duty to protect the interests of her child. Christie says that though she could not fight her husband for herself, she found the strength to fight him for Rosalind's sake. She knew how much Archie mattered to their daughter, and so she flatly refused to divorce him.

Agatha seems also to have been outraged by the manner of the divorce Archie was set on — that she should sue him for divorce on the basis of fabricated evidence of adultery, without any mention being made of Miss Neele. In *Unfinished Portrait*, Dermot is outraged when Celia implies that he and Marjorie, the woman he has fallen in love with, are lovers. Marjorie is far too "straight," says Dermot, to have sex with him before marriage. Celia's reaction to Dermot's sexual code is fascinating, and indicates the fundamental difference between Agatha's unorthodoxy — which is yet deeply religious — and Archie's respect for the accepted social mores. "If I loved a man I'd go away with him even if it was wrong. I might take a man from his wife — I don't think I would take a man from his child —

still, one never knows. But I'd do it *honestly*. I'd not skulk in the shadow and let someone else do the dirty work and play safe myself."

Archie Christie was not prepared for his wife's fierce resistance, and he fought back. Despite an initial agreement to try and patch things up with Agatha, Archie continued to see Nancy Neele on weekends at the homes of understanding friends. Rather than play on his wife's continuing love for him and appeal to her compassion (a strategy she says would have worked), he applied increasingly brutal pressure on her to agree to the divorce. The testimony of *Unfinished Portrait* is that the pressure amounted to psychological battering. Christie describes herself, in the character of her heroine Celia, as unable to eat or sleep, hardly able to walk, tortured by neuralgia and earache, and yet refusing steadfastly to agree to the divorce. Whereas before she had been outwardly robust and inwardly malleable, now she was physically weak but psychologically immovable. When her husband accuses her of being a "vulgar, clutching woman" who should be ashamed of her behavior, she seems outwardly untouched, though inwardly she bleeds at his cruelty and betrayal. Soon, Celia begins to feel she is going mad. She wakes up at night in panic, convinced that her husband is trying to poison her. As she locks up the weed killer kept in the gardening shed, Celia says to herself, "That isn't quite sane — I mustn't go mad — I simply mustn't go mad . . ."

Increasingly disturbed, Celia gets up one night and goes out into the rain. She is looking for her mother who is, in fact, dead. She wanders around in more and more distress, unable to remember her mother's name or her own. She stumbles into a ditch, wants to lie down in it, but finds the water too cold. She remembers the Gunman, realizes that Dermot is the Gunman, that he is stalking her down, that she must run and hide. Finally she returns home in crazy panic and is comforted and brought back to normal by her daughter's governess, Miss Hood.

How much of *Unfinished Portrait* is fact and how much fiction? Agatha Christie was the mistress of mystery and an acknowledged expert at dramatic dialogue and incriminating scenes, and it is probable that the events recounted in the novel are extensively dramatized. Some aspects of Celia distinguish her from her creator: Celia does not drive, she is not a detective novelist, she is in general far more depressed, dependent, and melancholic. Nonetheless, much of the detail in the crucial Chapter 18, entitled "Fear," fits Christie's own life. Clearly, Carlo Fisher is the Miss Hood of the novel. The London suburb Celia wanders about in is clearly Sunningdale, the kind of suburban landscape with potting sheds and deep ditches a desperate woman might drown in. Celia's removal of the poison in the potting shed makes much more sense if, like Agatha, she is an expert on murder with an awareness of poisons. Above all, *Unfinished Portrait* has a kind of emotional truth that throws light upon the events of 1926. Celia's physical weakness, her fear that she is going mad, her acts of madness, such as searching at night for a mother who is dead — all point to a state of mind and body that might lead to a state of total amnesia such as Christie's doctors attested she suffered from in December 1926. Mad Celia is fictional, but she is much more help in explaining the events of Agatha Christie's disappearance than the sad and depressed yet rational and normal Agatha we find portrayed in Morgan's account.

Now that the emotional background is in place, let us return to the actual events of 1926. The week before her disappearance, Agatha Christie appeared to be behaving normally. She spent a few days in London, saw her publishers about the still incomplete *Blue Train* manuscript, and, Gwen Robyns reports, bought an extravagant white negligee. On the morning of Friday, December the third, according to a press interview with the Styles maid, Agatha and her husband, who were still inhabiting the same house, had a violent row. This row occurs in Kathleen Tynan's novel, *Agatha*, as well as in the film, but Archie Christie denied to the press that any such scene took place. After lunching alone, Agatha went with Rosalind to visit her mother-in-law, Mrs. Hemsley. In an interview with the *Daily Mail*, Mrs. Hemsley said that Agatha had sung a few songs, joked with Rosalind, complained about her novel — "These rotten plots. Oh, these rotten plots!" — and said she was feeling less depressed. When her mother-in-law commented that Agatha was not wearing her wedding ring, Agatha "sat perfectly still for a some time, gazing into space, and giving an hysterical laugh, turned away and patted Rosalind's head." Agatha left her mother-in-law's about five, and returned home to dine alone, since Carlo had gone out to a dance and Archie was away for the weekend. At 11 p.m., according to Janet Morgan, or at 9:45 p.m. according to the original press reports, she told a servant that she was going out for a drive. She left behind a letter for Carlo Fisher, and possibly one for her husband.

The period between Agatha's departure from her home and her arrival at Waterloo Station early on the following morning is a blank. At about 8 a.m. on Saturday morning,

Agatha's car was found abandoned but unharmed off the road at Newlands Corner. The police report says that Carlo Fisher was alerted at about 11 a.m. to the fact that Agatha's car had been found abandoned. Carlo then telephoned Archie Christie, who was spending the weekend at the home of his friends Mr. and Mrs. F. James of Hurtmore Cottage, Godalming. Nancy Neele was also a houseguest of the Jameses. Press reports indicated that the weekend was planned as a kind of engagement party for Archie and Nancy by their friends the Jameses, though this seems unlikely, since Agatha writes that she only finally and unwillingly agreed to the divorce in the spring or summer of 1927. Newlands Corner is about five miles from Godalming, and at most an hour's drive from Agatha's home in Sunningdale, at the edge of Windsor Great Park. After hearing from the police, Archie immediately returned to Styles, and subsequently was taken by the police back to Newlands Corner to view the car.

Over the next ten days, the police forces of both Surrey and Berkshire concentrated on looking for the missing novelist, alive or dead. The hills around Newlands Corner were carefully searched by police and volunteers, who included Dorothy L. Sayers and her husband. The nearby Silent Pool, which Agatha had featured in one of her novels, was dragged. Press coverage of the Christie disappearance was intense. Reporters besieged Styles, plagued anyone involved in the case for interviews, haunted the police headquarters of two counties, and dogged the steps of those engaged in the investigation. Leading "crime experts" such as the famous detective novelist Edgar Wallace were encouraged to speculate on the case. Wallace analyzed Christie as a brilliant woman intent on "mental reprisal"

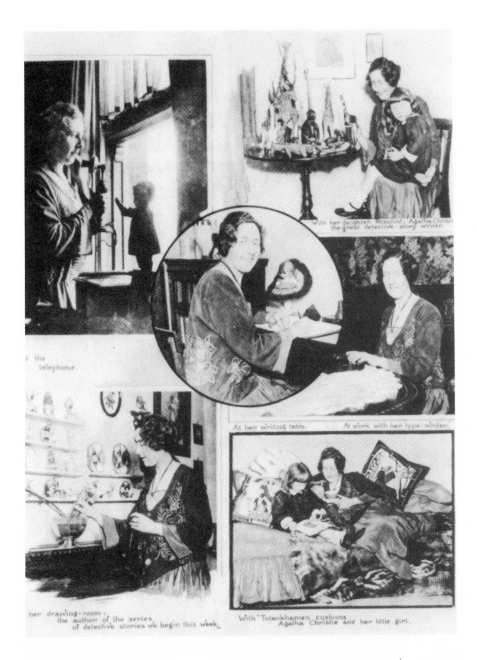

These 1923 pictures show an unusually relaxed and confident Agatha Christie at her Sunningdale home with her daughter Rosalind. (*The Mander and Mitchenson Theatre Collection*)

PUBLIC HUNT FOR MRS. CHRISTIE.

10,000 Motorists to Scour Surrey Downs.

POLICE VIEW.

"Convinced the Missing Novelist is Dead."

To-day the general public are joining in the hunt for the missing woman writer of mystery stories, Mrs. Agatha Christie.

MRS. CHRISTIE disappeared from her home, The Styles, Sunningdale, Berkshire, on the night of last Friday week. Later her abandoned motor-car was discovered in the road near Newlands Corner, a celebrated Surrey beauty spot in the Guildford district.

Police searches have been carried on incessantly ever since. The Downs have been exhaustively explored, ponds have been dragged, and woods combed and recombed in the hope of finding the missing woman. But all to no

Mrs. Agatha Christie—a photograph taken at her home at Sunningdale.

"I felt like a fox, hunted", wrote Christie of the press campaign waged around her disappearance in December 1926. (*The Mander and Mitchenson Theatre Collection*)

The Mallowans at Greenway House in 1952. Agatha's mother had once remarked that Greenway was the most perfect property on the Dart. (*The Mander and Mitchenson Theatre Collection*)

The *Mousetrap* parties were a trial as well as a triumph for Christie, here pictured in 1958 with actress Mary Law. (*Popperfoto*)

The woman and her mysteries at Winterbrook House. Note the modern sculpture on her desk. (*Popperfoto*)

on someone who had hurt her. Who that someone might be was hardly a mystery. The attention of both press and police was by now concentrated on Colonel Christie, who had metamorphosed from grieving husband to suspected adulterer and leading suspect in what many presumed to be a murder case. The press got onto the fact that Archie had been away from home on the fatal night and had been staying at Hurtmore Cottage. Journalists got little out of Mr. and Mrs. James, and there was a report that servants had departed before they could be questioned. There were rumors in the press that Archie had received a telephone call from his wife during dinner on the Friday night and even that he had gone out to meet her. These rumors were denied by the maids at Styles as well as by Mr. James.

Two interesting interviews were given to the press by members of the Christie family during the days Agatha was missing. Increasingly enraged by press insinuations and reporters' attempts to inquire more closely into his activities on the night of December 3-4, Archie told reporters that he doubted that his wife had committed suicide but thought it quite possible that she had deliberately staged a disappearance. Agatha had once claimed that she could successfully do so, and she seemed to be substantiating her claim. Archie was not alone in interpreting the disappearance as an elaborate joke by a past mistress of crime plots. Edgar Wallace came to the same conclusion, as did one of the reporters closest to the case, Ritchie Calder (in later life Lord Ritchie Calder), who was still rejecting the explanation of amnesia in the mid-seventies. Deliberate hoax to get revenge on her husband was the theory the sensationalist press was to adopt for some years after Agatha's reappearance. It was the press's vehement espousal of the hoax theory that sent the novelist into flight in the Canary Islands in February 1927 and, more importantly, occasioned her extreme and lifelong aversion to publicity.

Mrs. Hemsley, Archibald Christie's mother, saw things differently from her son. She seems to have been more cooperative with the press than any other member of the family, and she gave a fascinating interview to a *Daily Mail* reporter. Even though Mrs. Hemsley had not always enjoyed cordial relations with her daughter-in-law, she cast Agatha not as a scheming hoaxer, but as a victim, capable of taking her own life in order to smooth the path of the husband and child she adored. "I am inclined to think that my daughter-in-law planned her end and deliberately drove the car to where it was found. She knew the roads so well and even in the dark she would not lose her way. Although physically strong she could never crank up a car if it had stopped. She was devoted to her husband and child and would never willingly have left them. It is my opinion that in a fit of depression and not knowing where she was going or what she was doing, my daughter-in-law abandoned her car at Newlands Corner and wandered away over the Downs."

These rather scattershot remarks begin to make sense when they are placed in the context of the Christie family situation as known to us today and as known to Mrs. Hemsley in 1926. It seems clear that in the view of Mrs. Hemsley, who suspected a suicide plan, it was not an accident that Agatha Christie, an experienced driver who knew the roads well, went off the road at Newlands Corner, only a few miles from Godalming, where she knew her husband and Miss Neele were staying. Mrs. Hemsley is rather obscure when she says, on the one hand, that Agatha would never *willingly* leave her husband and child and, on the other hand, suspects that Agatha has wandered off to commit suicide and thus leave them forever. The remarks make sense if the situation between the Christies was in fact as Agatha will later describe it in her novel — if, that is, Archie Christie was putting brutal pressure on his wife to divorce him and if Agatha felt Rosalind would be much happier with her father than with her. The portrait of Agatha that her mother-in-law paints is convincing — the portrait of a loving and loyal wife and mother, a habitually rational and competent woman, who is in extreme distress of mind. Loving her daughter, deeply caring for her welfare yet unsure of Rosalind's love for her, Agatha, in her confused and neurotic state, may have felt that she could solve the problem through her own death. If she committed suicide, Archie and his new wife would take care of Rosalind, and the three could live happily ever after. Unable to resolve the problem of her husband's demands and the needs of her child, she determines to kill herself, first unsuccessfully by turning her car off the road down a steep embankment and then by wandering off across the Downs, perhaps in the direction of the Silent Pool she had already mentioned in one of her books.

While the police were beating the bushes, dragging the ponds, and interviewing the many people who claimed to have seen the missing woman, Agatha Christie was living quietly under an assumed name in a hotel in the north of England. Finally, hotel employees recognized "Mrs. Neele" as the missing novelist whose name and picture were plastered over the front pages of most of the dailies.

The police were notified, they called Colonel Christie to Harrogate, and he positively identified his wife.

The next day, the Christies left by the back door of the hotel and, hotly trailed by the press, took the train to Cheshire, where they escaped behind the iron gates of Abney, the home of James and Madge Watts. Two physicians were called in to examine Agatha, and in a special press interview, Archibald Christie stated that his wife had suffered from amnesia and remembered nothing of the events of the previous eleven days. After this interview, Christie's family and friends refused to cooperate at all with the press. At her sister's insistence, Agatha then went for a course of treatment with a London psychiatrist, who helped her to recover her memory of much that she had done in the missing days. Unimpressed by the amnesia story, the press attacked Agatha and her family bitterly for playing an elaborate hoax that had cost the taxpayer thousands of pounds and given police and volunteers hours of needless labor.

What happened on the night of December third and fourth? How did Agatha's car come to be beside the road miles from her home, with her coat and case still inside? How did Agatha get to Harrogate from Newlands Corner, and why did she not come forward and solve the mystery of her disappearance? In the authorized biography, Janet Morgan pictures Agatha on the evening of December third as a woman who has greatly suffered, who feels presently unable to cope with life at home, and who therefore makes a rational decision to get away for awhile. Thus, Agatha packs an overnight bag and leaves one or more letters, "letting her family know her plans." The haphazard nature of her packing and the facts that she takes an expired driving license, that she will leave at least one letter behind, and will later mail a third — these are considered by Morgan as random events, perhaps indicative of distress but of no wider significance.

Carlo Fisher found a letter from her employer when she returned to Styles around midnight on December 3-4. She showed this letter to the police, who perceived it as a suicide letter; she refused to discuss it with the press and much later gave it to Rosalind Hicks. From Morgan's phrasing, it is not clear whether she herself saw this letter or is merely repeating what Rosalind and her husband Anthony remembered of its contents. Morgan does not reproduce the letter for the reader. Part of the letter was a matter of employer-secretary business, asking Miss Fisher to cancel weekend reservations for accommodations in Beverley in Yorkshire that had been made for Agatha. Other parts of the letter were very personal. The letter was "exceedingly distraught," summarizes Morgan, but she adds that the police were quite wrong to conclude from it that Agatha had been suicidal. Its underlying theme was that Agatha had been treated extremely unfairly and needed to get away, but "was still in control of her own fate."

According to the newspapers, Agatha also left behind a letter for Archie, but the police report does not mention it. Campbell Christie, Archie's brother, certainly received a letter from his sister-in-law. The contents of the letter are not known, since Campbell Christie immediately lost it after he read it, though he forwarded to his brother the envelope, which was postmarked London, December 4. This would mean that Agatha put it into the mailbox on Saturday morning before taking the train to Harrogate. This whole business of letters is strangely reminiscent of one of

Agatha Christie's novels, in which textual documents such as letters play an important part. We need a Hercule Poirot on this case, discovering and analyzing documents that he lays before the reader, just as he did in *Styles*!

If we accept Morgan's account, Agatha left Styles late at night, very distressed but perfectly rational. She was going away by herself as life at home was simply too much to cope with. Where she was thinking to go is not known, though, according to the letter to Carlo, she had definitely decided not to go to Beverley as planned. The next hours, after Agatha drives away from Styles, are completely unaccounted for. Morgan has no theory to offer as to what Agatha was doing for some five hours or why, according to one apparently reliable witness, she ended up around six o'clock in the morning at Newlands Corner on the Guildford road. However, we are led to assume that Agatha was still essentially normal until she had an unfortunate accident. Morgan's detailed information about Agatha's car and her examination of the topography of Newlands Corner lead her to reconstruct the accident as follows: Agatha failed to make the complicated gear-change necessary to negotiate a tricky hill, went out of control, and rolled accidentally off the road down a steep embankment, into a quarry. This accident happened, if we are to believe Morgan, because Agatha was not only tired and upset but also a notably poor driver, "taught to drive when no tests were necessary, notoriously unmechanical." This statement about Christie's bad driving does not fit in well with Christie's own lyrical description of how much she loved driving and her car from the very start (cf. Chapter 3, p. 91) or her mother-in-law's comment to the *Daily Mail* about how well Agatha knew the roads around Newlands Corner.

Morgan surmises that although the car itself was essentially undamaged (the police later drove it away apparently without difficulty), Agatha suffered a severe concussion in the accident. This concussion in turn occasioned what Morgan calls an "hysterical fugue." Unable to start her car with the crank, Agatha walked off in a daze, abandoning her overnight bag and, despite the frosty weather, her fur coat. She then either walked or, possibly, took a bus the three miles or so from Newlands Corner to Guildford railway station, where she caught the milk train to London. Morgan writes, "She [Agatha] also recalled that, though she had blood on her face and was dressed only in a skirt and cardigan, no one [in the Waterloo Station buffet] seemed to notice." This memory has a distinctly dreamlike quality about it, and it is interesting to learn that Agatha reconstructed the events of her disappearance under hypnosis while being treated by a London psychiatrist.

In London, Agatha purchased a small case, some night things, and a coat, and then took the Pullman train to Harrogate. She chose Harrogate because, in Morgan's view, she had wanted to visit Beverley, also in Yorkshire, and may also have been influenced by the British Rail posters urging people to visit the Harrogate spa. In Harrogate, Christie took a small room at a large, conservative, and exclusive hotel, the Harrogate Hydropathic, registering under the name of Mrs. Teresa Neele of Cape Town. For the next ten days, she lived a very quiet life, breakfasting in bed, shopping, reading the newspapers, doing crosswords, and playing bridge in the evenings before retiring early. Christie was not short of money because she had "several hundred pounds in a money belt concealed around her waist." Morgan accounts for this large sum of money by the fact that Auntie-Grannie had always advised Agatha to keep money by her in case of emergency.

The interpretation of concussion-fugue is made on the basis of (a) Agatha's general state of distress in 1926; (b) the Harley Street psychiatrist's *post hoc* diagnosis that some trauma probably occurred to trigger amnesia; (c) Agatha's memory of the blood on her face; (d) the Hydropathic Hotel chambermaid's testimony that "Mrs. Neele" on the first days in Harrogate covered her face with her hand when the maid came into the room, which could indicate possible bruises or abrasions; (e) Morgan's own inspection of the Newlands Corner hill. How well does a diagnosis of "hysterical fugue" account for the facts of the case? To answer this question, we need first to have some good definition of "fugue."

A fugue is an extreme unconscious reaction to a situation someone cannot cope with consciously. Fugues, "wandering states followed by amnesia," were reported by the great nineteenth-century neurologists Charcot, Raymond, and Janet. According to historian of psychiatry Henri Ellenberger, fugues can be epileptic, traumatic, that is, occasioned by some external physical cause, such as a blow to the head, or hysterical, that is occasioned by long-term, essentially internal stress. A fugue is hysterical in that the patient enacts with the body such strong emotional responses as opposition, protest, retaliation, and punishment which he or she cannot express directly. Patients enacting a fugue have been known to disappear for days or months, sometimes going as far as from Europe to Australia. They appear to act normally, but in fact their actions are cut off from the continuity of consciousness. When, as usually happens, they suddenly return to themselves, they seem utterly unaware of what they have done during the period of fugue. Raymond and Janet note that the appearance and disappearance of the fugue state curiously responded to certain needs and demands in the patient's life. The fugue was also usually undertaken when the patient was in possession of a sum of money which permitted him or her to get away from a situation that had become irksome.

Agatha Christie was to present an exemplary case of mixed traumatic and hysterical fugue in *Giants' Bread*, a novel drafted, according to Morgan, in 1928 and published as the first Mary Westmacott book in 1930. Christie endows her male protagonist Vernon Deyre with much of her own childhood experience, and Vernon's love of music and of his family home are deeply illuminating about Christie's own feelings. After years in a Russian POW camp during the First World War, Vernon makes his way toward his beloved home, Abbots Puissants, and his adored wife Nell. By chance, he discovers that he has been officially listed as dead and that his wife has remarried, and is now living at Abbots Puissants, which she inherited, with her wealthy second husband. Stumbling out into the night in shock from the news, Deyre is knocked over by a car. He then adopts a wholly new identity and personality and lives for the next several years as a chauffeur with no conscious memory of the past. It should be stressed that Deyre's amnesiac fugue is both traumatic and hysterical in origin. When the fugue begins, he is in very poor physical shape; he is then knocked out by a car, but he also has very good reasons for not wanting to remember who he is or to return to his old life. Finally, Deyre is recognized not by his wife Nell, who is far from anxious to have him come back to life, but by his former lover Jane Harding. Treatment by an enlightened psychiatrist enables Vernon to regain his memory.

As Christie's presentation of Vernon Deyre indicates, amnesiac fugue is a very desperate state indeed. If we turn back to *Unfinished Portrait*, we find that the heroine Celia, who up to this point has been accepted by all commentators as Agatha Christie's self-portrait, is in just such despair. Following her mother's death and her husband's sudden request for a divorce, Celia has for some months been in a worsening state of distress that is close to madness. Then one day her husband subjects her to another barrage of invective on the subject of the divorce. Unable to contemplate any more abuse, at the end of her tether physically and mentally, Celia assures Dermot that when he returns from a two-day absence from home, "You won't find me here." By this, Celia means that she intends to kill herself. Dermot's verbal response indicates only that he assumes that she too is going away. However, from a flicker in his eyes, Celia is sure that her husband knows she will seek a solution in death.

Celia does not think Dermot is a bloodthirsty sadist. She knows that he would infinitely prefer it if she took the rational course and agreed to the divorce on his terms. However, she also knows that he will not prevent a suicide that facilitates his comfort and promotes his happiness. His very peace of mind will require him to deceive himself into believing that he was in no way responsible for her death. Chilled by this final proof of her husband's indifference to her, no longer even able to worry about her child, overcome by her own agony and her longing to escape, Celia jumps off a bridge into the river.

Agatha Christie did not attempt to kill herself by jumping off a bridge, but is Celia's suicide attempt a more than usually veiled account of Christie's acts and emotions on the night of December 3-4, 1926? It seems likely that in 1926 Agatha Christie went into a state of melancholia following the death of her mother and that this state was exacerbated by her husband's demand for a divorce and later harassment, that she experienced a severe mental breakdown so that she may even have tried to take her own life during the early morning of December 4. She then went into hysterical fugue, adopting a new identity in a new place, behaving with apparent normality but cut off from knowledge of her habitual identity and life. She did indeed suffer from amnesia and was not responsible for her acts.

It is not incidental that as a consequence of Agatha's disappearance, her practical, unemotional, self-centered husband endured the kind of emotional stress that she herself had for months been suffering impotently at his hands. Unconsciously or not, Agatha put Archie through hell by disappearing. A habitually quiet, good-natured, rational, compliant, loving wife caused her husband a kind of embarrassment and anxiety which he neither anticipated nor relished. In the eyes of the whole nation, Colonel Christie appeared not in his habitual role as a war hero and sober, God-fearing pillar of the establishment, but as a cold, unfeeling adulterer and probable wife-murderer. What is more, by registering at the Harrogate Hydropathic under the name of Neele, Agatha put onto every front page the name of the woman her husband wished to set in her place, a name he was solicitously trying to keep out of the divorce courts and the press. Agatha's unconscious mind exacted a kind of rough justice that her conscious mind could not sanction.

*

If 1926 had been a year of trauma and defeat, 1927 and 1928 would be years of reconstruction, of increased vitality and creativity. Perhaps the catharsis achieved by the fugue itself may have expedited this process. Certainly, Agatha was helped in her recovery by a band of loyal friends, those she lovingly called "The Order of the Faithful Dogs," and by the expert help of a psychiatrist. Christie took charge of her life once again, rejecting the role of victim and neurotic. On the advice of her brother-in-law James Watts and of Carlo Fisher, she accepted at last that Archie would not change his mind and agreed to give him a divorce on his terms. Rosalind, however, was to remain with her.

On April 28, 1928, goes a contemporary news report, "Mrs. Agatha Mary Clarissa Christie, the prominent woman novelist, was granted a decree nisi (a provisional divorce) before Lord Merrivale in the Divorce Court today. She petitioned for the dissolution of her marriage with her husband Colonel Archibald Christie D.S.O. on the ground of his misconduct at the Grosvenor Hotel, Victoria in November last with a woman unknown. There was no defence. The judge, after hearing the hotel evidence, said that Mrs. Christie had made her case. It was difficult to believe that a gallant gentleman would resort to a hotel on various occasions with some unknown woman and commit misconduct to get rid of a marriage which had become distasteful to him, but it had happened in this case. He had no alternative but to pronounce a decree nisi with costs, and he gave Mrs. Christie custody of the child."

Christie says in her autobiography that in 1927 she finally accepted that she was a writer, that she had a profession, and that by writing she could earn the money she needed to support herself and her child. Christie was in urgent need of money, since she had been unable to write anything since her mother's death and her small capital had been invested in the purchase of Styles, which Archie was having difficulty selling. Remarks Agatha makes about her "serious financial trouble" suggest that even before her divorce she planned to be financially independent as well as socially separated from her husband, and was not accepting any income from him. Conquering the writer's block that had plagued her in 1926, Agatha grimly completed two potboilers, to bring in some hard cash and keep her name before the public.

The first of these, *The Big Four*, was a novel that cobbled together four short adventures featuring Poirot and Hastings. The book was written in 1927 with the help of her brother-in-law, Campbell Christie, a lasting good friend to Agatha despite the trauma of the divorce but unfortunately no more in tune with Agatha's talents and themes as a writer than Archie had been. In *The Big Four*, Poirot starts hurling poison-gas bombs and falling in love with suspicious Russian countesses, while Hastings becomes almost an heroic character. Christie's own acerbic evaluation of *The Big Four* as "that rotten book" seems quite justified; however, it sold.

The second of these novels of expediency, *The Mystery of the Blue Train*, started in 1925, was completed in the Canary Islands in February 1927, when Agatha, Carlo, and Rosalind went abroad to try to escape the press. Christie never had a good word to say about *The Mystery of the Blue Train*, but it is far more interesting than *The Big Four*; and offers some insight into Christie's mind at the time of writing. Christie's heroine, Katherine Grey of St. Mary Mead, a mousy thirty-three-year-old spinster formed in the

Austen-Brontë school of cultured lady companions, inherits a small fortune from her late employer. She then updates her image with the help of a good couturier, sallies forth to visit aristocratic relatives in the south of France, and ends the novel choosing between the addresses of two dashing gentlemen. A new worldliness about sexual relations creeps gently into Christie's narrative, for example in the character of beautiful, hard-up fifty-year-old Rosalie, Lady Tamplin, who needs money to support her handsome, vacuous, and very young fourth husband. Had Christie started to read Colette? Everything in the plot points to the fact that Derek Kettering has killed his American heiress wife so that he can marry his actress mistress. However, any reader who uses knowledge of Mrs. Christie's recent marital problems and plumps for the husband as the murderer is due for a shock. Even here Agatha Christie's ability to make her readers' own prejudices and false assumptions lead them to the wrong solution does not desert her. Derek Kettering is not the murderer.

Two more rather second-rate and derivative books were published in 1929. *Partners in Crime* revives the Tommy and Tuppence characters first introduced in 1922 and exploits Christie's vast knowledge of contemporary detective fiction by parodying the styles, characters, and plots of some of her fellow writers. *The Seven Dials Mystery* uses Bundle Brent, Lord Caterham, "Codders" Lomax, and Superintendant Battle, whom Christie had used to good effect in *The Secret of Chimneys*. Unfortunately, Christie lets go of her warmly parodic treatment of the Bulldog Drummond and Rudolf Rassendyll traditions of English public school chivalry, and follows in the male tradition of popular writing for most of the book. Bill Eversleigh, the public school moron, is allowed to develop into a John Buchan type of hero — short on words, perhaps a bit slow on the uptake, but athletic, reliable, sure of always coming out on top in the end, and deeply attractive to the hapless heroine. As Bill's star rises, Bundle Brent's will fall. The young lady who had shamelessly ogled Anthony Cade will end up limp and breathless in Bill Eversleigh's strong saving arms. In a feeble, derivative version of the *Scarlet Pimpernel* plot, the silly young English ass turns out to be a dashing hero after all, and the end of *The Seven Dials Mystery* shows that Bundle Brent's efforts at detection have been hopelessly misguided and ineffectual throughout. Only the surprise denouement of the novel reassures us that tough-minded Agatha Christie has not totally caved in to the male myth. She is not after all asking us to accept that the apparently dim and lazy public school men who run Britain are in fact modest Supermen in disguise, and thus constitute the country's best defense against internal sedition and international crisis.

Nothing Christie published in the years 1927 to 1929 came even close to the excellence she had achieved in *The Murder of Roger Ackroyd* or even in her first novel, *The Mysterious Affair at Styles*. Nonetheless, the four novels sold quite well and enabled Christie to purchase a small, narrow, but pleasant house in Chelsea, to send Rosalind to private school, to retain the services of the devoted Carlo, and to regain her sense of achievement and self-esteem. Financially, she was making it on her own.

In September of 1928, Rosalind Christie went off to boarding school at Caledonia in Bexhill, preparatory to the exclusive private school Benenden. Agatha has been faulted as unmaternal in thus sending a nine-year-old away from home, but such an educational policy was now customary in her social class, for girls as well as boys, and Agatha tells us that to go to boarding school was Rosalind's special desire. It may well have been that mother and daughter needed some space between them. Agatha and her old friend from Torquay Eileen Morris visited a large number of schools before narrowing the choice down to two. The interviews with headmistresses and teachers, and Christie's subsequent experience as a parent of a boarding school child, were to prove useful to Christie much later in her work, notably in the 1959 novel *Cat Among the Pigeons*, which is set in a school like Benenden.

With money in the bank, continuing modest success as a crime novelist, and the fabric of her life patched back together, Agatha felt the need to escape England. By the fall of 1928 she was ready for a major change, and decided to go away for several months on her own. This seemed a fairly radical plan both to Christie and to her friends, and it became more radical. At first Christie planned to take the rather safe option of the West Indies and Jamaica. The tickets were bought and the travel arrangements completed when an apparently random dinner-party conversation with a couple who had just returned from Baghdad changed Christie's holiday plans and her life. Inspired by the idea of visiting the Persian Gulf area, Christie canceled all her tropic-island reservations and embarked on the fabled Orient Express from Calais to Istanbul. She planned to stay for some time in Istanbul and Damascus and then to journey across the desert to Baghdad.

At the end of the painful chapter of her autobiography dealing with the end of her first marriage, Agatha Christie sums up her reasons for traveling to the Middle East. This would be her first journey alone, without family and friends. For the first time she would be free to indulge her taste for travel, to do exactly as she chose, and to see how that freedom suited her. As a lifelong lover of dogs, she admits poignantly that up to that point in her life she herself had been like a dog, who waited for its master to go for a walk. "Perhaps," she writes, "I was always going to be like that. I hoped not."

As she set out on her first Middle Eastern journey, Agatha Christie was beginning a new phase in her life. New friends, new homes, new travels, new interests of many kinds lay ahead. There would be a cultural richness very different from the Sunningdale world of stockbroking and golf. Above all, there would be emotional security in a loving companionship of the kind that Agatha had dreamed of in vain with Archie and created between the men and women in her novels such as Tommy and Tuppence Beresford and Anthony Cade and Virginia Revel. More than thirty years of unusual creativity and productiveness in both the novel and the theater lay ahead. Just as Archie Christie had forced Agatha to learn to drive quickly because he needed a ride to work and wanted her to be independent of him, so Archie's decision to leave Agatha obliged her to construct a new, and better, life without him.

Nonetheless, despite all that she suffered during her first marriage, Agatha Christie never says that she regrets marrying Archibald Christie. Certainly she says that she would have been happier had she never met Archie but followed through on her engagement to that agreeable and devoted childhood friend Reggie Lucy. Nonetheless, even in sad retrospect, Christie accepted that she had actively rejected Reggie in favor of Archie, that she had wanted Archie, and that she had got him. She accepted both her desire and its sad outcome. As one of Christie's characters notes, rather obscurely in the context, "It's never a mistake to marry a man you want to marry — even if you regret it." Agatha regretted not her love for Archie, but what Archie had done with her love, and ultimately his actions were his own to answer for and live with, not hers.

CHAPTER
FIVE

Mrs. Mallowan
Last Trump for Skaitana

Agatha Christie visited the Middle East for the first time in the late fall of 1928. A highlight of her trip was a visit to the renowned excavations at Ur led by the English archeologist Leonard Woolley. To be invited to stay at an excavation site was quite an honor, since visitors were habitually regarded as nuisances by the working archeologists. Agatha was given the VIP treatment largely because Katherine Woolley, Leonard's wife, had greatly enjoyed reading *The Murder of Roger Ackroyd*. Agatha proved to be a model guest, interested in everything and getting in no one's way. Journeying abroad, for all the problems with travel sickness, fleas, and importunate British ladies, eager to advise, proved to be as delightful as Agatha had hoped. She became a new person, leaving the problems and the pain of the old one behind in foggy England.

In early 1930 she went again to Baghdad and on to Ur, where this time she met Woolley's young assistant, Max Mallowan, who had by chance been absent on her previous visit. Mallowan was quiet and serious and had the enviable talent of getting on well with everyone. The eldest son of an Austrian industrialist father and a French mother who had both emigrated to Great Britain, Max had been educated at Lancing and New College, Oxford. Despite taking only a second-class degree in classics, Max was an excellent classicist, with a deep love of ancient languages and literatures. He also spoke several modern languages fluently. After taking his B.A., the twenty-one-year-old Max was taken on as an assistant by Leonard Woolley, and he soon showed great talent for archeological field work. Max picked up Arabic fast, organized the Arab work force to everyone's satisfaction, and was a tireless worker. Perhaps most important of all, Max succeeded at Ur because he always managed to keep on the right side of his boss's wife. Katherine Woolley was a charming, creative, but imperious woman who ruled with an iron hand her husband and all his archeological associates. She found Max's efficient deference charming, and Leonard considered Max the perfect assistant.

When the dig party was breaking up for the season in the early spring of 1930, Katherine Woolley informed Agatha Christie that she was asking Max Mallowan to take Agatha on a tour of Nejev, Kerbala, and Nippur, the principal sights of the region around Ur, on the way back to Baghdad. Faced with what amounted to a royal decree, Agatha could only assent, though she felt some compunction about imposing upon a young man whom she barely knew who was due for some leave and time to himself, away from the exigencies of memsahibs. Life in the Middle Eastern desert was conducive to intimacy, and as they rattled and crashed about the countryside, Agatha and Max, accompanied by a local driver, soon found all their natural reserve and inhibition crumbling. Although the long hours of desert driving were hot and tiring, Agatha seems already to have loved the Arabian landscape, and she responded with enthusiasm to Max's expert talks on the sites. She was enchanted by the beauty of the pottery shards to be found on the surface of different "tells" (artificial mounds) and made a large amateur collection.

One evening was spent in a police post, and Agatha was obliged to summon Max to the prison cell she was sleeping in so that he might lead her through the darkness to the privy. On another day, coming upon a beautiful desert lake, Agatha and Max yielded to temptation and swam, clad decorously but unconventionally in their spare underwear. When, following the swim, it was discovered that the car had sunk into the sand and could not be moved, Agatha went to sleep in the shade of the car until the problem was resolved. Apparently this calm acceptance of events and failure to fuss and get in the way were perceived as a miracle of female cooperation, and Max decided on the spot that Agatha was the woman for him. Eventually the driver, a member of the Camel Corps, went off to get help and fortunately encountered a Model T Ford full of tourists. Agatha and Max were rescued from a possible one- or two-day wait in the desert, with very little water.

In Baghdad Max and Agatha rejoined the Woolleys, and over the next few weeks they all traveled back to Athens by train and boat via Kirkuk, Mosul, and Aleppo. Despite the despotic conduct of Katherine Woolley, who always insisted on having the first bath even if it had been run by someone else, and the best bed, even if it meant Agatha and Max's sharing the same room, this journey was a delightful one. The pleasure culminated in an afternoon on the beach at Mersin, where Max and Agatha bathed in the warm sea and Max hung giant daisy chains of wild marigolds around Agatha's neck. The party was scheduled to break up in Athens, with Agatha continuing with the Woolleys to Delphi and Max going off alone to see the Temple of Apollo at Bassae. However, at Athens Agatha found a series of telegrams from her sister in England, informing her that Rosalind was seriously ill with pneumonia and had been removed from school to Abney. This was before antibiotics, and pneumonia was potentially a killer disease, even among young patients. This was also before commercial air travel, and Agatha could not hope to be home in less than four days.

While Leonard Woolley and Max were out making travel arrangements for her, Agatha severely sprained her ankle in an Athens street, and was unable to walk. This accident gave Max Mallowan the opportunity to cancel his Greek plans and volunteer to accompany Agatha on the train journey home. In her incapacitated state, she was forced to accept Max's help. Despite Agatha's overriding anxiety about her daughter and the painful ankle, the journey on the Orient Express was again a pleasure, offering another excellent opportunity for Max and Agatha to deepen their acquaintance on an intimate yet casual basis. The trip back to England also had its comic moments, as when they managed to miss the train at an Italian station and had to catch up with it in a taxi at vast expense. Agatha was then obliged to hop out of the train at Paris and ignominiously beg Max's mother for an immediate loan to buy her ticket to London. What Mrs. Mallowan thought of this first introduction to her future daughter-in-law is not recorded. In any case, Agatha got back to England to find Rosalind very weak but on the mend.

Habitually, the paths of Agatha Christie and Max Mallowan would not have crossed in England, but before many months had passed, they had met in London, and then Agatha invited Max down to Ashfield to stay. Just as he had monitored her reactions to being marooned in the desert in the boiling sun, so she observed how he coped with a soaking family picnic on Dartmoor and romps with Rosalind and the aggressive little family dog, Peter. At the end of the weekend, Max came into Agatha's bedroom one night, ostensibly to return a book she had lent him but in fact to propose marriage. Christie insists that his proposal took her completely by surprise. "It had never occurred to me that Max and I could be on those terms. We were *friends*. We had become instant and closer friends, it seemed to me, than I and any friend had ever been before."

It took Agatha some time to decide to accept Max's proposal. The problem, quite simply, was that he was fourteen years younger than she. He had in fact been at Oxford with Jack Watts, Madge and James's only child, the nephew Agatha had cradled in her arms and taken swimming on her back! How could Agatha make herself ridiculous and again risk betrayal and unhappiness by marrying a man so much her junior? That Max was also a Catholic and still had his way to make in the world, while Agatha was a devout Anglican and already enjoying what she called the "plutocratic" phase of her career, did not make matters better. Madge Watts, Agatha's sister, did her sisterly duty and expressed the negatives of the proposed match clearly and relentlessly. James Watts was hardly more enthusiastic. Carlo Fisher and her sister, both loyal friends, were willing to back Agatha up in whatever she decided, but neither was urging Agatha to accept. Only eleven-year-old Rosalind, whom Agatha consulted as her "home oracle," was both pragmatic about the general idea of her mother remarrying and happy with the choice of Max as someone who might well prove useful for sailing and tennis, and was acceptable even to the irascible Peter.

Ultimately, Christie refused to worry about the world's disapproval. She listened to Max, believed him when he said that he loved her, that he thought they would suit each other, and that he had given their marriage very serious consideration. Max agreed that marriage would be a risk, but it was one he was very prepared to take if she would. On her part, Agatha gave Max all the practical reasons why they should not marry but never said the one thing that would have deterred him — that she did not love him. In fact, she realized very quickly that "nothing in the world would be as delightful as being married to him." In short, Agatha consulted her own feelings rather than the feelings of those around her and accepted Max's proposal. To escape the press, Agatha and Rosalind went for three weeks with Carlo Fisher and her sister Mary to the Isle of Skye. There the banns announcing the proposed marriage were read, as was customary in the Church of England, on three successive Sundays. Then in September Max traveled up to Scotland for the marriage in St. Columba's church in Edinburgh.

Max Mallowan was not the only man who courted Agatha Christie in 1927 and 1928. At the time of Max's proposal, two other, apparently far more suitable men were serious suitors. If her autobiography is to be believed, everywhere Agatha went on her travels, she found a man willing to escort her around a strange town, to help her with traveling problems, and to offer to keep her company at night. Obviously, even in her late thirties she was still a very attractive woman, despite her growing girth. Once, on a ship crossing, presumably on her first journey to or from the Middle East in 1928, Agatha innocently told an Italian gentleman her cabin number, and was indignant when he later appeared at the door, full of amorous intent. She was able to get rid of him at last only by explaining that she was English and "therefore frigid by nature." The incident is funny mainly because the excuse Agatha gave to the Italian was clearly so far from the truth. Agatha was not afraid of sex, or of men as lovers, even though she had quite decided not to live the "gay divorcee" kind of life, if only for the sake of her daughter. She records a conversation with an air force friend in Damascus who was having marital problems similar to her own. He told her that she would not be able to continue living without a man for long, and that she would eventually choose between taking one lover and taking several. Interestingly, Agatha was not shocked by this frankness, but rather recognized its accuracy. A lover — or lovers — might become necessary. What disturbed her about the prospect of new love and possible marriage was not the physical intimacy, but the emotional involvement. "Several lovers could not hurt you. One lover could, but not in the way a husband could. For me, husbands would be out. At the moment all men were out — but that, my air force friend insisted, would not last."

Max Mallowan got through the defenses Agatha erected after her divorce because his youth appeared to disqualify him as a suitor, because he approached her at first as a friend, one of "The Order of the Faithful Dogs," not as a prospective lover or husband. He proved to be someone she could rely on in time of trouble and someone who appreciated her for what she was — a very successful, independent woman, scarred by the past but nonetheless secure in her identity, dedicated to her calling as a writer, and confident of the future. Max and Agatha were very different, but their temperaments meshed, and Agatha felt at home with Max as she had not felt with even her close friends in the past. A shared life with her husband as lover, social companion, and economic partner was perhaps what Agatha remembered most fondly from the pioneer years of her first marriage, and companionship, based on a deep compatibility of body and mind, was at the heart of the Christie-Mallowan relationship.

Theirs was to be a very modern marriage. Both partners had well-developed independent personalities, interests, schedules, and projects, and a strong professional and cultural identity was part of the appeal each had for the other. Whereas after four or five years of marriage, Archie Christie had retreated into the traditional English male enclaves of City brokerage and golf, Max urged Agatha to share in his life as a practicing archeologist, and was overjoyed to find in her the seeds of a passionate love of ancient cultures comparable to his own. Furthermore, Max was not threatened by Agatha's international fame as a crime novelist and felt comfortable in the world of writers and publishers.

The Mallowans' honeymoon in Greece offers a good illustration of the way their marriage would work. It had little in common with the traditional relaxing two weeks in a Niagara hotel or a Cotswold cottage. Max organized for his new wife a fascinating introduction to the rapture and pain, scholarship and hedonism which for him were normal life outside of the British Isles. Skinnydipping in the sea at Dubrovnik and lyrical walks among the sacred groves of Olympia contrasted with long rides on buses infested with fleas (to whose bites Agatha was strongly allergic) and a fourteen-hour mule trek up and down ravines in the pouring rain which left her, she says, more dead than alive and wondering about the wisdom of marrying this young stalwart.

Despite, or because of, these adventures, Agatha and Max both seem to have been rapturously happy together during their honeymoon. However, all too soon their happiness was scheduled to be put on hold, since Max had promised the Woolleys to return to Iraq in October for his final season at Ur. Katherine Woolley had advised Agatha to wait a few years before marrying Max, and when this suggestion proved unacceptable, Katherine ordered her husband to inform Agatha that she would not be welcome as a guest during the five months of the dig and that her coming to Baghdad in October would equally be frowned at. Even the obliging Max found this interference infuriating, and he planned to join another archeological party the following year. In the meanwhile, his professional career depended to some considerable extent on the good will of Leonard Woolley, and it was not politic to protest too strongly. Therefore the Mallowans planned to end their honeymoon at Athens and take their separate ways, Max to set up the new camp at Ur for the Woolleys, and Agatha to return home to England.

In fact, the leavetaking proved even harder than anticipated, since Agatha indulged in a characteristic orgy of shellfish eating in Athens and contracted severe food poisoning just before Max was due to depart. Apparently, the Greek doctor was amazed and horrified at Max's decision to respect his professional commitment to be in Baghdad by October 15, rather than stay in Athens to nurse his sick wife. Agatha had her tongue firmly in cheek when she exploited this real-life incident in her 1935 novel *Death in the Air/Death in the Clouds*. One Christie character, the young French archeologist Jean Dupont, tells another, Jane Grey, that an Englishman thinks more of his job and even of his sport than of his wife. He knew of one case where a man had actually abandoned his sick wife in a little hotel in Syria and gone off to start work in another country. The English couple considered such barbarous and inhuman behavior quite normal! Dupont's moral is, of course, that the attractive Miss Grey should never marry a compatriot, but look kindly on civilized foreigners — such as himself.

Obviously Agatha did not enjoy being ill and alone in a strange country. Equally obviously she was far from happy to see her new husband leave for five months in Ur, and she resented Katherine Woolley's interference in her life. That resentment found expression in the little anecdote in *Death in the Air/Death in the Clouds* and more dramatically in the 1936 *Murder in Mesopotamia*, where Agatha cheerfully kills off a seductive but impossible archeologist's wife not unlike Katherine Woolley. However, despite her feelings, Agatha also understood Max's position and his dependence, as an ambitious young archeologist, on the established Woolley. Furthermore, she probably realized that Max was in some sense paying her a compliment in treating her not as a helpless female dependent, but as a competent adult who could be trusted to cope alone even in difficult circumstances. Theirs was to be an equal partnership, with each partner helping the other in time of need and also hacking it alone when possible. Agatha knew she could depend on Max to take care of her — he had proved that the previous year in the journey back from Athens. Max would not let her down in a moment of crisis as Archie had done. At the same time, Max did not aspire to a permanent role as knight errant. He loved Agatha not for her weakness and dependence, but for her strength, energy, competence, sparkling good humor, and her calm. She herself was convinced that it was terribly dangerous to love someone because that someone was dependent upon you, and she made this one of the central themes in her later work. By both offering Agatha his own strength when she needed it and by accepting hers when that proved necessary, Max was able doubly to reinforce Agatha's confidence and self-assurance.

1930 to 1939 were years of private happiness and increasing professional achievement for both Agatha and Max. Agatha's niche in publishing was secure in Great Britain, and her popularity was growing throughout the world, especially in the United States. Contemporary lists of the top English detective-story writers regularly included Agatha Christie, and she was asked to take part in several ill-paid but prestigious multiauthored mystery projects, either for broadcast on the BBC or for publication. Christie maintained an excellent relation with her agent Edmund Cork and the house of Collins, and agent and publisher performed an important liaison and courier service for the novelist as she moved around the country and, increasingly, the world.

Regular visits to the Middle East became an important part of Agatha's life. After his final season at Ur in 1930-1931, Max Mallowan signed up with the Campbell

Thompson party that was excavating the ancient Assyrian capital of Ninevah. Thompson was a notoriously stingy Scot, but he at least made no problems about Agatha's accompanying Max on the dig, once she had passed the test of walking for miles across the British countryside in bad weather without complaining. In late 1933, Max was for the first time able to get funding for a very modest archeological party of his own. After an encouraging year at Arpachiyah in Iraq, political difficulties inside Iraq induced Max to look for a suitable site in Syria. From 1935 to 1938, Max made a series of important finds at Chagar Bazar and then at the nearby Tell Brak.

Agatha and Max were both very hard-working. As Max remarked, "There are two sorts of people in the world, ladies and gentlemen, and both work until they drop." Agatha produced book after book, and Max worked endlessly to get funding and to plan and manage the highly complex operations required by archeological field work. He diligently published his findings, crafting a career in a difficult profession and laying the basis of an international reputation. The members of the archeological party Max put together for his excavations were exceptionally talented, and they remained lifelong friends to the Mallowans. The dig architect Robin Macartney made a career as a painter and produced several very successful covers for Agatha's books. Another architect, Guilford Bell, helped Agatha with her house-restoration plans.

Max may have given Agatha a new zest for work, but he was far from unresponsive to the pleasures and luxuries which life with Agatha brought his way. Agatha Christie found enormous pleasure living in a tent in the desert and eating meals cooked in a can over a primus stove, but she also loved gourmet food, sophisticated entertainment, and beautiful homes. The Mallowans took plenty of time out for play, and Agatha's money from detective fiction was used enthusiastically for acquiring property, for lavish entertainment of family and friends, and for travel. In December 1934, Agatha, who already owned several London properties as well as Ashfield, bought Winterbrook House, a fine Georgian property on the river Thames in Wallingford near Oxford. This was a part of the country that Max especially loved, and Winterbrook continued to be home to the Mallowans for the rest of their lives.

An era in Agatha Christie's life ended in October 1938, when she finally sold Ashfield. The house had been invaded by suburbia, there was a mental institution next door, and in many ways neither Ashfield nor Torquay were any longer the places Agatha had known and loved in her childhood. What was more important, Agatha had found her dream house, Greenway, a late-eighteenth-century Georgian house on thirty acres, set on the banks of the Dart estuary. Agatha's mother had always admired it, and when Greenway came on the market for the comparatively reasonable price of 6,000 pounds, Agatha was anxious to buy it and willing to sell even Ashfield to finance the purchase. The restoration of Greenway and its gardens was begun immediately, with the removal of the nineteenth-century additions to the building and the installation of new bathrooms, and it was to absorb much of Agatha's time and money after the war.

Simply owning, managing, and restoring their properties was a major job for the Mallowans, but they spent at least a third of their year abroad. On her journey around the world with Archie Christie in 1922, Agatha had loved the physical challenge, beauty, and excitement of new countries and cultures. Now such international adventures became a regular part of her life as she joined Max's excavation parties at Arpachiyah and Chagar Bazar. The months spent in the Middle East were deeply enjoyable and stimulating to Agatha, but they were also work. The success of an archeologist depends largely on his field work, and Max Mallowan's career was clearly helped by his wife's enthusiasm, energy, independence of spirit, and financial generosity. When she joined the excavation party, Agatha dived into the work, helping wherever possible and making her husband's parties among the most socially harmonious and culinarily pleasant. When Agatha tired of sleeping on a camp bed, getting sand in her hair, and developing endless boring photographs in the fierce heat, she could travel home under her own steam, and always had plenty of projects to keep her busy. Sometimes together, sometimes separately, sometimes with Rosalind, the Mallowans traveled extensively on their way to and from the Middle East, for example to Isfahan and Shiraz in Persia, to Cairo and Luxor in Egypt, to Petra in present-day Jordan, and to the south of the Soviet Union.

The yearly routine of journeying to the desert in the late fall and spring, of summers in Devon, Christmas at Abney, and intermittent sojourns in London and Wallingford, composed a varied and delightful life. Max and Agatha were a singularly loving and harmonious couple, enjoying being together, writing constantly to each other when apart. Their lack of children was a sorrow — Agatha miscarried in the first year of their marriage — but this apart, the Mallowans formed a pattern of marital life that most would envy. This halcyon period was celebrated in *Come, Tell*

Me How You Live, Agatha's highly entertaining account of excavation life with Max during the thirties. The book was started during the thirties, finished during the war with the help of diaries and letters, and published in 1946. *Come, Tell Me How You Live* is a tribute to Syria and Iraq, and to a period which Agatha had deeply appreciated and which she feared had ended with the war. The book was also a delicate and unsentimental homage to her absent husband, who was to spend much of the war far away from Agatha, serving as a civil administrator and magistrate in Egypt and Tripoli. Christie writes movingly of the beauty of the Near East, of the charm, humor, and rugged endurance of its people, and the intensity, hard work, and warm collegiality of archeological life in the field.

As far as Agatha Christie Mallowan herself appears in *Come, Tell Me How You Live*, it is not as the heroine or protagonist of the events described, but as an amused and admiring observer and willing, if inexpert, assistant in the work at hand. Agatha Christie's tone when writing of herself in letters, diaries, and autobiography is habitually comic and self-deprecating, and it is this same tone that prevails in *Come, Tell Me How You Live*. Agatha presents herself in several characteristically unassuming roles — as the middle-class wife intent upon buying sensible hats and lightweight dresses in regrettably large sizes; as the competent excavation photographer laboring long in the Syrian heat in an improvised darkroom tent; as the unflappable archeological assistant with her own techniques for cleaning precious artifacts with face cream; and as social wizard always able to get the best recipes out of local cooks. Agatha's craft of writer is referred to rarely. She talks affectionately of the sturdy typewriter table she insisted on buying on her first visit to Ninevah and of reading *Murder in Mesopotamia* to the members of the dig, but on the whole, the internationally famous persona "Agatha Christie" has been left, thankfully, back home in England. Even the arrival of tourists to take a look at the famous crime novelist is treated as a crazy aberration and a nuisance to the workmen, not as a threat to Agatha's jealously guarded privacy.

Christie's memoirs of digs in the Near East are in fact significant because they indicate a rare willingness to let the public back into her private life. Unlike the *Autobiography*, released for publication after Christie's death, and the fictionalized revelations of *Unfinished Portrait*, written under a carefully guarded pseudonym, *Come, Tell Me How You Live* was published in her lifetime, under her name of Agatha Christie Mallowan, and at her specific request. Christie's publishers were always very resistant to her attempts to write books that were not standard murder mysteries. They used the acute postwar paper shortage as an excuse for their unwillingness to publish *Come, Tell Me How You Live.* Christie was not deceived. She insisted on publication, and was quietly jubilant that all copies of the small printing were sold. Another strong objection came from one of Max's colleagues, who seems to have felt that the book was too irreverent about archeology. Christie's calm resistance to the opinions of publishers and friends is symbolic of the new confidence and security that she had gained at this stage in her life. This same self-confidence generated a veritable explosion of creativity and productiveness during the two decades after Christie's second marriage.

Christie's native energy and zest were released as she

opened up her life to new people, places, and ideas. Between 1930 and 1936, the modest housewife and lowly archeological assistant presented in *Come, Tell Me How You Live* produced no fewer than eleven best-selling novels and four collections of short stories. Also, 1934 saw the first professional production of Christie's play *Black Coffee*, which heralded her entry into a new and spectacularly successful career as playwright. The "sausage machine," as Christie lightly described herself, had now gone into high gear. In one single year, 1935, Christie came up with three innovative and interesting books. At least three novels from the thirties — *Murder on the Orient Express* (1934), *The ABC Murders* (1935), and *Death on the Nile* (1937) — are undisputed classics of the detective genre.

By 1934 Christie was well aware that her books ranked with the great detective works of the past, and she was enjoying her own preeminence. This awareness is apparent in Christie's interest in producing original treatments of classic detective problems such as the locked-room crime (notably in *Murder for Christmas*, 1938) or the mad, serial murderer (in *The ABC Murders* and *Murder in Three Acts/Three Act Tragedy*, both 1935). Even more significant is the increasing self-referentiality of her novels of the thirties, which "quote" and parody not only such worthies as Conan Doyle and Edgar Wallace but also Christie's own earlier work.

Unlike detective-novelist character Ariadne Oliver, who "wrote chatty (if not particularly grammatical) articles on *The Tendency of the Criminal; Famous Crimes Passionnels; Murder for Love, Murder for Gain*," Christie steadfastly refused to write any sustained commentary on the detective genre. However, her mature novels are full of remarks about the craft of detective-story writing. She portrays detective-story writers like herself as zany social outcasts and pokes fun at the stupid errors they make. She even gives solutions to her own earlier works with a recklessness that must have made her publisher shudder. For example, in *Death in the Air/Death in the Clouds*, Japp says, "I've questioned the passengers, too. Everyone can't be lying." Hercule Poirot replies, "In one case I investigated, everyone was." Christie fans young and old easily spot this reference to one of the novelist's most famous plots.

The habit of playful self-referentiality is particularly evident in 1935's *Death in the Air/Death in the Clouds*. This novel is interesting not so much for its solution — a reworking of a Father Brown classic — as for Christie's comic insights into detective fiction. Christie starts out by staging her murder in an up-to-date version of the locked room (an airplane cabin in flight). Then, with unabashed delight, she mixes the new and the hackneyed by laying her victim low with that classic of early crime best-sellers — the venom of a rare South American snake — administered, or so it seems, by means of a thorn from an Indian blowpipe! This blowpipe turned out in fact to be one of Christie's biggest bloopers, since all too many expert fans wrote in to complain that South American Indian blowpipes were far too long to hide in an airplane seat. With characteristic economy, Christie makes the most even of her errors, and in *Mrs. McGinty's Dead*, she allows her alter ego Ariadne Oliver to narrate the blowpipe incident with comically self-deprecating elan.

One of the prime suspects is passenger Daniel Clancy, a well-known detective novelist who, of course, can be counted upon to know all about deadly poisons, South

American snake venom, and blowpipes. Clancy is a male version of Ariadne Oliver, and like Oliver he has many of Christie's own idiosyncrasies. Like his creator, Clancy is both absent-minded and extremely observant, and he is prone to mutter to himself abstractedly and to make cryptic notes on odd scraps of paper. Rather than the apples preferred by Ariadne (at least up to the time of the deadly game of bobbing for apples in *Hallowe'en Party*) and by Christie herself, Clancy is addicted to bananas, and he lives in a chaotic banana-skin-strewn flat. Christie presents Clancy's habitual disorder sympathetically, since she herself seems not to have been guilty of meticulous neatness. Just after she agreed to marry Max Mallowan, she laughingly promised to practice "being tidy tomorrow and punctual the day after."

At the time of the "death in the air," Clancy claims to have been deeply absorbed in the Continental Bradshaw railway guide "dealing with the 19.55 at Tzaribrod" — a direct reference to Christie's earlier masterpiece *Murder on the Orient Express/Murder on the Calais Coach* which Christie throws in for the delectation of her dedicated fans. Clancy has his own unusual solution to the murder on the plane. This involves a girl snake charmer equipped with gas mask and parachute. Poirot greets Clancy's theory with that sardonic "Epatant" which he reserves for some especially, yes, stunning piece of nonsense or mendacity.

Mr. Clancy is used again in the same conversation to throw the spotlight of humor upon a classic narrative dilemma — the very one Wilkie Collins had to solve in *The Moonstone*. In so many novels, the author has to think up some new plausible reason why the idiotic heroine refuses to tell what she knows and thus allows the story to continue for another hundred pages or so. Continuing his critique of the detective genre, Mr. Clancy subsequently remarks to Poirot, "I have my methods, Watson. If you'll excuse me calling you Watson. No offence intended. Interesting, by the way, how the technique of the idiot friend has hung on. Personally, I myself think the Sherlock Holmes stories grossly overrated. The fallacies — the really amazing fallacies that there are in those stories."

Christie's self-confidence is apparent in her mockery of the great Holmes and of the gas-mask-and-parachute school of mystery writers. Her dissatisfaction with the "idiot friend" convention was to find practical confirmation. Christie's own Watson figure, Captain Hastings, narrates half of the 1935 *ABC Murders*, but after this he is sent firmly and definitively back to Dulcie and the South American ranch. Only Poirot's imminent death and his urgent need for his idiot friend's special qualities will bring Hastings back to Europe for *Curtain*.

In Chapter 3 of *The ABC Murders*, Poirot and Hastings are relaxing by the fire and discussing their ideal crime. Hastings plumps for the murder of "some big-wig" in an Edgar Wallace-style plot involving beautiful girls, curiously twisted daggers, and a damn fool of a detective. Poirot opts instead for "a very simple crime . . . very intime." He imagines four people sitting down to play bridge, while a fifth sits nearby close to the fire. At some point in the game, the player who is "dummy" gets up and murders the man in the chair. Intent upon the game, the other three players notice nothing amiss. "Ah, there would be a crime for you. *Which of the four was it?*"

Hastings is not impressed by his friend's perfect crime — "Well, I can't see *any* excitement in that!" he remarks indignantly — but this intimate set-up for murder is precisely the one which Christie lays before the reader in her next novel, *Cards on the Table*. She is gambling that this simple crime will appeal to aficionados of the detective genre, to those readers who do not have the "melodramatic soul" which Poirot derides in Hastings. *Cards on the Table* is not one of Christie's most famous novels, but it was one of her personal favorites, and it is a detective novelist's detective novel. In this book, Christie sets out technical rules for a narrative game of such difficulty that only the most brilliant writer — herself — can come out a winner. In *Cards on the Table*, Christie has all her wits about her, and she challenges the Actively Detecting Reader to keep up with her.

The novel begins with a highly unusual "Foreword by the Author" in which Christie takes issue with the commonly held view that the murderer should turn out in the end to be "the least likely person" involved in the crime and thus the person the reader is least likely to suspect. Christie writes in her characteristic almost telegraphic style, with its fondness for dashes. "There is an idea prevalent that a detective story is rather like a big race — a number of starters — likely horses and jockeys. 'You pays your money and you takes your choice!' The favourite is by common consent the opposite of a favourite on the race course." Her novel, Christie firmly assures her readers, will not be like this. Four suspects and only four will be presented, each of whom has not only the opportunity for murder but also the motive and an established track record as murderer.

Christie's eagerness to address the reader directly at the beginning of *Cards on the Table* indicates the special interest she has in this particular novel, and her anxiety for the public to appreciate it. It rankles with Christie that she is being associated with the "least likely" school of detective writers, and she is determined to rebut the charge. Christie defines the "least likely" strategy to mean that an author chooses as murderer the person who has least involvement in, and motivation for, the crime. A classic illustration of such a narrative strategy would be a story based on the old comedian's chestnut, "The butler did it." In the traditional country-house crime with its upper-class victim, the butler would be considered to have no motive, since, by definition, he cannot be the victim's heir, spouse, or lover. What is more, as a member of the lower classes, the butler is invisible to family members, guests, amateur sleuths — and upper-middle-class readers — and is therefore someone we are unlikely to suspect.

Christie is right in asserting that she is not guilty of resorting to the least-likely-suspect technique to achieve a surprise ending. She never keeps her readers in suspense for 200 pages only to cop out at the end by pinning the crime on a person whose motivation has been left wholly obscure. She does not choose her murderers among persons such as blacks, Jews, sexual deviants, or uneducated workmen who according to cultural stereotypes are supposedly predisposed to crime and hence become socially acceptable candidates for arrest, punishment, and even execution. In two of Christie's novels, a butler and a maid do indeed commit murder, and do in fact fail to arouse our suspicions largely because they never even make the reader's list of possible suspects. However, Christie's butler is not really a butler, but a rich gentleman actor playing the part — and some of the piquancy of the impersonation rests on the old "the butler did it" joke. The maid is acting as the cat's paw of another, highly motivated and "likely" public school product, and she has no suspicion of what she is doing.

Christie differs from, for example, Sayers since in her murder mysteries a range of mainly normal and well-motivated suspects are introduced from among whom the reader will by some authorial sleight of hand, choose the wrong one. In the image Christie chooses in her Foreword, the "winner" (or murderer) in one of her novels would never be an outsider, and the reader would never have to defy reason and "horse sense" to come up with a winner. Christie's art will consist in lining the horses up at the post, accurately listing their pedigrees and track records, and then letting the punting reader consistently bet on an outsider — only to watch the favorite romp home first past the post.

All Christie's ingenuity will go into devising variations on two basic plots. In the first, the prime suspect — the person who stands to gain most — has an apparently iron-clad alibi for a murder he or she in fact committed. In the second, a number of persons have excellent reasons to wish the victim dead, and no convincing alibi, and are thus equally likely murderers. *The Mysterious Affair at Styles* is an excellent example of the first plot: Alfred Inglethorp is by far the "most likely" suspect in the murder of his rich, elderly wife, but initial investigation seems to prove that he is the one person who could not have committed the crime. *Cards on the Table* is an excellent example of the second plot. We are informed authoritatively that either Dr. Roberts, Miss Meredith, Mrs. Lorrimer or Major Despard murdered Mr. Shaitana. We are told that all four have already committed murder without arousing suspicion, and that Mr. Shaitana knows this and has begun to flaunt his knowledge openly. All, therefore, have a motive for murdering Shaitana. The only question that remains, as Christie says in her Foreword, is which of the four is it?

As its name suggests, the novel *Cards on the Table* centers on a game — the game of bridge, which was immensely popular among the people of Agatha Christie's class and which is still a favorite, I should guess, with her readership. Bridge was just one of the games with which the British leisured classes occupied their time. As war, tournaments, and hunting receded from their everyday sporting experience, at least within their own isles, the idle Brits devoted their time and energies to cricket, golf, tennis, croquet, sailing, riding, and polo outside, and to billiards, whist, and bridge inside. Agatha Christie was too poor as a young girl to own her own horse, though she loved to ride sidesaddle, and she was unable to enjoy either flying or sailing because of extreme motion sickness. Nonetheless she was typical of her class and generation in her enthusiasm for sports and games of many kinds. Christie enjoyed swimming with a passion worthy of Lord Byron, played social tennis well into old age, and even liked golf until Archie became a links addict. She was, furthermore, an excellent card player and a devotee of the redoubtable cryptic crosswords and mathematical puzzles which the better British newspapers still offer their readers every day.

In many ways, Christie's approach to writing a detective novel had more to do with gamesmanship and problem-solving than with fictional verisimilitude and literary inspiration. Her characters are not so much imaginary human beings as they are game pieces to be moved across a textual board in a sequence of choices controlled by an elaborate set of rules. The structural constraints of a game and its economical elegance, the ordered sequence of moves that develops, delighted an essential part of Agatha Christie. She would have made a first-class computer hacker. Christie's ability to create a narrative that satisfies the same kind of problem-solving instinct in her readers is one of the major keys to her success as a detective novelist, and it is showcased in the murderous bridge game of *Cards on the Table.*

In *Cards on the Table*, Christie's plot and her cast of characters are set up by the structure of the game of bridge. Mr. Shaitana invites to dinner four persons, each of whom he believes on strong evidence to have already committed at least one murder. To match his four putative murderers, he also invites four persons associated with the world of detection, Hercule Poirot, the famous private detective, Superintendant Battle of Scotland Yard, Colonel Race of Military Intelligence, and Ariadne Oliver, the famous detective novelist. After dinner Shaitana sets up two bridge tables in two rooms, one table for the murderers and one for the sleuths. Shaitana chooses to sit by the fire close to the murderers' table, and at some point in the evening he is murdered. No one enters or leaves the room, the bridge party continues uninterruptedly, and it is certain that the murderer is one of the four bridge players in the room.

The opportunity to kill arises only as a result of an unusual feature of bridge. In contrast to other card games, during each hand of bridge, one player is "dummy," laying down his cards for his partner to play and, thus becoming free to move about the room. Had Shaitana proposed whist, poker, canasta, or Mah-Jong to his guests as after-dinner entertainment, he could not have been stabbed to death by the fire. Bridge has two further particularities that set up the structure of the murder of Mr. Shaitana and of the novel. First, a player's individual ability is peculiarly determinative of the course of play and can to a considerable extent overcome the luck of the deal. Second, bridge requires a complex system of written scoring.

In bridge, players are not as dependent upon the strength of the cards in their hands, or point count, as they are in simpler games. During the introductory bidding sequence, an expert player can direct the course of play and win a game against the odds. The murderer, Dr. Roberts, a shrewd, aggressive, and experienced bridge player, uses the structure of the game to create an opportunity for murder. When the right combination of cards comes his way, he exploits to the full a hand which will make him dummy and thus free to walk behind the cabinet that separates the players from the fire. Roberts makes himself an alibi drink, picks up the razor-sharp curio knife he has remarked on the nearby table, kills the sleeping Shaitana, and returns to the bridge table. While Roberts is thus occupied, the attentions of the other three players are fully engaged in an extremely exciting and difficult hand. Roberts has bid a highly audacious contract of seven diamonds, a grand-slam contract which the other team promptly doubles. Mrs. Lorrimer, Roberts's partner, an expert and passionately interested bridge player, has a slim but fascinating chance of making the grand slam. The defending pair, Miss Meredith and Major Despard, stand an excellent chance of defeating the contract they have doubled, provided they give all of their minds to the game. The risk Roberts takes in bidding seven diamonds, which will bring him either high gains or high losses, mirrors the risk he takes in thrusting a knife into the heart of a man sitting only yards away from three other persons.

The second particularity of bridge is that the game requires careful scorekeeping. The score card reproduces the course of every hand played, recording who played with whom, who won and who went down, and by how many points. The unusual and successful contract of seven diamonds doubled, made by the Lorrimer-Roberts partnership, is thus recorded by Miss Meredith, who acts as scorekeeper for that "rubber," or series of games. From the outset, the detective strategy pursued by Hercule Poirot centers on the reading, or exegesis, of the bridge scores. The bare text of the scores is fleshed out in the interviews in which Poirot asks the suspects to comment upon the style and skills of the others and to reconstruct the events at and around the card table. Facsimiles of the bridge scores are included as part of the text of *Cards on the Table*, and Poirot's interviews are conducted verbatim. Thus, the reader, or at least the bridge-playing reader, has the same opportunity as Poirot to deduce how and when the murder was committed, and by whom. The bridge scores in *Cards on the Table* are a superb example of Christie's textual clues. When Christie lays the bridge scores out in front of us, when we find Hercule Poirot carefully explaining that he sees in the scores the essential clue to the character of each of the four suspects, Christie lives up to her own detective-writer rules, throws down a challenge to the reader, and scrupulously "plays fair."

Bridge is a small, intimate game, and *Cards on the Table* is, as Hercule Poirot desired, a very intimate mystery. Apart from the eight bridge-playing dinner guests and the plot catalyst Shaitana, only one other character of more than incidental interest is introduced, Anne Meredith's friend and companion, Rhoda Dawes. One person notable by his absence from this novel is Poirot's chum Captain Hastings. The old-boy badinage and pipe-and-slippers intimacy of the Holmes-Watson archetype never held much appeal for Agatha Christie. She had a distinct preference for mixed company, and was always more interested in exploring relationships between the sexes than within one sex. What is more, there were real problems in presenting novel after novel through the eyes of an "idiot friend." Ultimately, it becomes boring when unperceptive people like Hastings stand between the reader and the protagonists in the story, and Agatha Christie never cared to be either bored or boring.

In the 1926 novel *The Murder of Roger Ackroyd*, Hastings had already been discarded, and the story is told by Sheppard, Ackroyd's doctor and friend whom a mysterious phone call summons to the scene of Ackroyd's murder. In a stunning twist, the novel exploits the advantages of looking at events through the eyes of a character intimately involved in the mystery. In her later years, Christie was to have great success with believable young male narrators like Jerry Burton in 1942's *The Moving Finger* or Charles Hayward in 1949's *Crooked House* whom she endows with her own understated intelligence, quiet humor, courage, and physical attractiveness. Oddly enough, in 1936's *Murder in Mesopotamia*, Christie is much less successful with her female narrator Amy Leatheran, an uninspiringly down-to-earth woman whom Christie seems to have modeled upon Mary Roberts Rinehart's famous nurse detective Miss Pinkerton. Christie also experimented with mixed narrative and diaries à la Wilkie Collins in *The Man in the Brown Suit* (1924) and *The ABC Murders*. Subsequently, however, she seems to have shaken off the influence of her Victorian detective forebears and opted to tell her stories in a very straightforward, unobtrusive form of third-person narration.

Thus, *Cards on the Table* can begin with an economically dramatic meeting between our by now beloved sleuth Hercule Poirot and Mr. Shaitana, a rich, foreign gentleman whom Poirot knows and whose moustache he evaluates competitively.

"'My dear M. Poirot!'

"It was a soft purring voice — a voice used deliberately as an instrument — nothing impulsive or unpremeditated about it.

"Hercule Poirot swung round.

"He bowed.

"He shook hands ceremoniously.

"There was something in his eye that was unusual. One would have said that this chance encounter awakened in him an emotion that he seldom had occasion to feel.

"'My dear Mr. Shaitana,' he said.

"They both paused. They were like duellists *en garde*.

"Around them a well-dressed languid London crowd eddied mildly. Voices drawled or murmured.

"'Darling — exquisite!'"

(Opening to Chapter 1 of *Cards on the Table*) No third person needs to witness this meeting but the writer and we readers. The words said are recorded directly, the situation is succinctly established, the tone of Mr. Shaitana's voice is evaluated by the author-narrator. No dulling Watsonian screen is interposed between ourselves and the story, and, for the first time, we reach directly, though only for a brief instant, into the mind of Hercule Poirot.

Poirot does not like Shaitana. We readers also tend to dislike him, since Shaitana epitomizes the kind of exotic, alien, nonpukka, Dr. No character that British popular writers have enjoyed casting as villain. Our reader prejudices seem at first to be confirmed when we learn of Shaitana's "collection" of murderers and his amoral interest in finding out about successful killers who are never brought to trial. In a manner reminiscent of Thomas De Quincey's famous essay on the aesthetics of murder, Shaitana remarks to Poirot that doing anything, even murder, supremely well is its own justification. Instead of being arrested and hanged, "a really successful murderer should be granted a pension out of the public funds and asked out to dinner."

Shaitana seems a thoroughly stereotyped villain, but, interestingly, Christie casts him as victim, not villain. Though so often accused of using cardboard characters, Agatha Christie is in practice far more inclined to subvert the stereotypes invented by her male compatriots than to support them. In Christie's world view and in the world of her fiction, evil is both real and hard to spot. It does not advertise itself with elaborate dinner jackets, sinister moustachios, and wicked repartee. As Poirot remarks, more in sorrow than anger, Mr. Shaitana's cultivated Mephistophelian aura is an "enfantillage." By presuming to set himself up as a man able to control and manipulate the forces of evil, Shaitana in fact merely makes himself into an easy victim.

Placed squarely center stage from the first words of

the novel, Hercule Poirot is a more distinguished, subtle, and varied man than the one presented to us by Captain Hastings, and a more weighty opponent of evil. No longer the poor refugee we met at Styles or the comical cultivator of vegetable marrows of *Ackroyd*, Poirot now appears as a distinguished foreigner of refined tastes, whom it is natural to find at an élite charity exhibition of antique snuff boxes. In the chic London haunts of rich men like Mr. Shaitana, Poirot's impeccable black clothes and patent-leather shoes are proper, his formal manner correct, his foreign accent and mannerisms charming. And of course, Poirot is now in his thirteenth major murder case since settling in England, and has become the defender of national security, the savior of the innocent, and the darling of the popular press. Poirot's vast self-confidence, so often ridiculed by Hastings, now seems deserved rather than vainglorious. It mirrors Poirot's creator's increasing cosmopolitanism and cultural assurance, her new awareness of her own preeminence within the detective genre.

Superintendant Battle, also, has gained in interest as well as in years and rank. The officer first met in *The Secret of Chimneys* had been cast in the solid, stolid, but not unintelligent model of the Victorian Sergeants Cuff, Bucket, and Gryce. *Cards on the Table* allows a more relaxed, humorous, yet still impressive representative of law and order to emerge. Battle is the man officially charged with the investigation of Mr. Shaitana's murder, but he has none of the rigidity and silliness of Conan Doyle's Japp. Battle welcomes not only the help of fellow law officer Colonel Race but also the informal aid of crime novelist Ariadne Oliver. Toward Hercule Poirot, Battle always shows an attitude of deference mixed with humor. The two men rejoice in the complementarity of their resources and approaches to crime and in the congeniality of their professional relation.

Throughout her long career, Christie will continue to invest in the legend of the great private detective, but the successes of Poirot and Miss Marple will almost always be achieved through cooperation with the officers charged with the case, not through rivalry or hostility. Christie's policemen may sometimes be cocky, overspecialized, and vulgar like Inspector Crome in *The ABC Murders*, but they are basically efficient and caring, never venal, corrupt, or violent. If it is typical of conservative British middle-class values to trust the police and subscribe to the myth that every citizen can find justice, then Christie can aptly be accused of being a British bourgeois conservative. By the same token, her continuing popularity today among readers young and old, far removed from her in time and space, argues that this myth has not lost its power.

Unlike the theatrically villainous victim Shaitana, Christie's murder suspects appear to be pillars of middle-class male respectability and genteel female distinction: Dr. Roberts, a highly successful doctor of impeccable reputation; Major Despard, an explorer, big-game hunter, and writer in the grand old public school tradition; Mrs. Lorrimer, an elegant, highly intelligent lady of advanced years; Miss Meredith, a sweetly pretty and modest young gentlewoman in slightly distressed circumstances. Who could believe that all of these had already deliberately taken the life of at least one person and that at least one of them had the brutal audacity to steal up on a man sleeping by his own fireside and stab him to death in the presence of three other persons?

With hindsight, it is easy to see that a trail of clues as well as a strong psychological profile should lead the reader infallibly, and at an early stage, to select Dr. Roberts as the murderer of Shaitana. Christie plays impeccably fair with her readers, and yet even when the available suspects have after Mrs. Lorrimer's death been narrowed down to three (or even two, if we accept the evidence of Major Despard's innocence), it is still easy to bet on the wrong horse. Ariadne Oliver's feminist instincts — as well as her comically idiosyncratic dislike for Welshmen — lead her to point to Roberts as the obvious suspect from the start, but of course, the very illogicality and immediateness of Mrs. Oliver's "J'accuse!" is well calculated to make the reader assume that she cannot be right. Roberts is so exactly the bluff, jolly, efficient medical man whom many of us trust with our lives, and the idea that our doctor might use his skills to murder rather than save is a sinister one. Yet, of course, doctors and nurses and even dentists have invaluable expertise and excellent opportunities to kill people without attracting suspicion, as Christie shows us in several of her novels and stories.

Must we accuse Christie of stereotypical class solidarity when she reveals that of the four suspects, one at least, the handsome and dashing Major Despard, is in fact no murderer, whatever Shaitana's informants may have said? No, for as we look through all of Christie's novels, we find that the British officer and gentleman cannot automatically be ruled out of the category of murderer. In one Christie story, a gallant military man uses his legendary expertise with a rifle to shoot his bride and her lover as they embrace in the garden. Another retired major kills his oldest friend, because the latter not only achieved higher rank and a larger fortune but was also better at crossword puzzles.

Major Despard is, in many ways, a reprise of the younger Colonel Race we met in *The Man in the Brown Suit*, a grizzled but still handsome and virile man to whom every woman gives a second glance and who seems as much on the search for the right woman to share his adventures as for the right jungle to explore. Colonel Race and Major Despard come from a long and distinguished literary race which originated, in turn, in such fearless, real-life, stranger-than-fiction English public school adventurers as Sir Richard Burton, master linguist, sexual experimenter par excellence, and translator of *The Arabian Nights*. Murthwaite, the old India hand Wilkie Collins introduces in *The Moonstone*, is a bowdlerized version of Sir Richard Burton and a kind of nineteenth-century predecessor of today's movie hero Indiana Jones. Such men are eagerly welcomed by top hostesses, deft with a dessert fork, handsome in a dinner jacket, able to make excellent drawing-room conversation, and yet most at home in the untamed regions of Africa or Asia or South America, surrounded by admiring natives, faithful dogs, and wild game. Rudyard Kipling, a key popular writer in Christie's youth, is famous for celebrating and elaborating that old English form of "right stuff" associated in Kipling's day with Empire-building. Isak Dinesen and Beryl Markham, two higher-caste women contemporaries of Christie who were also writing in the thirties, both testify in their lives and their works to the exasperating charm exerted by such men and their seductive blend of culture and courage, classic quotations and physical resilience. The ease with which in the film *Out of Africa* an American actor, Robert Redford, could be cast as Denis Finch Hatton, in real life a quintessentially upper-crust Englishman (or indeed the German actor Klaus Maria von Weber could be cast as Danish count Bror Blixen) indicates the durability and international appeal of this aristocratic male type.

Agatha Christie's own susceptibility to the Finch Hatton variety of sex appeal can perhaps be seen in her decision to offer the eligible Despard as hero-husband material to her two attractive young women in *Cards on the Table*, Anne Meredith and Rhoda Dawes. Despard seems to have a difficult time choosing between the two, and even a dedicated Christie specialist will, like Rhoda Dawes's charlady Mrs. Astwell, have trouble deciding which girl he is "sweet on." On the one hand there is Anne, with her wide gray eyes, curly brown hair, and damsel-in-distress manner, and on the other hand the "tall, dark, and vigorous-looking" Rhoda, who has a directness of manner, a social independence, and a private income reminiscent of Charlotte Brontë's Shirley. Rhoda is cast in the same "female adventuress" mold as several other Christie women, such as Anne Bedingfeld of *The Man in the Brown Suit* or Tuppence Beresford. However, as Rhoda herself remarks wistfully, such resilient young women are far from certain of capturing their men in either life or literature. Jo March loses Laurence to little sister Amy, Annie Oakley could not get a man with her gun, and in *The Murder of Roger Ackroyd* the enchantingly pretty but morally weak Flora has irresistible charm for good old Major Blunt, while strong and independent Ursula Bourne has difficulty bringing Ralph Paton up to scratch.

Christie puts the affections of Despard to a dramatic test by forcing him to choose on an impulse which of the two women he will save from death. The very same format with a very different outcome was used in the tragic shipwreck scene of her first Mary Westmacott novel *Giants' Bread*, where Vernon Deyre saves the wrong woman from drowning. In *Cards*, Christie presents us with a tableau vivant emblematic of Rhoda and Anne's contrasting styles and activities. We see a punt moving down the river, with Rhoda perched on the back, pushing vigorously on the punt pole, while Anne lies passively at her feet. Suddenly the two women are thrown into the water; neither can swim, only one can be saved. As Rhoda and Anne both struggle for their lives in the river, we readers stand with Poirot and Battle on the bank, anxiously waiting to see whom Despard will dive in after. Has Despard seen Anne's hand reach up and jerk her unsuspecting friend into the river? Does he still find it impossible to believe that brown curls, "wide, limpid eyes," and girlish shyness can mask a murderous heart?

Unlike almost all her English mystery-writing contemporaries, male and female, Agatha Christie does not assume that murder is essentially a masculine business or that women murderers exude the naked female sexuality loved and feared by the American "hard-boiled" school. She is ready to make the charming Anne Meredith a murderer even though, as Ariadne Oliver remarks in *Cards*, "they [the readers] don't really like the young and beautiful girl to have done it." Moreover, Anne Meredith is not shot dead by the male private eye or turned over to the vengeful hands of law officers intent on maintaining patriarchal order. Providence, not Hercule Poirot or Superintendant Battle, intervenes in the shape of a rocking boat, and Anne Meredith falls out of the punt to die the death she had planned for Rhoda, her loving friend and selfless protector. Meanwhile, Prince Charming, in the sunburned shape of Major Despard, arrives in the nick of time to save Rhoda, and the two live happily ever after. An almost Victorian and melodramatic sense of justice emerges in Christie's resolution of the Anne-Despard-Rhoda love triangle. Nonetheless, by pairing the frank, open, resolute Rhoda with her male counterpart, Despard, Christie is making a statement about equality and compatibility in heterosexual relations that is the antithesis of Victorian. Christie is featuring in her novels the kind of equal relation between husband and wife that she was developing with Max Mallowan.

In Ariadne Oliver, author of such classics as *The Death in the Drain Pipe, The Affair of the Second Goldfish*, and *The Clue of the Candle Wax*, creator of the fabulous Finn Sven Hjerson, Agatha Christie offers a self-parody that is both comical and confident. Oliver is the kind of large, untidy, scatterbrained, middle-aged woman whom society tends to ridicule or ignore and whose professional aspirations were anathema to eminent Victorians like Charles Dickens, W. S. Gilbert, and Conan Doyle. In the fictional world of Agatha Christie, Mrs. Oliver, is not "that singular anomaly, the lady novelist" who finds her place on Koko's list of those who won't be missed in *The Mikado*. Neither is she a Dickensian Mrs. Jellyby who neglects children, home, and husband in favor of her Borrioboolan correspondence. She is, on the contrary, an accepted part of the social and cultural landscape like Roberts the doctor, Battle the policeman, and Despard the soldier.

Mrs. Oliver is funny with her scrambled grammar, her crazy hair styles, her mismatched shoes, her showers of apple cores, and her love of small, low-slung, fast cars apparently at variance with her sex, age, and ample figure.

However, whereas Agatha Christie obviously develops Ariadne Oliver partly as a form of comic relief, she writes the comedy in such a way that we find ourselves laughing *with* Ariadne, rather than at her. A good example of this humor occurs when, in her first conversation with Anne and Rhoda, Mrs. Oliver pooh-poohs the idea that Major Despard may be suffering because he is under suspicion of murdering Shaitana. "'Pah!' said Mrs. Oliver. 'He's a man! I never worry about men. Men can look after themselves. Do it remarkably well, if you ask me. Besides, Major Despard enjoys a dangerous life. He's getting his fun at home instead of on the Irrawaddy — or do I mean the Limpopo? You know what I mean — that yellow African river that men like so much." Just as Poirot has his odd little affectations but is nonetheless the Great Detective, so Ariadne has hers and is nonetheless the Great Detective Novelist. Ariadne is so famous and talented that she can afford to get so enthralled with a new plot line that she forgets to make her appearance as guest of honor at an important literary luncheon.

The humor which Ariadne extracts from her literary trade, with its "untraceable poisons and idiotic police inspectors and girls tied up in cellars with sewer gas or water pouring in (such a troublesome way of killing anyone really)," is produced *by* her, not at her expense, and becomes indeed one aspect of her talent. In her relations with the other characters, Ariadne is as adroit and successful as in the plot lines of her novels. Without ever being less than herself or striving to appear more, Ariadne wins the admiration and confidence of Rhoda, the respect and fear of Anne, and a collegial acceptance from Poirot and even Battle. Why? Because she is able, intelligent, and reliable as well as fun to be with — a good friend and associate who happens to be a woman. The happiness and social confidence that Christie was concurrently enjoying in her professional and private life is amply expressed in the character of Ariadne Oliver.

In a novel of essentially ten characters, it is unusual to have four of the ten be women, and two of those women neither young nor beautiful. Rhoda Dawes can be seen as an established stereotype — the young adventuress beloved of popular story and film. Anne Meredith also appears to be a stereotype, but here the stereotype acts to trip the reader up, since it is inverted for maximum mystery and shock appeal. The damsel in distress is actually a vicious killer. Ariadne Oliver and Mrs. Lorrimer may also now appear to be two more in Agatha Christie's stock cast of characters. However, Christie did not inherit this particular female stereotype, she largely invented it and imposed it upon popular fiction.

Mrs. Lorrimer has none of the comic flakiness of Ariadne Oliver. The fact that we never learn her first name is indicative of the reserved dignity and elegance of her social presence. All of the characters in *Cards on the Table* find Mrs. Lorrimer a charming and yet formidable woman, whose superb bridge skills are indicative of her general intellectual acuity. Major Despard compares Mrs. Lorrimer to "one of my God-fearing aunts." Ariadne Oliver is impressed by Mrs. Lorrimer's powers of survival in the world of competitive bridge, where the very structure of the game sets one partnership to take advantage of the vulnerability of the other. Hercule Poirot holds an extremely high opinion of Mrs. Lorrimer, whom he sums up as the best brain of the four players and the most dominating personality. Possessed of a cool, mathematical brain, Mrs. Lorrimer is capable of murder despite her advanced years. Poirot considers Mrs. Lorrimer an unlikely suspect mainly because so thoroughly rational and efficient a person would be more likely to plan a crime ahead of time rather than act on the spur of the moment, as in the Shaitana murder.

Of all the characters in *Cards on the Table*, Mrs. Lorrimer is the one Agatha Christie invests with the most individuality and invites us most to respect. It is true that Mrs. Lorrimer has killed her husband, but she refuses to confess to Poirot or to offer any reasons or excuses. Christie's habitual spareness of characterization works well here. Mrs. Lorrimer's self-reliance and reserve, her refusal to use idle words to palliate what in Christie's world view is the ultimate sin against God and man — the taking of human life — add to the respect we, with Hercule Poirot, feel for this woman. In the end, Mrs. Lorrimer, as it were, symbolically atones for her past sin by interposing herself between the law and Anne Meredith, and dies at the hands of Roberts. In this way, Christie solves the narrative problem of creating a character who is certainly a murderer in the past as well as an excellent murder suspect in the present, and who yet commands our sympathy. Mrs. Lorrimer is a successful character whose nature, ability, and way of life refute habitual preconceptions of the role of elderly women in our society.

With the youthful Max by her side, Agatha entered into an Indian summer of renewed energy, of enjoyment heightened by an awareness that only experience can bring. The fortieth and fiftieth birthdays that most of us dread came and went, and yet life was, on the whole, better as time marched on. Christie was clear-sighted in her perception of the advantages and opportunities we have when we have passed middle age. She writes of the excitement of finding that life at fifty can mean new challenges as well as a renewal of old pleasures that had been laid aside to accommodate lovers and husbands and children. There are paintings to see, books to read, concerts to attend, journeys to be made, and once past middle age one has the energy, the time, the attention, and the resources to enjoy things as never before. "It is as if a fresh sap of ideas and thoughts was rising in you." This deep, joyful conviction of the new possibilities of life when one is no longer young informed the even, undramatic, yet marvelously full and varied life that Christie was to lead for the rest of her life.

CHAPTER
SIX

Mary Westmacott
Death Comes as the Beginning

The Second World War left few lives in Great Britain untouched. Agatha Christie and Max Mallowan were among the more fortunate of their compatriots, but for them too the years 1940 to 1945 brought sorrow, separation, and material difficulty. Whereas the Mallowans had been almost wholly wrapped up in their own personal and professional concerns during the thirties, in the war years both did what they could to assist the national effort. Both Greenway and Winterbrook House were requisitioned, the London house at 48 Sheffield Terrace, Kensington, which the Mallowans had bought in 1934, was made unsafe by bombing, and so the property-rich Agatha Christie was obliged to spend most of the war years in rented accommodations in the Lawn Road Flats. She chose to live in London, initially to be with Max, who was working at the Air Ministry and trying to get an overseas posting, and later to be close to the center of things. After renewing her training as a dispenser in Torquay, Agatha volunteered to work in the dispensary of University College Hospital. For about three years she put in a regular two full days, three half days, and Saturday mornings, and filled in when other workers were unable to get to the hospital.

Central London was a somewhat dangerous place to live, and Agatha might have taken refuge with friends or relatives in the country. It is true that nowhere in Britain seemed wholly safe from attack. At the beginning of the war, two bombs delivered by a Messerschmidt landed close to Greenway, much to the fascination of a little boy who had been sent by his mother to live with Agatha so that he would be out of danger. Later in the war, Abney, Madge and James Watt's huge house in Cheshire, came under attack by incendiary bombs, one of which was discovered, unexploded, in the center of the billiard room. Nonetheless, Londoners were significantly more at risk than people in other parts of the country, as the mass evacuation of London children indicates. Showing the kind of physical courage she admired in others, Agatha stayed in Hampstead, ignored the air raids, and slept in her bed with a pillow over her face to protect against broken glass, refusing to go down to the shelter. Only when Rosalind and the baby Mathew had to stay with her in London for a few weeks in 1943 did Agatha appear anxious about the danger.

At the beginning of the war, Max Mallowan failed to secure any war work, in part because of his age (he was thirty-five in 1939), in part because his father was Austrian. Inactivity at a time of national emergency was a bitter pill for the patriotic and energetic Max to swallow. He continued to write letters, make calls, and pull every string to ensure he got "a proper job" that used his considerable talents as an administrator and a linguist, particularly an Arabist. At last, Max was sent abroad as a colonial administrator, first to Cairo, where he found his younger brother Cecil, and then to Tripolitania. In certain ways, Max had a not unenjoyable war after 1942. He liked the work and proved good at it, he was at home in the Middle East, and was surrounded by the great antique sites that were his life's passion.

Agatha, living in cold and dangerous London, eating sausages and mash at the stall on the way to work and traveling on crowded, erratic, and unheated trains, often thought with longing of Max with his bungalow by the sea, warm climate, and diet of fresh fish and vegetables. Separated from her husband and missing him deeply, Agatha kept herself very busy. Though all her efforts to get permission to visit Max abroad failed, she seems to have managed quite a lot of travel within Britain. She visited her sister, whose huge house in Cheshire was occupied by the military, checked her own houses in Devon and Berkshire, visited friends in various places, and, especially after the death of Hubert Prichard, Rosalind's husband, spent time with her daughter at the large and at that time dilapidated Prichard estate at Pwllywrach in South Wales. Agatha was increasingly involved in the theater, adapting her works (notably *Ten Little Indians/And Then There Were None*) to the stage, attending rehearsals and first nights, and going to as many other plays as she could. Despite the stringent wartime rationing, Christie and her friends still from time to time managed to pool culinary resources and have a good dinner together, toasting those far away in prewar wine or, in the case of Agatha Christie who hated all alcoholic drinking, plain water. Without Max, the wartime was lonely for Agatha, but there was a strong support group of friends, who all helped each other pull through. A colleague of Max's, professor of Egyptology

Stephen Glanville, spent many hours with Agatha, and found in her a sympathetic companion and loyal friend. It was Glanville who urged Christie to write her ancient Egyptian detective story, *Death Comes as the End*, and gave her the necessary expert information on the period.

Despite all the friends and the visits and the work, Agatha was much alone. She read voraciously, boned up on her algebra for fun, composed a letter to Max every day, and knitted endless warm, woolly garments, but above all she wrote. Between 1939 and 1945 Christie published ten books, wrote two more to put into cold storage — in case a bomb should have her name on it — and wrote and adapted three plays. She used her fiction to shut out the cold and the gloom and the sorrow not only for herself but for the thousands of her readers.

The most intense experience Christie had during the war was perhaps her writing of *Absent in the Spring*, the novel she would publish in 1944 under the Mary Westmacott pseudonym. Christie's description of how she came to write this novel is one of the most enlightening passages about her experience as a writer. The whole fifty-thousand-word novel was written in three days flat. On the third day, the habitually conscientious and reliable Agatha called the hospital with an excuse for not coming to work. She felt the imperative need to finish the book, a book that had been "growing inside" her for a long time. So fearful was she of losing the flow of inspiration that she wrote the last chapter immediately after the first. At the end of it all, Christie was completely exhausted and fell down on her bed to sleep uninterruptedly for some twenty-four hours. When she went back to work, her fellow workers at the hospital commented upon how ill she looked, but despite her weary and haggard appearance, Christie's emotions at that time were of relief and exultation. All the fatigue and effort had been worth it. She had brought her book into the world.

Here is unusual and fascinating testimony to the role of the unconscious in the life of the popular writer. The experience of writing the Westmacotts was for Christie a release, a self-indulgence, a pleasure, that she allowed herself only rarely but could not wholly renounce for more than twenty years. Christie presents the experience of writing *Absent in the Spring* as a kind of literary childbirth. The mixture of exhilaration and exhaustion Christie describes after finishing the book is very much the state of mind of the woman immediately post partum. The traditional and poignant metaphor of literary creation as childbirth was perhaps all the more real to Christie in 1944 because Rosalind had recently given birth, reminding the author of her own experience in pregnancy and labor. Like a mother-to-be, the writer presents herself as intensely involved in her literary labor and yet feeling only partly responsible. The literary child is both herself and another.

In contrast to the organic and sexual imagery she uses about writing *Absent in the Spring*, Christie elsewhere refers to the act of writing her mystery novels as an immense chore, a bore, a painful and uncongenial effort, which she persists in for purely external reasons — to help her mother keep up Ashfield, to support herself and Rosalind after the divorce, to permit the purchase of luxuries and treats. She never satisfactorily explains why, once the material wants that she acknowledges have clearly been met, she should have gone on with what she claims is dry labor. Perhaps the psychological rewards she admits to when writing a Westmacott were not so much absent as deferred when she was hatching a new Poirot or Marple story since the yoking of her fantasy world to the singularly rational, material, cut-and-dried world of the post-Holmesian detective novel was taxing. The inner fantasy world had to fuse with the world of outer reality. Nonetheless, it was the challenge and striving of that fusion which gave birth to the Christie mystery, that marvelous amalgam of fact and fancy, floor plans and fairy tales.

Intense productivity was Christie's way of coping with loneliness and stress during the war, but this explosion of literary products brought little immediate financial reward. The war was a disaster for Christie, since she no longer received any of her increasingly large American royalties, and was yet required by the British authorities to pay taxes on money she had not received. Falling deeper and deeper into debt, Christie thought seriously about selling Greenway, which seemed like a huge and unnecessary extravagance. Fortunately no suitable buyer came forward, and the house was occupied for much of the war by an admiring and respectful group of American naval officers. Christie's agent and publishers could only be happy that their most valuable client was so active, but it was already becoming clear to Christie's family and financial advisers that, from a short-term financial point of view, there would be little profit for her in writing more than one novel per year, since after a certain point all additional earnings were eaten up by taxes.

The saddest part of the war for Agatha Christie came in 1944. Whereas in the First World War, both Agatha's young husband and her brother had come through alive, Rosalind was not to be so fortunate as her mother. News came that her husband Hubert Prichard had been listed as missing in action, and after some weeks of agonizing suspense, a telegram came in August announcing his death. Rosalind was stoical, and Agatha as usual relapsed into silence. Christie writes, "The saddest thing in life and the hardest to live through is the knowledge that there is someone you love very much whom you cannot save from suffering. . . . I thought, I may have been wrong, that the best thing I could do to help Rosalind was to say as little as possible, to go on as usual." The grief for Hubert's death was in some sense balanced, at least for Rosalind, Agatha, and Max, by joy in the life of Mathew, who was born at Abney on September 21, 1942. Mathew was Christie's only grandchild, and he was to play an increasingly large role in her life. During her own pregnancy with Rosalind, Agatha had hoped for a son, and from the start she delighted in Mathew's size and strength and joie de vivre. When in 1949 Rosalind married Anthony Hicks, a man greatly to the taste of both Agatha and Max, the wounds of the war healed over, and a new era of happiness for the Christie-Mallowan-Hicks family was inaugurated.

As for Max and Agatha, after their three-year wartime separation, they appear to have picked up their lives where they left off. Agatha had worried how it would be when Max came back from the war. In 1945 she was fifty-five, gray of hair and stout of waist, and she must have remembered how easily Archie Christie had found a new young love when separated from his wife for only a matter of weeks. As it turned out, when Max stumbled up the stairs to Agatha's Lawn Road flat in Hampstead, as covered with jangling impedimenta as Alice's White Knight, the two fell into each other's arms and ate burned kippers in glorious unity. Max too had gained weight—over twenty pounds! Three years of separation had changed their bodies but not their hearts.

The immediate postwar years showed a slow and laborious return to normal. On Christmas Day, 1946, the Mallowans took possession once more of Greenway from the Admiralty, and found it essentially sound despite the row of fourteen new and superfluous lavatories at the back and the riotous growth of the gardens. Despite his gloomy forebodings, Max Mallowan's career as an archeologist had not been aborted by the war. In 1948, in his newly created position of professor of Western Asiatic archeology at the Institute of Archeology of London University, Max began his life's great work, the excavation of the huge mound of Nimrud in Iraq, site of the ancient city of Calah, military capital of Assyria. The excavation of Nimrud was to take over ten years, and it brought Max Mallowan fame, a knighthood, and the respect of the international archeological community. The Mallowans purchased a comfortable local-style house in Baghdad, and became accustomed, if not resigned, to the prosaic air travel that replaced the romantic world of the Orient Express, small cargo boats, and car rides across the desert.

Agatha continued to write her novels and her plays, though at a slower pace than during the thirties and forties. She often traveled with Max to Nimrud, and she continued to work as excavation photographer as well as help care for the pottery and art objects retrieved from the dig. Her pleasure in cleaning and reconstructing these beautiful artifacts was intense. She delighted in these examples of ancient human creativity, which she saw as mirroring the divine creation. At Nimrud, Agatha petitioned to pay to have a special room built onto the excavation house for her exclusive use. The room was called the "Beit Agatha" (Agatha's house), and a name placard in cuneiform was put on the door. At home in England, Agatha delighted as ever in family and friends, in picnics and elaborate restaurant meals, in tennis games and Wagner operas, in the flowers and fruits of her gardens, the fine silver and glass in her homes. She avoided the press and photographers as much as possible, refused to give interviews or to appear on radio and television programs, and was regularly outraged by what was written about her.

After the war, Agatha's financial situation improved enormously, as the American and British tax authorities reached mutual agreements. Edmund Cork decided that Agatha was being taken for granted too much at Collins and Dodd, Mead, her American publishing house. He negotiated a sharp increase in royalties for his client, and this stirred the publishers to do more promotional work to recoup their expenses. Sales and revenues increased all round. Agatha's plays, which by the 1950s included *The Mousetrap* and *Witness for the Prosecution*, were a whole new source of revenue, and the motion-picture world was beginning to show interest in acquiring film rights. Far from losing its appeal, Agatha's work was reaching out to vast new audiences, and her fame and her wealth increased commensurately. She was a goose who continued to lay golden eggs of increasingly high carat, and her publishers gave her kid-glove treatment, flying special delicacies and copies of *The Times* to Iraq and supplying her and her family with books, elegant private parties, and tickets to special events like the Bayreuth festival and the Oberammergau Passion Play.

*

When Christie began her career in the twenties and thirties, she was just one of the numerous writers associated with the so-called Golden Age of British detective fiction. In the postwar world, however, as the fame of many of Christie's contemporaries waned, she remained popular. In fact, the world she had first created in her novels reached new audiences through the stage, film, and, at last, television. This success, which continues unabated today, points to a deep and remarkable consonance between Christie's world view and that of an enormous public, yet the definition of that world view proves to be enormously difficult.

Christie's continuing success relies to an extreme degree on her ability to hide behind her fictional characters and plots. Unlike most of her male contemporaries and even the later Sayers, Christie does not use her detective novels as a means of biographical exploration, personal analysis, or ideological exegesis. Readers enjoy an Agatha Christie because — not in spite of the fact that — she so rarely says what she thinks, makes general statements, or expounds her ideas about the meaning of life. The very success of Christie's hidden-author strategy means, however, that it is very difficult to establish what it is about her that people find so effortlessly congenial. To understand the meaning of Christie's popularity, we need to be able to define the structures of her imagination, the fantasies she incarnated in her fiction, the value system that she saw as operative — or desirable — in the world. Yet these are precisely what she seeks in her detective fiction to withhold from us.

Solving the mystery of Agatha Christie, in fact, turns out to be less like history than archeology. Instead of simply evaluating the remarks that the author makes to the reader directly in the novels themselves, as is the case even with popular writers such as Edgar Wallace, John Buchan, or Ian Fleming, we have to dig below the surface of Christie's fiction, unearthing structures, extracting small, fragmented objects, and correlating them with others found in other sites.

The archeological methods of researching Agatha Christie's mind can be assisted by the historical — through the Mary Westmacott books. These are works of fiction, but they stand in a very different relation to their author's life and mind than the works published under her own name. They are privileged because written under a pseudonym that the author protected with peculiar zeal. None of Christie's friends was told that she was Mary Westmacott, though one old friend Nan (Watts) Kon guessed the truth from internal evidence. Christie used a further pseudonym, Daniel (first Nathaniel) West, for the Westmacott publishing contracts. When, in 1946, the identity of Mary Westmacott was revealed in an American review article of *Absent in the Spring,* Christie was wounded and outraged. As she was later to remark to her agent, Edmund Cork, "The people I really minded knowing about it were my friends. Cramping to one's subject matter. It's really all washed up . . . An author's wishes should be respected." Through the elaborate self-masking device of Mary Westmacott, Agatha Christie felt free to speak to the reader more directly and openly than anywhere else. The woman who had hated to "part with information" and who had changed herself into the Mistress of Mystery felt an imperative need for at least one outlet for the expression of her own personality, experience, ideas, and emotions.

Just as the first two Westmacott books, *Giants' Bread* and *Unfinished Portrait*, offer the best published testimony to the events and emotions of Christie's childhood, youth, and first marriage, so the best key to her mature years is offered by the four later Westmacotts, most especially *The Rose and the Yew Tree*. This novel was published in 1947 but written before the American reporter uncovered Christie's pseudonym. Max Mallowan gave it as his opinion that *The Rose and the Yew Tree* is "the most powerful and dramatic" of all the Westmacotts, "one in the classical vein . . . and not destined for oblivion." Christie herself testifies to the importance she gave to this novel. As with *Absent in the Spring*, though not quite so imperatively, Christie felt the need to write this book that had been in her mind for years and that she was to entitle *The Rose and the Yew Tree*. She thought books like these were "a must" and that they seemed to come from God and allow the writer to feel something of God's joy in creation. "You have been able to make something that is not yourself."

In *The Rose and the Yew Tree* and to a lesser extent in *The Burden*, Christie made a vital attempt to set down her ideas on life and death, success and failure, love and lust, man and woman, mankind and God. Where the background of Christie's detective plots had been woven of threads from Jane Austen and Charlotte Brontë, Dickens and Trollope, Arthur Conan Doyle and Anna Katharine Green, the plot of *The Rose and the Yew Tree* comes out of Christie's reading of the New Testament, Thomas à Kempis, and T. S. Eliot.

The teller of the tale, the fictional first-person narrator of *The Rose and the Yew Tree*, is Hugh Norreys. His is the voice of the upper-class British male, a kind of modified Major Thompson or Colonel Blimp, with a public school-regimental background and an independent income — from unspecified sources, of course. The voice is a stereotyped one: a thousand books, films, and television shows have taught us how the Hugh Norreys of England dress, where they live, how they clip their vowels, eliminate their "r's," and perhaps even, like Lord Peter Wimsey, drop the final "g's" off present participles. It is a voice Agatha Christie has already used to excellent effect in her first great mystery novel, *The Murder of Roger Ackroyd*, and which she uses again and again, with variations, throughout her career. It is, by definition, not the voice of a woman, since all its markers refer to the male world of Eton, the Guards, the club. It is, thus, not Agatha's voice, but it is a voice she feels comfortable with, whose conventionality she can enjoy, exploit, and, at certain times, subvert.

If, as the narrator of *Unfinished Portrait* remarks, a novelist is God to his characters, Agatha Christie, even at her most personal and explicit, is a *deus absconditus*, a hidden God. In *The Rose and the Yew Tree* as in her mystery novels, Christie reveals herself only at one remove, through the intermediary of a narrative mask. The unusually confessional nature of this book, in comparison with the mysteries, is apparent in the fact that, contrary to her custom, Christie comments on the mask and its implications. She says through the voice of her narrator Hugh Norreys, "I can choose from which angle I will view my life — from the angle of frustration, or as a triumphant chronicle. Both are true. It is, in the end, always a question of selection. There is Hugh Norreys as he sees himself, and Hugh as he appears to others. There must actually be, too, Hugh Norreys as he appears to God. There must be the essential

Hugh. But his story is the story that only the recording angel can write."

Something of the essential Agatha Christie is revealed here. Knowledge of the human being is, in her view, neither the privileged, preverbal self-knowledge — or self-fiction — each of us has of himself or herself and which the unbelievers among us assume will die with our death. Neither is it that locus for the multiple shifting perceptions of others, which continue in our absence or after our death, rather as a text does. Christie maintains a theological perspective, within which each person exists as an ultimate reality in the mind of God and will continue to exist after death. Since this is so, the unknowability of the self to others, of others to the self, and even of the self to the self becomes, perhaps, acceptable. In the words of Thomas à Kempis, whom Christie admired deeply, "You are just what you are, the thing God sees in you — there is no going beyond that."

Intimations of this "essential" self are one of the most important threads in the later Westmacott books. In *Absent in the Spring*, Joan Scudamore, a woman suddenly and unexpectedly deprived of entertainment and occupation, begins to doubt her own identity and the validity of her whole understanding of life. Who is she? Does her family love her? Do they see her as she believes they do, and as she sees herself? Joan begins to sense that the literal desolation of the Iraqi desert that surrounds her replicates the spiritual desolation she has lived in for many years. For a moment she is reluctantly made to see herself as she is, to see the patterns she has forced upon those nearest to her, to recognize the hollowness of her aspirations and achievements, to acknowledge that she lives in hell, in the hell of the loneliness of the self in which other people are "merely projections," in T. S. Eliot's phrase.

Joan Scudamore of *Absent in the Spring* is too weak to build on her moment of self-understanding, but John Gabriel of *The Rose and the Yew Tree* and Llewellyn Knox of *The Burden* are not. Moved by a dissatisfaction and a searching he is unable either to define or to reject, Llewellyn Knox goes into the desert for three weeks, has a series of visions of the future, and returns to civilization convinced that God has chosen him for a special mission. The exact nature of that mission is revealed to him when he attends a revival meeting, stands up to speak as if in a trance, and finds himself greeted as the new great evangelist. Christie makes no attempt to impart any precise theological content to Knox's message, but she makes it clear that she believes in charismatic evangelism, believes that God and man may communicate directly at certain rare moments, and that certain people are chosen by God to speak his word. Knox is an idealistic figure who puts aside all personal desires and ambitions, whose body is almost consumed by his divine mission, and who remains uncorrupted by the commercialism of the modern American evangelical ministry. What Christie tells us about the mystic experience of Joan and of Llewellyn helps us to understand how, in *The Rose and the Yew Tree*, the selfish materialist John Gabriel can metamorphose into Father Clement, a fictional twentieth-century version of St. Dominic or St. Francis of Sales.

Hugh Norreys is the narrator of *The Rose and the Yew Tree*, but as he makes very plain, he is not the protagonist or hero. The book opens in Paris with a framing account of how the middle-aged and somewhat disabled and antisocial narrator is called imperatively to the bedside of Father Clement, a man of whom he has heard much. Norreys discovers that the heroic and saintly father is in fact John Gabriel, an Englishman he knew years earlier and for whom he conceived a passionate dislike and contempt. Norreys arrives at Gabriel's bedside soon enough to hear his final words, the words that end the novel. However, instead of developing the relation between the two men in the Paris present or telling the story of Gabriel's life since the two last parted, Christie takes us back some fifteen years to the time when Norreys and Gabriel met. First, however, Norreys lays down the cross stitch against which the figure of John Gabriel will stand; that is, he tells us about himself and how he came to "know" Gabriel.

The two men first meet in the fictional Cornish seaside town of St. Loo, where Gabriel is running as the Conservative Party candidate in the general election of 1945. The Germans have been defeated, and although there is still fighting in the east, the British servicemen are returning home and the country is turning to the problems of peacetime. Unlike Gabriel, Norreys himself is no longer running for anything, literally or figuratively. He has had a nearly fatal motor accident which has left him crippled, pain-wracked, sexually impotent, and deeply withdrawn and depressed. The depression is all the deeper since, on the morning of the accident, Norreys had been starting out on a new life with Jennifer, the woman he passionately loved. There is a deep irony in the fact that Hugh has returned unscathed from his wartime soldiering only to be crushed and humiliated by a delinquent lorry in the unheroic Harrow Road. Norrey's recuperation has been complicated by his and Jennifer's mutual discovery that in fact they have nothing in common but physical passion. Each was in love with a projection of his or her desire — Hugh's the desire to save and care for someone weaker, Jennifer's the need for someone to respond passionately to her self-perpetuating and not unenjoyable projection of wounded guilt.

Hugh sends Jennifer away and agrees to go down to Cornwall, where his brother Robert and sister-in-law Teresa now live in Polnorth House, the house Teresa has inherited from her aunt. When Hugh comes to Polnorth House, his mind is set on suicide, and he has carefully and, he believes, secretly saved enough sleeping pills to allow him to exit life on his own terms. However, Hugh's hopelessness and longing for swift death are matched by the detached and impassive but relentless will of Teresa, who watches over him and challenges him to find some new meaning in life even if, in the world's view, he is only half a man. Through Teresa, Hugh gets to know the "county" set of St. Loo, in particular the inhabitants of St. Loo Castle — the dowager Lady St. Loo, her widowed sister Lady Tressilian, her widowed sister-in-law, Mrs. Bigham Charteris, and her nineteen-year-old granddaughter, Isabella Charteris. Hugh also finds himself involved in the general-election campaign whereby the Conservative Party — to which the county set inevitably belongs — hopes to regain the seat lost to the Labor Party in the previous election.

Agatha Christie has chosen a very interesting moment to frame the major part of her story in *The Rose and the Yew Tree*, since the 1945 general election was a turning point in modern British history. Winston Churchill, the leader of the Conservative Party, had headed the wartime coalition government and inspired the whole nation through the Second World War. Nonetheless, Churchill and his party were decisively defeated in 1945, and the Labor Party under Clement Attlee was given a mandate to change British society. Christie's prewar interest in politics had been virtually nonexistent, and the fact that even she became interested in electoral issues is in itself a political indicator. As an intelligent but sceptical political neophyte, she offers us in the fictional St. Loo election a surprisingly insightful microcosm of British society at this time. Christie shows us a Conservative Party at a crossroads, deeply uncertain as to the road to take. The traditional equation of political power with high social caste and economic ascendancy no longer holds. The aristocratic and hereditary Conservatism of Lady St. Loo and Lady Tressilian, with its doctrine of noblesse oblige, is as old-fashioned as the dirty but real diamond jewelry that the old ladies like to wear. On the other hand, the slick, efficient party machine, as represented by the lower-middle-class Conservative Party agent Carslake and his wife, is intellectually and morally bankrupt. In such Tory strongholds as St. Loo Castle it is of course inconceivable that "dear Mr. Churchill" may lose, yet even there an unstated agreement exists that for St. Loo a sound but inarticulate candidate of the old school will not do, that something new must be tried.

The St. Loo Conservative Parry establishment has, therefore, mobilized behind the candidacy of John Gabriel, a man who, before the war, would never have entered through the front doors of Tory homes or been received in their drawing rooms. Gabriel is the son of a plumber, a small, dark, sallow man who speaks in the "flat" tones which then clearly labeled persons of the lower social orders. He has, however, one qualiry which Conservatives traditionally find invaluable, and which at the Second World War achieved even greater cachet: he is a twenty-four-carat, one hundred and ten proof, bona fide war hero. Gabriel has been awarded the Victoria Cross, the country's highest honor for valor in action, won by a handful of soldiers usually posthumously! Gabriel is the living symbol of the courage, the *virtus*, that, at least in military mythology, wins wars, and as such he is irresistible to the Tories, and, they hope, to the St. Loo voters.

Just as we saw Christie trying to confront her own racist prejudices in her presentation of Sebastian Levinne in *Giants' Bread*, so in John Gabriel she seems to be trying to say something about class. Critics have ridiculed Christie's unwillingness to portray any characters outside her own middle-class, and have seen the few working-class characters she does include, notably the domestic servants, as exemplifying the author's grotesque class prejudice. The characterization of John Gabriel still manifests the condescending attitudes these critics object to. For example, Christie seems seriously to believe that "gentlemen" have more attractive legs than working-class men, and she builds part of her unfavorable physical comparison between the plebeian Gabriel and the aristocratic Rupert, Lord St. Loo, on the fact that Gabriel has "common legs." Other disquieting examples of Christie's middle-class mythology can be found in the short stories, which tend in general to be less carefully controlled than the novels. For example, in the 1934 Parker Pyne collection, Christie has her sociological Mister Fixit solve the boredom and depression of a rich widow of humble origins by kidnapping her and marooning her on a Cornish farm. Obliged to do hard physical labor,

Mrs. Abner Ryan thrives, makes friends, finds a second husband, and determines at last to hide the bulk of her enormous fortune and spend the rest of her life as a modest farmer's wife. There seems here to be a grating assumption that working-class women are naturally happier slaving on the farm with a somewhat delinquent husband than lounging in a yacht with the smart set at Biarritz.

On the other hand, in two of the Harley Quinn stories as well as, preeminently, in *The Rose and the Yew Tree*, Christie's explicit message is not that the working classes are intrinsically different from and inferior to the bourgeoisie, but that charm, brilliance, talent, charisma, political insight, and spiritual vision are God's gift to individuals regardless of social class. Christie seems convinced that, at least in modern Great Britain, men of the right caliber can rise to positions of power and prestige, however "flat" their accents or "common" their legs. Such belief in the equality of talent and opportunity is perhaps a more salient part of American political ideology than of British, and one is tempted to divine here the influence of Christie's American father, Frederick Alvah Miller. The rags-to-riches myth has perhaps been realized on a larger scale in the U.S.A. than in any other culture, and the Millers had certainly risen far up the social scale.

Christie shows her belief in equal social opportunity in the Harley Quinn story called "The Face of Helen." The narrator, Mr. Satterthwaite, goes to the opera and notices the working-class couple Gillian West and Philip Eastney. As Colin Watson has noted, these two stick out like sore thumbs in the well-dressed London opera set, and the rich and aristocratic Satterthwaite sees Gillian and Philip almost as alien beings. However, Satterthwaite looks upon the two young people not with superiority and disdain, as Colin Watson implies, but with deep admiration, wonder, and understanding. Christie's idea in this story is not to ridicule the pair's uncultured accents or their tawdry and ill-fitting evening clothes, but to highlight, on the one hand, the girl's extraordinary beauty — hers is the mythic face that could launch a thousand ships — and on the other hand the man's genius, as musician and scientist. In "The Dead Harlequin," Satterthwaite meets a similarly talented young artist who carries a large chip on his shoulder because of his working-class origins. Satterthwaite advises the man to trust firmly in his own genius and to disabuse his mind that "birth has any significance at all in our modern conditions." Similarly, in 1967's *Endless Night*, Christie adopts as her narrator a young man from very humble origins but endowed with superb natural aesthetic taste as well as personal magnetism, who moves effortlessly into the sophisticated transatlantic set of his rich young wife.

It is certain that Agatha Christie moved in a narrow social circle, had few opportunities, as she herself remarked, for rubbing shoulders with miners or their ilk at the local pub, and retained conventional and probably prejudiced ideas about people from "the lower classes." It must equally be said that, just as her social anti-Semitism led her to endow her Jewish characters with extraordinary wealth, intelligence, and taste, so her class prejudices led her to attribute to her rare working-class characters, particularly men, an almost Lawrentian intelligence, sensitivity, and dynamism. These characters stand in sharp contrast with the many boring, undistinguished, muddled public school clones Christie presents from her own social class.

In the Christiean gallery of charismatic lower-class men,

John Gabriel of *The Rose and the Yew Tree* is the most complex, the most ambitious, the most articulate, the most realized. Gabriel's physical courage is real. He is that rare man who is not afraid to die. Agatha Christie had known at least one such man — her brother Louis "Monty" Miller. However, Gabriel, like Monty, has little in common with the idealistic and noble hero of military mythology. As he himself tells Hugh Norreys at one point, he has seen the war as his opportunity to capitalize on his one talent — physical bravery — a talent that has virtually no currency in peacetime. As ambitious and unscrupulous as he is brave, Gabriel has looked for the chance to be a hero. As the bullets whizzed round his head, as they smashed into his arm and leg, as he agonizingly dragged his companion to safety, he knew that, if he could only survive, this was his ticket out of the ranks of the powerless.

Gabriel shows the same calculation in miniature during the St. Loo campaign when he jumps unhesitatingly into the sea after a drowning child. Unlike any public schoolboy, Gabriel cannot swim; his jump into the sea is PR staged for the benefit of the eyewitnesses and for the next day's press reports. Nonetheless, the risk is quite real — Gabriel could drown as easily as the child, but, as he says, "you can't have it both ways. You can't go in for heroism unless you're prepared to be more or less heroic." His search for fame, moreover, is not at the expense of the drowning child, whose needs are his first concern. He assures Norreys that, had there been no one but himself present, instead of throwing himself uselessly into the sea, he would have run round to the beach, taken out a boat, and hoped to get to the child in time that way. However, in the situation that exists, he calculates that there are enough spectators and boats available to give both the child and himself an excellent chance of survival, and in fact survive they both do. Gabriel's campaign is a modern campaign, in which appearance matters far more than substance. Doing something pointlessly brave, like jumping into the sea after a child when you can't swim, gains you voters. On the other hand, being honestly kind and understanding toward a woman who is being battered by her husband is taboo, since any hint of sexual misconduct is the electoral kiss of death.

Gabriel has no ideological preference for conservatives over socialists or liberals. He simply decides that in the post-war Britain which he assumes — correctly — will be ruled by a Labor government, an ambitious young proletarian like himself will stand out much more strongly against a background of what he calls "nice, mealy-mouthed English gentlemen" than of other ambitious proletarians. If we think of John Gabriel as a fictional Edward Heath or Margaret Thatcher — postwar British prime ministers who came out of Gabriel's class and did indeed rise in the Tory hierarchy through sheer ability and dynamism — we note that Agatha Christie has her finger on something interesting here.

Gabriel's political philosophy is similarly prophetic in its cynical understanding of how the right wing can maintain its hold over the electorate in a democratic society. "There are only two things that ever stir people politically. One is to put something into their pockets. The other is the sort of idea that sounds as though it would make everything come right and which is extremely easy to grasp, noble but woolly — and which gives you a nice inner glow." A cynical spokesman for Reaganite America or Thatcherite

Britain could hardly have put the matter more clearly.

If the male Conservatives of St. Loo are governed in their choice of John Gabriel as their electoral candidate by the thought that "if you can't have a gentleman . . . a hero is the next best thing," the ladies look upon Gabriel with a much warmer eye. Though small and ugly, Gabriel likes and desires women, and his charm is felt by every woman he meets, even the nasty Mrs. Carslake. Only two women resist his attraction, or appear to do so, the redoubtable old dowager Adelaide, Lady St. Loo, and her granddaughter, the beautiful, remote, and silent Isabella Charteris.

Isabella is the third side of the triangle that links John Gabriel and Hugh Norreys. Of the three, she is the one we readers know least about. We are never permitted to enter Isabella's mind, but merely observe her from the outside. The other two protagonists are also strange and impenetrable on many occasions, but in her capacity as God in the story, the author does admit us to some extent to their thoughts. By choosing a first-person narrative, Christie is obliged to endow her narrator Hugh Norreys with some kind of self-perception to lie alongside other people's reported perceptions of him. John Gabriel is convincingly portrayed as a man of many words as well as many actions, a man who, even on his deathbed, needs for his inner truth to be known. Isabella, on the other hand, remains a beautiful enigma, loved and admired but understood by no one except God.

Much is made of Isabella as a beautiful object: she is variously likened to a figure from a stained-glass window, to a Tang statuette, to an Italian primitive virgin, to an archaic Greek *kore*. She answers shortly and directly to questions, but, unlike John, Hugh, or even Teresa, Hugh's sister-in-law, she almost never volunteers any comment or shows any curiosity about people and events. What we know about Isabella we know through her relation not with John Gabriel, with whom she goes off, not with her fiancé and cousin Rupert St. Loo, whom she leaves virtually at the altar, but with the narrator, Hugh Norreys.

Hugh's enforced stillness matches the natural stillness of Isabella. Reduced to pseudo-womanhood by his accident, Hugh must learn to live at ease in the world of the senses, largely unmediated by language, which is Isabella's natural kingdom. Taking Isabella at first for a beautiful moron, Hugh is surprised to learn that she was one of the most brilliant students at her school, excelling in mathematics and astronomy as well as in Latin and French. Then he discovers almost by accident that the slow, sedate, absent Isabella can act with great swiftness and effectiveness if need arises. When Norreys, to his terror, spills his precious supply of sleeping pills out on the grass in full view, Isabella moves with instinctive complicity to cover the pills with her scarf and distract the attention of the watchful Teresa. Gradually, Hugh learns to enjoy simply being with Isabella in silence, and experiences through her an unspeculative, unmanipulative, contemplative oneness with the natural world.

On only one point does Isabella show animation and express emotion, and this is when she talks of her terror of death. It is not dying that terrifies her, for the final agony is still part of life, but death itself, separation from the body, the "literal," being no longer able to touch and smell and hear and see. Challenging her assertion that it is the nothingness of death, not the torture of dying, that terrifies her, Gabriel presses his lighted cigarette end to Isabella's arm. Gestures like this, common in the works of existentialists like Sartre or political novelists like Koestler, are rather surprising in the fiction of Agatha Christie. Certainly, the conventional Norreys is horrified by the brutality of Gabriel's gesture, by the incongruous invasion of the torture chamber into an English drawing room. Yet Isabella not only withstands the pain of the burn without complaint, she understands, and supports, Gabriel's reasons. "I don't see," she says to Norreys, "why you should be so upset. Major Gabriel was only seeing if I could stand pain. Now he knows I can."

The scene with the cigarette is paradigmatic of what will be the permanent pattern of relations between John Gabriel and Isabella. He will push harder and harder to find a limit to her self-understanding, to her value system, to her physical resistance. Just as Norreys is outraged when Gabriel burns Isabella's arm, so he will be horrified to learn, first from John himself and then from Isabella, that John has made violent and passionate love to Isabella, not so much out of physical desire as from a metaphysical need to try and force her into expressing repugnance and contempt for him. Gabriel deliberately oversteps the mark set by the gentleman's code of lovemaking, but, as always, both he and Norreys are quite wrong in their anticipation of Isabella's reaction. When Norreys asks Isabella whether she was shocked, frightened, or upset by Gabriel's action, she replies, "No, I don't think so. Ought I to have been?" This reply turns the tables on Hugh, who is forced to reconsider what a normal woman ought to feel when she first arouses passion in a man, as opposed to love and tenderness. Teresa has told Hugh that Gabriel is attractive to women, yet he wonders if it is Gabriel himself Isabella has found attractive, or his lovemaking. In other words, has Gabriel been simply the instrument through which Isabella has come to discover her own capacity for sexual passion? Certainly, it is a capacity that she accepts and acts upon in a way not usual with the virgin heroines of conventional romance. What is more, by her calm and uncomplicated acceptance of her own sensuality, Isabella confounds not only Norreys's conventional chivalrousness, but John Gabriel's classic male-chauvinist tendency to divide women into two classes — those who resist and are therefore frigid teases, and those who respond, who are therefore hypocritical sluts.

Stupid yet brilliant, passive yet capable of dramatic action, conventional yet willing to throw her whole life away on what seems a whim, Isabella is profoundly mysterious. At no point does she explain precisely why she gives up what she herself describes as certain married happiness with the handsome and eligible Lord St. Loo, as well as the chance to fulfill her beloved grandmother's aspirations, for a man she knows does not love her. Buried in the fictional story of John and Isabella is the real-life story of Agatha and Archie. Christie is affirming once again through her created character that she herself does not understand why she married the inscrutable, alien Archie, not the eligible and comradely Reggie. She has, however, learned to live with and accept the consequences of her own mysterious act. The nature of sexual attraction is quintessentially a mystery in Agatha Christie's fiction, and the passion between a man and a woman is something that must always be taken into account even as it is unaccountable.

Conventional Christian morality has tended to condemn sexual relations outside of wedlock as "living in sin," but in this case as in many others Agatha Christie is not a conventional Christian. In her fictional world, the women and the men whose actions are motivated by sexual passion are not castigated, though they are rarely rewarded. Christie's scorn and condemnation are reserved not for the Paolos and Francescas who are consumed by passion, but for those, like Dermot in *Unfinished Portrait* — and presumably like Archie Christie in real life — who feel sexual desire and will go to any lengths to secure the object of their desire, but conceal their passion from the world and perhaps from themselves behind a cloak of propriety. When Isabella Charteris goes away with John Gabriel, her action is wrong in the context even of Christie's eccentric Anglo-Catholicism, but it is also, in some sense, disinterested. Neither of the two is married or has any primary responsibility to another human being. Both are free to act on their desires and ready to accept the consequences of their action. Strangely, by not marrying, they do not sully the sanctity of what Christie believed to be the sacrament of marriage.

Through the mysteriousness of Isabella's nature and of her relation with Gabriel, Agatha Christie is not primarily trying to tell us about female masochism or men's tendency to make beautiful women into objects, though these issues are touched upon. Teresa Norreys, who in some ways performs the function of chorus in the novel, interprets Isabella as a person uniquely attuned to the real world and thereby also uniquely in touch with the divine pattern. Unspeculative, unphilosophical, devoid of a desire to change the world and earn her place in heaven by good works, Isabella is, without her knowledge or anyone else's, a fit instrument for God's purpose. Resistant to pain, unaffected by degradation, accepting even of her lover's sadism, Isabella fears death, but when she sees the assassin preparing to fire at Gabriel she reacts as swiftly and decisively as Gabriel himself once had done on the battlefield. She has chosen this man, she has made him the center of her world, she is able to save him, and she does.

Fairy tales had a very special importance for Agatha Christie, as age-old fables incarnating some kind of essential, unchanging truth about human life. The fairy-tale motif is sounded again and again in *The Rose and the Yew Tree*. When Hugh Norreys is first introduced to the inhabitants of St. Loo Castle, he describes them as unreal, "pure fairy story. The Three Witches and the Enchanted Maiden." When he learns that Isabella is unofficially engaged to marry her first cousin, Rupert St. Loo, the heir to the castle, Norreys says again, "This place becomes more like a fairy story than ever. . . ." When Norreys witnesses the meeting of Rupert St. Loo and Isabella after nine years' absence, he comments, "It was idyllic — unreal — a fairy story's happy ending. It was Romance with a capital R." The relationship between Isabella and her cousin seems in fact both idyllic and real, idyllic because real.

Yet Norreys's view of Isabella is limited and partial, not simply because he is immobilized on a sofa in one room, but because his conventional male morality and indeed his own romantic love for Isabella preclude him from understanding the active force of God-given desire in her life. The fairy tale in which Isabella Charteris has been so convincingly cast as heroine-princess opposite her cousin's hero-Prince Charming, with the romantic ruins of St. Loo Castle as backdrop, is both real and imperfect. It is a story told by humans by Adelaide St. Loo, notably, with the active cooperation of Rupert and satisfies human criteria for perfection as defined by Hugh Norreys. However, Agatha Christie juxtaposes this human pattern with another pattern, which she identifies with God. In this pattern, it is not Isabella's relation with Rupert St. Loo or with her aunts or Hugh Norreys or conventional society that will count, but her relation with John Gabriel. In this pattern, every aspect of Isabella's strange character will play a part — her self-containment, her physical quietude and metaphysical anxiety, her flashes of activism, her awakening desire — and both her life and John Gabriel's will take on a meaning that transcends the value systems of the Hugh Norreyses of the world. What had seemed a fairy story married to a sketch of contemporary political life becomes an allegory of the divine purpose.

This conviction that human beings are part of a divine purpose is stated quite overtly in *The Rose and the Yew Tree*. Perhaps the central issue that Christie grapples with in the postwar Mary Westmacott books is how to reconcile Christian activism — the imperative to use one's God- given talents to promote God's purpose in the world and protect his creatures — with Christian receptivity. In *The Rose and the Yew Tree*, Christie achieves this by splitting the functions between her two protagonists, making Isabella the apparently passive, inward-turning mystic and Gabriel the active, outward-turned militant. In *The Burden*, Llewellyn Knox is active and passive at different stages in his life. He has some fifteen years of active evangelism during which all considerations of self are sublimated, but then he is given leave by God to develop his own free will and his own desires in the private realm as lover, husband, and, potentially, father. Laura Franklin, in the same novel, has in the end to accept that her own active benevolence was one important thread in the events leading to the tragic death of her adored younger sister Shirley. Not content with saving the life of the baby sister whom she had at first hated and longed to kill, Laura then devotes her life to Shirley's welfare. She does not hesitate to enable the death of Shirley's husband, Henry, whom she considers responsible for wrecking Shirley's happiness, health, and fortune. In a very odd twist of theological logic, Llewellyn tells Laura that Shirley is dead and that the burden she must henceforth bear is the burden of happiness and of being loved. The debt Laura had incurred in allowing Henry to die cannot be paid, or rather it has already been paid, by Shirley herself.

The idea that one can use one's death actively to pay for some sin recurs again and again in Agatha Christie's novels. This, together with the generally sensationalist and melodramatic quality of the Westmacott books, betrays the strong influence on Christie of nineteenth-century popular fiction of the *Uncle Tom's Cabin* variety. A commonplace of such works was the death of a young innocent being, usually female, to secure the conversion and redemption of other people, usually powerful adult males. The death of Isabella Charteris to save John Gabriel, both literally and spiritually, is the foremost example of this theme, but Christie develops it in other ways. In *A Murder Is Announced*, Philippa Haynes's life has been darkened by her no-good, deserter husband. Finally, however, the husband is allowed to repay all he has received in love and help by giving up his life to save a child. Similarly, in *Cat Among the Pigeons*, Miss Chadwick, who, on jealous impulse, has killed a fellow teacher, redeems herself by moving in the way of a bullet aimed at her beloved friend Miss Bulstrode.

These cases of what might be called redemptive suicide must be balanced against Christie's insistence in several books that no one has the right to commit suicide for selfish reasons simply because he or she finds life unbearable. Mr. Satterthwaite, in *The Mysterious Mr. Quinn*, insists that "your life is your own. Nobody can alter or influence the use you make of it." But he also asks a woman intent on suicide, "Can you dare ignore the chance that you are taking part in a gigantic drama under the orders of a divine Producer? Your cue may not come till the end of the play — it may be totally unimportant, a mere walking-on part, but upon it may hang the issues of the play, if you do not give the cue to another player. You, as you, may not matter to anyone in the world, but you as a person in a particular place may matter unimaginably."

When John Gabriel comes to tell Hugh Norreys of Isabella's death, Hugh's reaction is the natural human one. He cannot accept without bitterness that the young, innocent woman he loved should die in place of her debauched and corrupt lover. He cannot forgive Gabriel for putting Isabella in a place where such a thing could happen to her. He wishes Gabriel in hell, and Gabriel seems ready to accept such a fate. Yet the message of the novel, conveyed with all the suddenness and unexpectedness of Christie's murder-mystery solutions, is quite different. Isabella has followed her pattern faithfully, if blindly, and *sub specie aeternitatis* her short life has as much meaning as if she had lived a hundred years. To quote the novel's opening epigraph which together with her title Christie borrows from T. S. Eliot's "Little Gidding": "The moment of the rose and the moment of the yew-tree/Are of equal duration." Furthermore, the almost mythical goodness and great actions of Father Clement are the direct result of Isabella's action. By taking on death in his place, she convinced him not only of her love — which he had never wholly been able to trust in before — but in the worth of his life. Isabella's death is thus, literally, in imitation of Christ.

The Rose and the Yew Tree, like the other Westmacott books, is usually referred to as a "romance," but its plot, its message, and its characters have little in common with a Harlequin novel or the more ambitious narratives of a Danielle Steel, Margaret Mills, or Judith Krantz. John Gabriel has certain of the traditional qualities of the romantic hero — wit, energy, sensuality, sexual magnetism — but he does not bow down before the charms of the heroine or devote his life to loving service of her. Isabella looks like a traditional heroine and draws men to her in the traditional way, but she very deliberately does not marry Mr. Right and refuses even to repent her decision not to live happily ever after. Rupert, Lord St. Loo, who has been given every attribute of a Prince Charming, is left at the altar and obliged to find a prosaic happiness with an American heiress. Constructed more like a medieval morality play — or a T. S. Eliot drama — than a modern romance, *The Rose and the Yew Tree* uses a story about the loves of three men and one woman to carry a message about the relations of man and God, a message that is at once political and theological.

The political element is both the less important and the more carefully realized. All of the characters in the novel

are Conservatives; all except the painter Robert Norreys
are shown working in the electoral campaign, canvassing,
attending meetings, licking envelopes, driving workers to
the polls. None, however, except the elderly ladies from
the castle, profess any ideological conviction that the
Conservative Party is better. As so often in the novel,
Teresa Norreys is used to articulate the general authorial
position. Before 1945, Teresa has had no role or interest in
politics, confining herself to voting for the candidate who
seemed likely to do the least harm. In the current election
she does not see that there is anything to choose between the
parties. However, having recently inherited Polnorth House,
she cannot see herself as anything else but a Conservative
supporter. "The late Miss Amy Tregellis would turn in her
grave if the niece to whom she has bequeathed her treasures
was to vote Labour."

Clearly, Teresa is a stout defender of the status quo —
and thereby her own interests as a property owner — but
at the same time she is tolerant of those who for similar
reasons of tradition, social caste, and financial interest will
support other political parties. She would never question
that should the Conservative Party she supports fail to get
a majority, the opposition Labor Party will govern the
country and determine policy. The suspicion, not unmarked
by admiration, with which Teresa and Lady St. Loo regard
John Gabriel is occasioned by their seeing that his political
affiliation is governed by personal ambition, not by any
class solidarity. Teresa is similarly tolerant toward her
husband who refuses to undertake any political activity
at all. She excuses Robert to the Tory establishment by
stating firmly that he is a communist — a fiction that, in
Christie's view, places him outside the political arena of

British politics. When Mrs. Carslake starts to indulge in Red bashing, pointed reference is made to the major role communists played in the heroic French Resistance.

Obviously not someone who will seek to revolutionize society or fight for the interests of the poor and downtrodden, Teresa Norreys, like her brother-in-law Hugh, or indeed John Gabriel, is equally resistant to the siren songs from both communism and fascism. For all their faults, these are not the kind of people either to turn into Ionescan rhinoceroses or to join the pigs of Orwell's *Animal Farm*. In fact, John Gabriel vigorously defends the materialism and greed for which the old-fashioned British Tory party stood accused both by the left wing and by the new ideological right wing. Stung by Hugh's accusation that he is greedy for power, John exclaims, "Who do you think I am — Hitler? I don't want power — I've no ambition to lord it over my fellow creatures or the world generally." Gabriel insists that the world is threatened not by greedy materialists, who feather their own nests but are content to let their fellow countrymen be, but by the fanatics who will happily rape, murder, and pillage in pursuit of their ideal.

The cynicism and distaste for politicking Agatha Christie displays so overtly in *The Rose and the Yew Tree* are not new. Although Christie was a lifelong Tory whose class background and ideological orientation opposed her to liberalism or radicalism, hers was always a conservatism with a small c. She was as conscious of the clay feet of conservatism's political organ as she was philosophically unconvinced of the possibility of any greater-minded political movement emerging. A *faute de mieux* Tory, Agatha Christie was congenitally suspicious of all political structures and arguments. She was above all committed to tolerance and compassion in all aspects of life. Not without reason, she feared that the militant orthodoxies of the twentieth century, fascist as well as communist, would prove less tolerant and less compassionate than the old tired orthodoxies of her nineteenth-century origins.

Christie's apoliticism is a hidden theme in mystery novels written throughout her career. In 1922's *The Secret Adversary*, Christie's surprise denouement depends on a very unusual twist on the old "least likely" concept. In this early novel, Christie relies on the fact that, at least for her own generation of readers, an outstanding member of the Tory establishment, a Member of Parliament and King's Counsel, a man touted as the next Prime Minister, is one person who will never be suspected of being a criminal mastermind. *The Secret Adversary* is by no means a classic of the adventure-mystery genre, and its denouement has been dismissed as mere cleverdickery. All the same, one wonders what comparable male author of popular fiction at that period or later — Edgar Wallace, William Le Queux, John Buchan, Michael Innes, Ian Fleming — would be capable of turning the narrative tables in this particular way?

Christie returns to very much the same idea in a later and far more successful novel — *The Patriotic Murders/One, Two, Buckle My Shoe* — where an explicit ideological justification is offered for essentially the same denouement. In *The Patriotic Murders*, published, significantly, in the opening year of the Second World War, Hercule Poirot refuses to be influenced by the argument that the end justifies the means, that "the safety and happiness of the whole nation" depends on one illustrious public servant remaining active and honored whatever crimes he may have committed as a private citizen. Poirot says to the great politician, "I am not concerned with nations, Monsieur. I am concerned with the lives of private individuals who have the right not to have their lives taken from them." At the end of *The Patriotic Murders*, Poirot talks to two fiery and intemperate young radicals upon whom suspicion, "naturally," has fallen. Poirot's words are simple, unusually heartfelt, and ring strangely from such an apparently dyed-in-the-wool conservative: "The world is yours. The New Heaven and the New Earth. In your new world, my children, let there be freedom, let there be pity . . . [sic]. That is all I ask."

Humility and brotherhood are virtues worn by the antiestablishment representatives of the Christian religion, among them Jesus Christ himself, and it is clearly as a devout Christian that Agatha Christie opposes political morality on right and left. Religion is a subject rarely discussed in Christie's mystery novels, but it provides the framework for all her writing. Unlike her great mystery-writer contemporary Dorothy L. Sayers, Agatha Christie wrote no Christian mystery plays or Anglican polemics. Christie had had no formal education in philosophy or political thought, was no linguist, had none of the scholarly talents needed to write about religion and theology. All the same, Christie was as serious about her religious faith as Sayers, and, unlike Sayers, as she grew old, she saw her work as a humble but acceptable way of expressing certain values she held dear. Her talent was to make plots, tell stories, weave fantasies, write modern fairy tales. Such a talent had little standing in the world, but it was God-given and Christie did not hide it in the earth.

The Rose and the Yew Tree is a modern fable, with all the

fable's directness and simplicity, all its unexplained twists and turns. It tells us that the experience of physical passion, in either man or woman, is part of the human condition, of the spirit made flesh, and can be acceptable in God's sight if it is joined with love. It tells us that what matters is how we live, not how long we live, that death is not the end but a kind of beginning. As Mr. Harley Quinn says so oddly, "Is death the greatest evil that can happen to anyone?" It tells us that a man or woman can sin greatly, in the eyes of God and of the world, and still repent and make good and be redeemed.

Agatha Christie always kept her mother's copy of Thomas à Kempis's *The Imitation of Christ* by her bedside, and the literal lifelong proximity to Christie of this most famous text of the mysticism of "humble labour and charity" is deeply suggestive. In *The Rose and the Yew Tree* the woman entrusted with explicating much of the meaning of the events is called Teresa, and this character's matter-of-fact energy, her detachment and clear-sightedness, her benevolent noninterventionism, her willingness to leave things and people to God are a kind of modern view of how the mystic life advocated by Thomas à Kempis might be lived in a twentieth-century, secular setting. The name Teresa, as well as the final scene when the narrator finally looks at his sister-in-law and sees her "high cheekbones and the upward sweep of black hair that seemed to need a mantilla and a big Spanish comb," indicates that Christie is thinking of the great Spanish mystic St. Theresa of Avila.

This unexpected trail of mysticism leads us in turn to that nineteenth-century unrealized St. Theresa — George Eliot's *Middlemarch* heroine Dorothea Brooke. *Middlemarch* ends with the following sentence, which may serve to sum up one of the fundamental messages that Agatha Christie conveyed in her novels: "But the effect of her being on those around her was incalculably diffusive: for the growing good of the world is partly dependent on unhistoric acts; and that things are not so ill with you and me as they might have been, is half owing to the number who lived faithfully a hidden life, and rest in unvisited tombs."

CHAPTER
SEVEN

Dame Agatha
Murders in St. Mary Mead

Death Comes as the End was the title of the ancient Egyptian mystery that Agatha Christie wrote during the Second World War. Christie loved life and was to live long, but she also prepared in many different ways for the death that would inevitably come as the end. She tidied up as many loose ends as she could while still in full possession of her senses and tried to make the administration of her legacy as simple as possible for her loved ones.

As the novelist grew older and wealthier and her legal and tax position became more complex, careful provisions were made to protect her earnings from super tax and from eventual death duties. In 1955 and 1957, trusts were set up to guarantee the novelist an annual salary, cut her tax rate, and still enable her to be generous in her support of others. Christie's relations with the Inland Revenue — the British tax authorities — were stormy and involved considerable legal expenses. Until the very last years of her life, Christie claimed that she had cash-flow problems that necessitated her writing a new book each year. Given the fact, however, that any newly generated income from royalties would be taxed at the same high rate as the old, it seems far more likely that she kept writing not to keep the family fortunes afloat, but because she enjoyed writing and because her sense of self was intimately bound up with her work as a writer. Until the end of their lives, Agatha and Max lived comfortable, even luxurious lives, though they were certainly not millionaires. Agatha was generous, donating the royalties for different works to Max, Rosalind, Mathew, and one of Max's nephews, supporting various charities, endowing a new stained-glass window for a local church. As is not infrequently the case with happy, successful, and affluent people, Agatha's last years were not packed with drama and suspense, but there was much quiet enjoyment. Three things especially — food, gardens, and young people — seem to have gladdened the novelist's heart even as her energy and physical resilience waned.

Food was always one of life's greatest pleasures for Agatha Christie. She recalls in fond detail her delight as a child in an illicit forkful of steak offered her in the night nursery by her nanny, in the crisp, flat, curranty, oven-hot rock buns made by the Ashfield cook Jane, in the smell of pear drops being cooked at the local sweetshop, in the handful of French plums from a jar in Auntie-Grannie's cupboard in Ealing. As an adult, Christie became a diligent collector of recipes, an accomplished amateur cook, a devoted fan of professional chefs. Even when living in the Arabian desert in a tent, she dressed for dinner, had Stilton cheese and chocolate truffles imported by the long-suffering Edmund Cork, and prevailed upon local cooks to produce éclairs with cream from water-buffalo milk and walnut souffles cooked in a square tin can. A celebration in Agatha Christie's life always meant a first-class meal, usually with an abundance of seafood in cream sauce, garden-fresh vegetables, fruit desserts, elaborate chocolate cakes, and for Agatha, who never touched alcohol, a cup of cream to drink. It is hardly surprising that Christie fought all her life against overweight, and was almost happy when, after some slight illness, she lost her appetite and shed a few pounds. Active, creative, in control until the very last of her eighty-five years of life, Agatha Christie is something of an advertisement for the high-cholesterol diet.

Losing herself contentedly in the gardens at Ashfield, gazing in silent rapture at the glory of the family's great beech tree, sitting in a field of yellow buttercups, inhaling the rose-scented air of Auntie-Grannie's small suburban plot — these too were formative experiences in Agatha Christie's childhood, and she remained passionately fond of gardens all her life. In the postwar years, as chatelaine of Winterbrook House and Greenway, Agatha took delight in superintending the establishment of extensive kitchen gardens and ornamental gardens. In the early fifties, when the Mallowans were at Nimrud, poor Edmund Cork found himself trying to get the large market-gardening operation Christie had authorized at Greenway onto some kind of sound financial basis. The people running the operation were producing exactly the kinds of exclusive products their employer liked to eat, but their talents at marketing were virtually nonexistent, and Christie was losing money hand over fist. Also at Greenway, Agatha spent a great deal of time as well as money in bringing the gardens back to their pristine glory with much new planting, often of rare shrubs. The gardens at Greenway are still a local treasure, and are regularly opened to the public by Mrs. Hicks.

Christie's love of gardening had always shown itself

in her novels, where herbaceous borders, potting sheds, bedding plants, and shrubbery figure prominently. However, in the novels written in the author's old age, gardens and horticultural expertise come center stage. Christie's increasingly popular spinster sleuth, Miss Jane Marple, personifies Agatha's growing passion for gardening in her later years. From the first of her mysteries, *Murder at the Vicarage*, 1930, Jane is shown as a dedicated and expert hands-on gardener, whose suspicions are aroused when a young man offers quite unsuitable rocks for her rock garden. In her last mystery, *Nemesis*, Miss Marple is signed up for a Homes and Garden Tour, during which it becomes quite obvious that she is rather bored with architecture but fascinated with gardens. Miss Marple is immediately affected by the sinister profusion of the beautiful but invasive Polygonum Baldschuanicum in the neglected garden of the Bradbury-Scott sisters. This gardener's sensitivity enables her to deduce the location of Verity Hunt's body. As she advances in years and declines in vigor, Jane Marple is forced to give up the active pleasures of weeding and pruning. She has to rely on the dubious industry of jobbing gardeners who, moreover, have a horrid preference for asters over pompom dahlias. These changes in Miss Marple's life parallel the real-life experience of the aging Christie, who still rejoiced in her glorious spreads of rhododendrons and white peonies but had increasingly to rely upon the services of a staff of trained, and prize-winning, gardeners.

In 1969's *Hallowe'en Party*, Christie transports even Hercule Poirot into a horticultural setting. Poirot finds his investigations centered on an extraordinarily beautiful quarry garden designed by professional landscape architect

Michael Garfield. As Miss Marple so often does on her Homes and Garden tour in *Nemesis*, Poirot sits down on a strategically placed bench and notes how the garden has been designed to be beautiful in every season. "There were young beech trees and birches with their white shivering barks. Bushes of thorn and white rose, little juniper trees. But now it was autumn, and autumn had been catered for also. The gold and red of acers, a parrotia or two, a path that led along a winding way to fresh delights. There were flowering bushes of gorse or Spanish broom — Poirot was not famous for knowing the names of either flowers or shrubs — only tulips and roses could one approve and recognise." Here Agatha's real-life expertise in flowers and shrubs almost carries her away into an exotic vocabulary (acer, parrotia) most unusual in her prose. She is forced to drag herself back from the detailed delights of this imagined garden with the thought that the urban Poirot would be quite unable to do it justice.

The Englishness of Agatha Christie is perhaps nowhere more apparent than in her deep interest in the designing of gardens and nurturing of plants and in her lyrical response to that unique blend of the wild and the cultivated that is the southern English landscape. She writes in *Hallowe'en Party*: "A drive through Devon lanes. A winding road with great banks going up on each side of it, and on those banks a great carpet and showing of primroses. So pale, so subtly and timidly yellow, and coming from them that sweet, faint, elusive smell that the primrose has in large quantities, which is the smell of spring almost more than any other smell."

Food and gardens had been perennial delights in Agatha Christie's life, but a new factor in her old age was her delight in the new generation, as chiefly represented by her grandson Mathew Prichard. Mathew seems to have been an ideal grandchild, and Agatha's relationship with him was perhaps less complicated than that with her own daughter. Handsome, active, sociable, achieving, confident in the public world, Mathew gave Agatha in her old age the invaluable gift of youthful acceptance, companionship, and admiration. When Mathew captained the victorious Eton side at the annual Eton-Harrow cricket match, Agatha was very proud. She was happy in 1960 when with Rosalind and Anthony he joined her and Max for a vacation in Ceylon and vigorously defended her from attacks by paparazzi. She was overjoyed to find in Mathew someone who enjoyed opera and modern art as much as she did and who could introduce her to people like jazz musician John Dankworth and artist Oskar Kokoschka.

When Mathew married Angela Maples and settled down with his family on his father's estate, she enjoyed paying ritual visits to Pwyllywrach as she had once enjoyed the Christmases at Abney. In her eighties, Christie was demanding that Cork send her copies of Fanon, Chomsky, and Marcuse because "Alexandra [Mathew's first child] *must* have an intelligent great-grandmother." Mathew succeeded admirably on those public occasions that Agatha so feared, and she loved this in him. Though separated by fifty-three years of life, the two seem to have been friends and allies as well as respectful grandson and doting grandmother. In some ways, being with Mathew enabled Christie to be a child again. The famous novelist was often more at ease and more open when talking to people a third her age or younger, than with her contemporaries. She would gladly abandon the adult company in the drawing room to play snap and tell stories with a visiting child, and gave a happy welcome to an unkempt teenager hitchhiking to her door with the inevitable friend in tow.

In the 1970s Agatha Christie was recognized as one of the greatest detective-story writers of all time. Agatha's creative energies were remarkable even in advanced old age. She was over seventy when she wrote the haunting and innovative mystery *Endless Night*. A Christie for Christmas was a must purchase for many a person across the world, and in the last decade or so of the author's life even the hardback editions of her novels sold between forty and fifty thousand copies in the first weeks of publication. The demand for rights to reprint Christie's early work was hot. This success, coming in her eighth decade, was the result of unrelenting hard work. Christie talked all her life about the glories of uninterrupted leisure and of liking above all to do nothing, but in practice she was a miracle of professional diligence. She continued making notes and thinking about new stories until the very end. Christie constantly surprised much younger collaborators by her ability to produce new material on time and adaptations to order with the minimum of explanation and fuss.

Christie's increasing international fame did not mean that the novelist became transformed into a modern media personality. Agatha Christie, famous novelist, consistently took refuge behind the persona of Mrs. (later Lady) Mallowan, wife of the famous archeologist, and she used her wealth and literary clout to keep her life as far as possible out of the limelight. This resistance to public attention is shown very clearly in her decision to write an autobiography that would be published after her death. The assembling of material for the autobiography in the early sixties was probably the most important literary labor of her eighth decade. It reflected both a natural desire to relive the happiness of the past and a learned intent to maintain in the future the kind of control over biographical information Christie had maintained in the past. Christie wished for nothing better than to remain hidden behind her work, but she had been forced to recognize the public's insatiable thirst for personal information about her. She had seen that where no accurate material was available, it was invented, and she determined to allow the public to have details about her life — but on her own terms. At the end of 1965, she said, "I am delighted that if I die, everything is ready for me to be first in the field with my own life, cutting the ground from under the feet of others." In one sense, *An Autobiography* was Christie's final revenge against the reporters she hated.

In 1971, Agatha Christie was made a Dame of the British Empire, the female rank that is the equivalent of a knighthood but awarded much more rarely. In her last years, Christie was much flattered and pleased by the attention paid her by the British royal family, and admitted that a crowning event in her life was the evening when, in the words of a well-loved nursery rhyme, she "went up to London to look at," and indeed dine with, the Queen. Buckingham Palace had long contained some devoted Christie fans, and the original radio-play version of *Witness for the Prosecution* had been written as a birthday gift to Queen Mary. Her very last public appearance was at the premiere of the Albert Finney film version of *Murder on the Orient Express*, attended by Prince Charles. The film had been produced by Lord Brabourne, the son-in-law of Lord Mountbatten, Prince Charles's godfather, so the event was something of a family celebration for the royal family as well as for Christie. One somewhat sour note was sounded in Christie's life by Lord Snowdon, at one time the husband of Princess Margaret. Trading on his royal connections as the Queen's former brother-in-law, the photographer was admitted to Wallingford in the last years of Christie's life and took a series of devastatingly candid pictures of the aged novelist and her husband. The Christie family was assured that the pictures would be made public only on Agatha's express approval, and was shocked and upset when the pictures appeared in the *Sunday Times*, as well as in an "interview" in an Australian newspaper.

Organized and collected in all matters and strong in her love of God, Christie faced up to death well in advance. She carefully left written word for her family of the inscription she wished to have on her tombstone: "Sleep after Toyle, Port after Stormie Seas/Ease after Warre, Death after Life, Doth greatly please." To this quotation from Spenser she later added a phrase from the psalms — "In Thy Presence is the Fulness of Joye." She requested that the Bach Air in D from the third Suite and the "Nimrud" variation by Elgar be played at her funeral.

Having suffered increasing ill health after a heart attack in the fall of 1974, Agatha Christie died in Wallingford on January 12, 1976, and was buried in the churchyard in the nearby village of Cholsey. At a London memorial service in May at St. Martin in the Fields, the music she had requested was played, and there was a reading of the Twenty-Third Psalm and of a passage by Thomas à Kempis.

After 1946, Christie was unable to hide behind her pseudonym of Mary Westmacott, and it is probable that having achieved personal security as well as professional clout, Christie no longer needed anonymity to express the things close to her heart. Instead, she developed in her mystery fiction two female sleuths, Jane Marple and Ariadne Oliver, whom she could use where needed as authorial spokeswomen. If the character of Miss Jane Marple is by no means a fictional self-portrait of Agatha Christie, it has played the role of stand-in, holding the spotlight of public attention, deflecting attention away from the author who stands, contentedly, in the darkness behind the scenes. In Miss Marple, Agatha Christie was to create the world's most famous woman detective to date.

Agatha Christie was about thirty-eight when she first started to sketch the character of Miss Marple, who was to make her publishing debut in 1930. She does not immediately seem to have realized Jane Marple's potential. Twelve years separate the first full-length Miss Marple mystery from the second, and ten years separate the second from the third and fourth. It was during the postwar period that Miss Marple began to attract more and more popular attention. By this time Poirot was in great disfavor with Christie: she had killed him off in *Curtain*, one of the wartime manuscripts that were prudently laid away in a vault, and she cheerfully eliminated him from the 1951 stage version of *The Hollow*. As Poirot's star waned with his creator, so Miss Marple's rose. When Poirot does appear in the postwar novels, he is usually paired with Christie's detective-story-writing alter ego, Ariadne Oliver. After the 1950s, when Christie herself was in her sixties, Miss Marple novels became more frequent, no doubt because an increasing congruence had developed between the aging author and her elderly female sleuth. The Miss Marple novels tell us a great deal about the way Agatha

Christie lived in the postwar era, about how she perceived herself and her family and British society in general. Two Marple novels, in particular, *The Body in the Library*, 1942, and *Nemesis*, 1971, are excellent examples of Christie's development of the craft of mystery-story writer.

Agatha Christie tells us that her spinster detective was a development both of the Caroline Sheppard character she had enjoyed introducing in 1926 in *The Murder of Roger Ackroyd* and of the kind of old women she had known in her childhood in her surrogate grandmother's house in Ealing. Christie insists that Miss Marple is not at all a portrait of her Auntie-Grannie, being far too "fussy and spinsterish." However, Jane Marple was like Auntie-Grannie in one important respect: "Though a cheerful person, she always expected the worst of everything and everyone and was, with almost frightening accuracy, usually proved right." Christie related several anecdotes showing how her Auntie-Grannie — i.e., Margaret West Miller — could apparently spot a wrong'un at a hundred paces because the person would remind her of deviant characters she had met in the past. "I've known one or two like him," she would exclaim in a manner her adoptive granddaughter would immortalize in one of the world's most famous fictional sleuths.

When we compare Miss Marple with the two portraits Christie gives of Margaret Miller in *An Autobiography* and in *Unfinished Portrait*, we understand what Christie means by Miss Marple's fussy spinsterishness. Margaret Miller had an eye for the men, and a way with them, that Miss Marple never displays, though she is prone to make statements about the "gentlemen." "Gentlemen," Miss Marple will say, "so easily feel neglected" or "are usually rather selfish," and again, "with her old maid's way of referring to the opposite sex as though it were a species of wild animal," as Christie describes her, "Gentlemen are frequently not so levelheaded as they seem." Miss Marple may be unshockable, but her words are always extremely circumspect, and she displays none of that lively interest in medical histories, obstetric minutiae, and sexual misbehavior that Agatha Christie remembers in her Auntie-Grannie. "'My sister Jane was so small she was put in a soap box,' said Grannie." 'A soap box, Grannie?' 'They never thought she'd live,' said Grannie with relish, adding to Mrs. Mackintosh in a lowered voice, 'Five months.' Celia sat quietly trying to visualize a baby of the required smallness. 'What kind of soap?' she asked presently." Later in the novel, Grannie refers with relish to old Admiral Collingway, who "gave his wife a bad disease," carried on with the governess, and leaped out on the maids stark naked. "Naturally they couldn't stay." Vignettes like this remind us why Agatha Christie never thought of the Victorians as naive and sexually constrained. It is really too bad that Agatha Christie did not develop the Auntie-Grannie vein of humor more widely in her detective novels.

Miss Marple's life story, though skimpy, has probably been told more accurately and more sympathetically than Agatha Christie's. Thanks to the devotion of fans like Julian Symons and Ann Hart, it is common knowledge that Miss Marple came from a respectable upper-middle-class family with strong ecclesiastical connections (two uncles were canons of Ely and of Chichester), that she had a sister (the mother of novelist Raymond West and of the lesser-known Mabel), and a good-for-nothing brother. Of Miss Marple's parents we know no more than that her mother was called Clara, though we may presume that

Jane owes her slim independent income to her father. As a girl, Jane attended a school in Florence where she became friends with the rich American heiress sisters Ruth and Carrie-Louise Martin. Julian Symons has imagined the young Miss Marple as "tall and elegant, with fair hair . . . a peaches-and-cream complexion, and innocent china-blue eyes." In *Murder at the Vicarage*, however, the first novel bringing Miss Marple to public notice, she is already an elderly white-haired woman whose "gentle appealing manner" is balanced by a reputation as "the worst cat in the village," who "knows every single thing that happens — and draws the worst inferences from it." The eyes are indeed large and china-blue, but they are now either directed deceptively at some elaborate piece of crochet or else scanning the neighborhood for mischief through powerful bird glasses.

Where Hercule Poirot is essentially an urban soul, happily ensconced in the geometric neatness of his London flat at 203 Whitehaven Mansions, Miss Marple is essentially part of the life of the English village. St. Mary Mead has long been Miss Marple's home, and as might be expected of a Georgian structure, her small but charming cottage Danemead stands right on the High Street. There seem to be some correspondences between Danemead and Agatha Christie's Wallingford house, Winterbrook.

The Mystery of the Blue Train, 1928, first introduced the reader to St. Mary Mead as the village where heroine Katherine Grey lived a dreary but useful life as companion to Miss Vine, very much as Lucy Snowe did to Miss Marchmont in Charlotte Brontë's *Villette*. St. Mary Mead is located in the fictional Radfordshire, a few miles between Much Benham and the larger town of Market Basing, as well as eighteen miles from the nearest coastal resort of Danemouth. Its topography in the high Marpelian period of 1928 to 1971 has been established in considerable detail. Apart from the largely anonymous denizens of the Development — the housing complex built after World War II on the open fields between Vicarage and Hall — the inhabitant of almost every house and shop has traditionally been known by name. All the same, society in St. Mary Mead is far from static. As Miss Marple will have occasion to remark in 1950, "Fifteen years ago one knew who everybody was" because one had known their parents and grandparents. Now everything was different, people came and went, and all one knew of one's neighbors was what they chose to tell.

Closely woven into the traditional social world of St. Mary Mead, with its teas at the Vicarage and sherry parties at the Hall, its Women's Institute meetings, bring-and-buy sales, and perennial canvassings for charity, Miss Marple is also blessed with a far-flung group of friends, most of them at least one generation younger than herself. Of roughly the same age as Miss Marple herself are Elspeth McGillicuddy, Ruth (Martin) Van Rydock, Carrie-Louise (Martin) Serrocold, and Sir Henry Clithering, sometime assistant commissioner for Scotland Yard, as well as fellow villagers Dolly Bantry, Miss Wetherby, and Mrs. Price Ridley. More typical, however, of those important in Jane Marple's life are her nephew, the successful novelist Raymond West — together with his wife, artist Joan (sometimes also referred to as Joyce) Lempriere West — Dr. Haydock and the Reverend Clement, both of St. Mary Mead, and a trio of vicar's wives — Griselda Clement, Maud Dane Calthrop of Lymstock, and "Bunch" Harmon of Little Cleghorn. Time passes, and the elderly lady sleuth claims yet another generation of young friends. All the knitted baby garments Miss Marple produced for friends' offspring seem to have had excellent results in binding the generations together. Though much the poorer financially, Miss Marple is notably richer in friends than her fellow sleuth Hercule Poirot. Here again we may note a difference in sociability in Miss Marple's life, as opposed to Poirot's, that reflects the difference in sociability in Christie's own life once she married Max Mallowan.

One personal trait that Agatha lent to Jane Marple and Ariadne Oliver, and to a lesser extent the postwar Hercule Poirot, was an ability to get on with people much younger than herself. In the course of her adventures, Miss Marple will rely on the collaboration and friendship of men and women young enough to be her grandchildren — Dermot Craddock, who is Sir Henry Clithering's godson, young Leonard Clement, son of the Reverend Leonard and Mrs. Griselda Clement, David West, Miss Marple's great-nephew, and that formidably efficient lady mathematician *cum* home help, Lucy Eylesbarrow. Those fictional relationships created for Miss Marple parallel similar relationships in Christie's own life.

Seeing life from a child's point of view was one of Christie's skills that she exploited chiefly in her Westmacott books and that she inherited, in part, from her nineteenth-century novel-writing predecessors. Both the young Celia in *Unfinished Portrait* and the young Laura Franklin in *The Burden* are unconventional, unsentimental child portraits of considerable dynamism, and the youthful fellowship of Vernon, Josephine, Sebastian, and Nell in *Giants' Bread* is one of the finest things in Christie's fiction. Child characters are rarer in the mysteries, but Josephine Leonides of *Crooked House*, for example, is a compelling figure who moves in unexpected directions. Christie also introduces into her detective fiction as well as her Westmacott novels a number of interesting friendships between young children and elderly people. Both *The Burden* and *A Daughter's a Daughter*, for example, feature a relation of rare confidence and affection between a septuagenarian and a teenager. The combination of youthful, hands-on energy and elderly, detached wisdom is often invoked as a peculiarly successful partnership in detective novels such as *What Mrs. McGillicuddy Saw* (Miss Marple and Lucy Eylesbarrow) and *The Clocks* (Hercule Poirot and Colin Lamb).

In her novels of the forties, fifties, and sixties, Christie introduces several sets of youthful sleuths — the schoolgirls in *Cat Among the Pigeons* and schoolboys in *What Mrs. McGillicuddy Saw*, for example — whose dialogue and letters are well realized and seem based on shrewd observation. All of these fictional examples of excellent relations between old and young are surely based on Agatha Christie's real-life experience. Here again Christie's characters and plot structures defy novelistic stereotypes, by moving away from the adult peer-group relationships that dominate popular fiction. For Christie, the interesting and challenging part of life does not necessarily begin with puberty and end with menopause, and satisfying relationships are not necessarily between actual or potential sexual partners.

Servants and interior decoration were two major concerns in Agatha Christie's life, and these are reflected, on a small scale, in Miss Marple's. Miss Marple's small family inheritance has exempted her from paid work, graced her life with some nice pieces of antique furniture and china, and given her for much of her life the services of a maid. Florence, the first and longest-employed of Miss Marple's maids, is a "tall grim-looking woman" of the old school, devoted to her mistress even after she has retired from service to the spotless comfort of her own home at 4, Madison Road, Brackhampton. Later come a succession of rather anonymous young girls from St. Faith's Orphanage, whom Miss Marple trains in the old-fashioned household arts. Perhaps the least intelligent and able of these young women, Gladys Martin, has the part of the maid to play in a murderous reenactment of the rhyme "Sing a Song of Sixpence." In the 1953 novel *A Pocket Full of Rye*, Miss Marple travels posthaste from St. Mary Mead to ensure that the person guilty of killing her former maid,. poor Gladys, in so contemptuous a manner does not get away with it.

After the war, when even the orphans from St. Faith's have presumably found better career options than domestic service, Miss Marple is provided with a live-in companion, Miss Knight, through the kindness of her affectionate nephew Raymond. Unfortunately, Miss Knight's lower-middle-class gentility grates far more on Miss Marple's nerves than Gladys's adenoids and clumsiness ever did, and she soon trades in Miss Knight for the services of a daily help, Cherry Baker. Cherry comes from the same class as Miss Marple's prewar orphaned Amys and Alices, but she is a married woman with her own husband and cramped, thin-walled home in the Development.

When Agatha Christie has the Bakers move into the spaces over the kitchen and stables in Danemead, she considerately provides Miss Marple with the postwar, cut-price, woman's equivalent to the care rich old Hercule Poirot gets from his valet, Georges, and his secretary, Miss Lemon. Miss Marple cannot afford two full-time employees to look after her, but she and the Bakers are willing to trade services for space and privacy, and the assumption is that both parties to the plan will enjoy the company of the other. Having surrogate grandchildren living in a separate apartment in one's house is, surely, an ideal solution to old age's problem of loneliness and increasing infirmity. One can understand that Miss Marple is prepared to put up with a little dust on the stairs and with the Bakers' booming stereogram (an extraordinarily prescient touch for 1962!) in exchange for youthful company, humor, and energy.

As the story of Miss Marple and St. Mary Mead unfolds in eleven novels and twenty short stories, it mirrors the accelerating pace of change in English society, especially after 1945. The fishmonger refrigerates his slab, a supermarket opens on the High Street, various taxi companies succeed Inch, and the faded leather and chintz comfort of Gossington Hall under Dolly Bantry and her husband Arthur yields to the multi-bathroomed glitz of a movie actress and her producer husband. Yet even as changes in English society are mirrored in Christie's fictional world, a sociopsychological bedrock remains. The patterns of character development and of social interaction which Miss Marple recognizes in Much Benham, Little Cleghorn, Brackhampton, Lymstock, and Dillmouth as well as in St. Mary Mead, and upon which the sleuth will base her famous intuition, are rooted in the English past and in literary tradition. The topographical interaction of village street, country lane, and farmer's field; the social interaction of gentry, professional men, tradespeople, and farm folk; the rapid spread of gossip; the nostalgia for a mythical golden age when village life was stable and reliable; the resistance to, yet dependence upon, outsiders moving into the village — all these are features of English village life recorded by Agatha Christie that had already been immortalized in the nineteenth century by Jane Austen, Mary Russell Mitford, and Elizabeth Gaskell, to name only the most illustrious.

When Christie refers to the elderly ladies she met "in so many villages where I have gone to stay as a girl," she sounds remarkably like Elizabeth Gaskell, whose girlhood visits in the 1820s to the village of Knutsford became the subject for her most famous novel, *Cranford*. In Agatha Christie as in her nineteenth-century predecessors, all serious financial or industrial activity is peculiarly displaced to a shadowy, almost legendary metropolis, and the basic village dramatis personae is amazingly the same — squire, vicar, apothecary and/or doctor, solicitor, land and/or estate agent, retired military man, rich retired merchant, refined but impoverished spinsters, widows, potentially marriageable young persons, respectable shopkeeper, hearty innkeeper, domestic personnel, jobbing gardener, and occasional "local yokel." The precisely scheduled occupational patterns of getting up after morning tea, going out each morning to do the shopping, taking meals at home, and meeting in the evening for private social events or public meetings is remarkably constant between Jane Austen's Highbury of 1816 and Agatha Christie's Chipping Cleghorn of 1950. To take one small precise example, Miss Bates of *Emma*, Miss Matty Jenkyns of *Cranford*, and Miss Emily Barton of *The Moving Finger* are all remarkably similar spinster ladies of genteel education, draconian families, and reduced circumstances whose hold on "modern" life is sadly tenuous. Literary tradition is strong here, but equally, each of us today can no doubt still find a real-life contemporary version of Gaskell's Miss Jenkyns, the vicar's daughter, Mrs. Jamieson, the merchant's widow, and Captain Brown, the retired naval officer.

One feature characteristic of Miss Marple's St. Mary Mead, and conspicuously absent from Miss Bates's Highbury or Miss Matty Jenkyns's Cranford, is the high murder rate. That pillar of local society and stern guardian of Anglican values Colonel Protheroe is found murdered in 1930 — in the vicar's study, no less! A mere twelve years later the body of a young blonde woman in full evening dress is discovered in the library at Gossington Hall, home of Colonel Arthur Bantry, local magistrate and stalwart member of the Much Benham Conservative Association. Male establishment figures are something of an endangered species in Agatha Christie's St. Mary Mead, and it will take all Miss Marple's skill to clear Colonel Bantry of suspicion.

Obviously the Colonel denies all knowledge of the sexy young miss lying dead on his carpet, but equally obviously he would have to! Given that the Colonel has shown some tendency to flirt with young ladies over the tennis net, and that his wife has been very preoccupied with her herbaceous borders, the Miss Wetherbys, Mrs. Price Ridleys, and Claras of St. Mary Mead have no hesitation in coming to their own conclusions about the relations of Colonel to corpse. In fact, even the chief constable, Colonel Melchett, reads the mystery of the dead blonde in the Bantry library in the same way as the village gossips.

While Colonel Bantry denies all knowledge of the blonde in his library, takes comfort, in P. G. Wodehouse fashion, around the pigsty, and throws suspicion on that insubordinate young blighter Basil Blake, Miss Marple and Mrs. Bantry sally forth to Danemouth to prosecute their own inquiries. Danemouth, like Agatha Christie's native town of Torquay, has a Riviera flavor, and the world of the Majestic Hotel, Danemouth, bears a certain resemblance to the Nice or Cannes hotels of E. Phillips Oppenheim and William Le Queux. It was in a hotel such as the Majestic that Agatha Christie's Auntie-Grannie, Margaret West, worked before her marriage in 1863 to the rich American widower Nathaniel Miller. It was to a hotel such as the Majestic that Agatha Christie took flight in her famous disappearance in 1926. It was a milieu in which Christie felt at home both in fact and fiction.

In the 1940s of Agatha Christie, the rich and leisured of the world, as represented by financier Conway Jefferson and his entourage, still maintain large suites, as they did in the 1920s or even the 1880s. Silly young asses like George Bartlett still motor down for a little golf and tennis during the day, a little dancing and dalliance in the night. Attendant upon the wishes of the guests at the hotel are a staff including the handsome tennis pro and expert dancing partner Raymond Starr, the intelligent, efficient, and well-groomed bridge and dancing hostess Josephine Turner, and the young blonde dancer Ruby Keene. It is Ruby who is identified by her cousin Josie as the dead girl in the Gossington Hall library.

The character of Conway Jefferson is one we have become familiar with in Agatha Christie's novels since *The Mysterious Affair at Styles*. In a pattern repeated in such novels as *Crooked House, Hercule Poirot's Christmas*, and *Appointment with Death*, Conway Jefferson is an elderly, rich, and disabled person surrounded by dependent relatives whose affections, by the logic of murder mysteries and indeed traditional nineteenth-century fiction, are only with great difficulty to be differentiated from their financial needs. These financially successful family autocrats are portrayed with an increasing warmth and sympathy as we progress through Agatha Christie's writing career. This is not surprising, given that Christie's own situation had grown to resemble the fictional one. When *Styles* was written in 1917, Agatha Christie was a young married woman of limited means. Her treatment of the elderly victim, Mrs. Emily Cavendish Inglethorp, is perfunctory, if showing a prophetic interest in the possibilities of marriage between an older woman and a younger man. In the post-World War II period, Christie is herself an elderly matriarch, increasingly rich and famous, and exerting that familial power accruing to the person who has made the family one fortune and still seems capable of making another. Thus, it is not surprising that Conway Jefferson of 1942's *The Body in the Library* and, even more, the multimillionaire Jason Rafiel of *A Caribbean Mystery*, 1964, and *Nemesis*, 1971, should emerge as interesting, unusual, and sympathetic people, and that they have a talent for making large sums of money, even when old and sick.

Jason Rafiel is on the surface a stereotypical irascible millionaire with no time or energy for anything but making money. Nonetheless, it is to the antisocial and crippled Mr. Rafiel that Miss Marple turns in *A Caribbean Mystery* when she is desperately seeking to prevent a murderer from striking again. Rafiel is essentially a cold man but also a just, quick-thinking, courageous, and reliable one, and Miss Marple recognizes in him the partner she needs.

In *Nemesis*, Miss Marple discovers elaborate arrangements Mr. Rafiel has made to induce her to investigate the murder for which his son Michael has been imprisoned. Rafiel has no illusions about his son, a minor embezzler and sexual offender, whom he deems incapable of going straight. How far Jason Rafiel's coldness toward his son as well as Michael's incurable delinquency may result from the early death of the beloved wife and mother are issues Agatha Christie touches on but does not pursue. Rather, Christie indulges in a rare piece of theorizing and presents criminality as a kind of inborn defect, like epilepsy, which favorable circumstances or special influence may modify but not eradicate. Whatever Michael's past errors, however, his father has always offered material support and an unbiased mind, and Jason Rafiel is not convinced, despite all the evidence, that his son Michael did in fact murder Verity Hunt. His last act of cold justice will be to employ Miss Marple to seek out the truth of Verity's death.

Conway Jefferson, though not endowed with Jason Rafiel's fabulous wealth, has the resources to support a large entourage in comfort and to satisfy his every whim. Just as all Rafiel's money cannot give him a son he can love and respect, so Jefferson's fortune is at the heart of insoluble personal problems. When his private plane crashes eight years before the opening of *The Body in the Library*, Jefferson loses his beloved wife, his daughter, Rosamund, and son, Frank, and is himself permanently paralyzed from the waist down and confined to a wheelchair. Jefferson can make more money to keep his mind busy, pass the time, and replace the fortune he has already bestowed on his children at the time of their marriages. The harder task is to replace the children themselves, however unsatisfactory they may have been. Rosamund Jefferson had married a charming ne'er-do-well who, we discover in the course of the novel, lost all her money, now sponges on her father, and is willing at the end to collude in his murder. Frank Jefferson had been dominated by his father, and in a vain attempt to show that he too had the paternal Midas touch, had lost the fortune his father had given him. Whereas Agatha Christie shows increasing respect and affection for old entrepreneurs like Jason Rafiel, Conway Jefferson, and Aristide Leonides of *Crooked House* and stresses their good relationships with a promising generation of grandchildren, she consistently presents the generation of the entrepreneurs' children as at best charming and attractive dependents, at worst as unprincipled rogues.

Conway Jefferson's son-in-law, Mark Gaskell, and daughter-in-law, Adelaide Jefferson, appear for a while to fill the shoes of their dead spouses, but at the beginning of the period covered by the novel, each has been showing signs of restlessness and a need to move on to new relationships. Conway Jefferson is, in any case, not blind to the degree to which their willingness to devote themselves to him is likely to be occasioned by pecuniary interest rather than love. His solution is to adopt a young person who needs his money, who will owe him everything, and who may thus be counted upon to lighten the pain-wracked end of his life. At the Majestic Hotel, Jefferson meets the eighteen-year-old Ruby Keene, a chirpy, attractive working-class girl employed at the hotel as a dancer, who is radically different from the people Conway usually comes across and also bears a tenuous resemblance to his dead daughter Rosamund. Where the rest of the world sees Ruby as common in every sense of the word, Conway Jefferson enjoys her chatter, admires her pluck, basks in her admiration, and determines to play fairy godfather to her Cinderella. Miss Marple understands Jefferson's motivation thoroughly and sympathizes with his preference for someone young and funny and irreverent when all around him are gloomy or abstracted. She also notes the demands for exclusiveness which underlie Jefferson's magnanimity and which, even if not directly sexual in nature, may prove dangerous should Ruby find a boy friend.

Unlike earlier rich patriarchs in Christie's fiction, both Jason Rafiel and Conway Jefferson are fated to die in their beds. Their money will serve as an incentive to the murder of other people and as the means by which murderers are brought to justice. Thus, when Conway Jefferson announces that he intends to adopt Ruby Keene and leave her the fortune he has amassed since the tragic plane accident, it is Ruby who disappears and is subsequently found dead.

Ruby Keene and Pamela Reeves, the two victims in *The Body in the Library*, and the co-murderer Josephine Turner — as well as one of the suspects, "gigolo" Raymond Starr — come from a social class very different from the Jeffersons'. That class is clearly indicated by their names. Josephine Turner is a name that can pass muster at the Hotel Majestic. Similarly, "Raymond Starr" is a well-researched pseudonym that the young tennis pro claims as his own with enough authority to convince even the skeptical ex-policeman Sir Henry Clithering. In contrast, Josie's young cousin earns her reputation for stupidity by adopting a professional name, Ruby Keene, that is only marginally more classy than her real one, Rosy Legge. Earning their livings as professional entertainers and facilitators, these characters spend their lives in the company of the rich, upper-class Jefferson types, and their aim is to become so indispensable to the class employing them that they are adopted into it. Ruby's combination of blonde prettiness, prattling naiveté, and shrewd self-interest has brought her close to realizing this ambition — when she is murdered. Her cousin Josie, who, we discover in the final pages of the novel, is the second but secret Mrs. Mark Gaskell, seemed to be only one step away from the same goal when Ruby got in the way. Similarly, it is the lure of fame and fortune, as represented by a mythical film contract, that brings Girl Guide Pamela Reeves to the Majestic Hotel, where she willingly submits her hair, face, and nails to the rituals of modern glamour that are in fact preparations for death.

It is not Josie's or Ruby's or Pamela's ambitions that Agatha Christie condemns or derides. Christie's view is that all too many young women have only their youthful attractions, their energy, and their desire as assets in the game of life, and she in no way blames them for making the most of these assets in an unjust world. As Miss Marple says gently when she gazes at the body of the girl in the library, "She's very young," and the tragic loss of two young lives mobilizes Miss Marple as much as the tarnished reputation of Colonel Bantry and the danger to Basil Blake. Nonetheless, once greed turns to murder, exposure and retribution are ensured by the arrival of Miss Marple, who can forgive lust and ambition but not disregard for human life.

The murder plot in *The Body in the Library* is as absorbingly intricate as that in *The Mysterious Affair at Styles*, which it resembles in many ways. Josephine Turner and Mark Gaskell are the kind of murderers we have come to expect in Agatha Christie's work. First, like Evelyn Howard and Alfred Inglethorp in *Styles*, they are a pair of lovers whose collaboration makes the murder possible and whose relationship is extremely difficult for either fellow characters or the reader to uncover. In each pair, one member has a very large and obvious motive for murder and a correspondingly large alibi. Dr. Haydock decrees that the girl in the library was killed not earlier than 10 and not later than midnight, and from 10:40 p.m. to 12, Mark Gaskell and Adelaide Jefferson — the two characters with the most obvious motive for wanting Ruby dead — are seated at the bridge table with Josephine Turner and Conway Jefferson in the public lounge of the Majestic Hotel, some thirty minutes' drive from Colonel Bantry's library. Mark's partner in murder thus also has a good alibi, but she is protected from scrutiny above all by her apparent lack of any motive for murder and apparently good relationship with the victim. In *Styles*, Evelyn Howard appears to be so concerned for her employer Mrs. Inglethorpe's welfare that she risks dismissal by warning that lady against Alfred Inglethorpe's evil intentions. Similarly, in *The Body in the Library*, on the surface, Josephine Turner seems, if anything, more likely to gain than to lose from her cousin Ruby's inheritance of a fortune from Conway Jefferson, and is therefore an unlikely suspect in her murder.

Certain patterns of plot and character recur in Agatha Christie's work, and these are highly indicative of her essential mind set. Thus, if Josephine Turner is a working-class version of Christie's favorite young-woman-on-the-make character, Mark Gaskell is a fairly undeveloped version of the charming, devil-may-care, upper-class rapscallion, whom Christie can turn into unprincipled villain or romantic hero at will. In the fifteen Christie novels in which murder is committed by a man-woman team, it is interesting to notice that either the male or the female conspirator can come from a lower social class, that either the man or the woman can be the elder, that the wealth the conspirators seek to appropriate can be held by either a patriarch or a matriarch, that the actual act of murder can be committed by either partner, but that the brains and energy behind the murder plot are usually supplied by the female partner, whereas the charm and good looks are more commonly the male's. Josephine is a rather typical Christie murderer in that she is young and female and "the strong character" who plans the complicated murder plot. She also has the strength to carry a dead body down several flights of stairs and, at the end of the novel, the agility to enter Conway Jefferson's room via the window.

It is also important to see development as well as continuity in Christie's fiction. Thus, by 1942, when Agatha Christie is writing *The Body in the Library*, she has dropped her early Watson-style narration in favor of an unobtrusive form of omniscient narration, and enjoys playing with the detective-story genre and with her own fame. Young Peter Carmody proudly shows Miss Marple and Sir Henry Clithering the signatures of famous crime writers he has collected including that of Agatha Christie. The title and opening sequence of the novel are a spoof on the English country-house murder story. Already in 1935's *The ABC Murders*, Captain Hastings, composing his ideal murder, had declared to Poirot, "Scene of the with two potential male accomplices — Raymond Starr and also Adelaide's faithful Dobbin lover, Hugo McLean. Adelaide also has two potential motives, first, financial need, and second, love of Peter Carmody, her son by her first husband, whom Conrad Jefferson has passed over when making Ruby his heir.

Doubling of the victims so as to give an alibi to the murderers, especially the murderer with an obvious motive, is the heart of the plot elaborated by Josephine Turner to eliminate her rival for Conway Jefferson's fortune. Young woman A, Pamela Reeves, is lured to the Majestic by Mark Gaskell for a spurious film test and bleached, made up, and dressed by Josie Turner so as to resemble as far as possible young woman B, Ruby Keene. Young woman A is drugged, and finally strangled by Gaskell at around 10 p.m. and left first on the hearthrug in Basil Blake's pseudo-Tudor house in St. Mary Mead. Young woman B — alive and kicking before a host of unbiased witnesses until she leaves the Majestic's dance floor at about 11:40 p.m. — is also drugged and then killed by Josie Turner at about 12:15 a.m. when Josie is changing for the exhibition dance she will perform with Raymond in Ruby's place. Some time after 2 a.m. Josie moves Ruby's body out of the back door of the hotel and into silly young ass George Bartlett's car, drives to a nearby quarry, sets car and body on fire with gasoline, and walks back to the hotel in time to start seeming worried about Ruby's disappearance. As Ruby's next of kin, Josie is the person asked by the police to come and identify the body of the girl in the library. This identification-of-the-body stage in police murder procedure is one exploited over and over again by mystery-story writers. When Josie says the body crime — well, what's wrong with the good old library? Nothing like it for atmosphere," and *The Body in the Library* is obviously Christie's attempt to take a hoary old detective-story chestnut and give it a complicated new twist. The point is made quite explicitly in the first chapter when Colonel Bantry, roused reluctantly from deep sleep, says to his wife, "You've been dreaming, Dolly. It's that detective story you were reading — *The Clue of the Broken Match.* You know, Lord Edgbaston finds a beautiful blonde dead on the library hearthrug. Bodies are always being found in libraries in books. I've never known a case in real life." As far as the clue of the broken match goes, we note that by 1950 Christie has decided to prune her clues and concentrate her effects. The clutter of coffee cups, cloth fragment, wax droppings, and footprints from the flower bed found in *The Mysterious Affair at Styles* is eliminated, and the plot is set out with elegant simplicity and economy.

The murderous plan whereby Josephine Turner and her husband-accomplice Mark Gaskell seek to ensure the Jefferson inheritance involves a duplication of suspects and motives as well as a duplication of victims. Both Adelaide Jefferson and Mark Gaskell have pressing financial reasons for wanting Ruby Keene dead. What is more, Adelaide's overt relationship with the handsom tennis pro and dancer Raymond Starr, which seems like to lead to marriage, is the double of the covert relationsh of attractive dancer Josie and Mark, whose secret marri: is already on record at Britain's invaluable Somerset Ho record office. In fact, Agatha Christie sets the Mark-J relation in shadow by throwing the spotlight on Adel Christie multiplies the likelihood that Adelaide Jeff is the murderer of Ruby Keene by providing Ad in the library is Ruby, there is no reason to disbelieve her. Contrariwise, as Humpty Dumpty would say, once it is known that Josie has falsely identified an unknown young girl as her cousin Ruby, Josie herself becomes identified as the murderer.

Unlike the body in the library, the body in the car in the quarry is so efficiently burned as to make any identification impossible. Both the police and the victim's family are satisfied that a shoe and a Girl Guide badge should identify the corpse in the car with Pamela Reeves. The murder of Ruby Keene seems meaningful, if sad, because it is explicable in terms of familial jealousies and financial imperatives. The murder of Pamela Reeves, to the contrary, appears to be senseless, attributable, at best, to the random viciousness and madness conventionally deemed characteristic of our modern world. The corpse of the girl in Colonel Bantry's library, identified as Ruby Keene, provides the novel's title and is placed in the full searchlight of police investigation, amateur sleuthing, press reporting, and private gossip. The disappearance and violent murder of Pamela Reeves, on the other hand, like her unidentifiable corpse, is an almost anonymous item in a list of silly, minor, routine disappearances, an item that Colonel Melchett irritably dismisses, and that even the Actively Detecting Reader probably passes over in the rush to get on to the next chapter. ("Pamela Reeves, sixteen, missing from her home last night, had attended Girl Guide rally, dark brown hair in pigtails, five foot five . . .")

Miss Marple is able to sort out the doubled murder plot because she alone looks carefully at the body in the library, and has a female framework into which she fits the visual evidence of bitten, varnished fingernails and tawdry, rather worn finery. Where Colonel Melchett and Inspector Slack read blonde hair, flimsy ball gowns, and garish nails as London glamour with overtones of sexual promiscuity, Miss Marple reads them as class markers, age indicators, and items of fashion, with no necessary moral connotations. Perfectly conscious of the way her own appearance affects her public image, Miss Marple views costume changes as image creators that a young woman, in particular, may put on according to her game plan. As a later Christie heroine Ginger Corrigan says in *The Pale Horse*, "Different clothes and lots of make-up, and my best friend wouldn't look at me twice." Just as murderess Josie can mastermind a plot depending on the transformation of Pamela into Ruby, Miss Marple can defeat that plot because she is able to visualize that the brash, sexy young adventuress Ruby is only a hair-do, a make-up job, and a change of clothing away from the brown-haired, pigtailed, Guide-uniformed schoolgirl Pamela. Given an average face and figure, any young girl in the kitchen, in the schoolroom, in the drugstore, can metamorphose into a Cinderella, a Gigi, or a Lana Turner, or so the myth goes, and Miss Marple is not so old and spinsterish as to have forgotten the real-life power of such myths.

Dinah Lee, the third young "peroxide" blonde introduced in *The Body in the Library*, smokes, drinks, and drives, inhabits the racy world of the film industry, and sunbathes shockingly on the front lawn in a two-piece bathing suit. Where St. Mary Mead and the police see a young floozy flaunting her illicit relationship, Miss Marple sees an inexperienced girl going through an uncomfortable stage in her hesitant transformation from young society sexpot into happily married woman. Basil Blake and Dinah Lee Blake are, in fact, the young contemporary versions of middle-aged Colonel and Mrs. Bantry. Hence the attraction-repulsion the two couples exert over each other, culminating in Basil Blake's "joke" — his quick decision to transport the body he finds on his floor to the Colonel's library — and the Colonel's equally quick decision to divert police suspicion to young Basil and his blonde companion.

Heterosexual passion, joined to financial greed, is the motivating force behind many Agatha Christie novels, and the success of the mystery depends in large measure not on the manipulation of clues, but on the concealment of intercourse between the murderous pair. The Actively Detecting Reader experienced in the ways of Agatha Christie learns to read every expression of extreme dislike as a possible expression of the opposite, to pick up any hint that a character may be romantically involved, to connect any two characters in physical proximity, even if they are divided by age, class, or style. However, it is not until 1971's *Nemesis*, written when the author was already eighty, that Agatha Christie takes one more logical step and joins three characters together in a murder triangle on the basis of mixed heterosexual and homosexual desire.

Homosexual and homosocial characters, whether overt or covert, probably play a smaller part in the work of Agatha Christie than in that of any of her contemporaries. In *The Moving Finger* the retired antiquarian Mr. Pye seems a stereotypical gay man, and Christie introduces a most sympathetic lesbian couple, on the "Ladies of Llangollen" model, in *A Murder Is Announced*, 1950, probably the greatest of the Miss Marple novels. Miss

Hinchcliffe and Miss Murgatroyd are a devoted pair who fit effortlessly into the social scene of Chipping Cleghorn. When Murgatroyd is brutally murdered, Agatha Christie does an excellent job of conveying "Hinch's" savage but largely silent grief. The Murgatroyd-Hinchcliffe pairing interestingly doubles the novel's central relationship of Miss Blacklock and Miss Bonner. With these few exceptions, however, through most of Christie's writing career, her characters are heterosexual. Their sexual identity as men or women seems to be as fixed, conventional, and secure as the social and criminal roles allotted to them are shifting and context-defined. In Christie's fictional world, a male character or a female character can be slotted into either side of the traditional binary pairing — active-passive, desiring-desired, rich-poor, indolent-striving, victim-murderer, murderer-detective. However, a poor, indolent, beautiful, sexually desirable male in Christie's work is always desirable to a rich (or intending to be rich), active female, not to another male, and vice versa. It is because of these apparently lifelong patterns in Christie's work that *Nemesis* confounds the assumptions of the Actively Detecting Reader. When Miss Marple reveals that the respectable spinster Clotilde Bradbury-Scott has killed her young ward Verity Hunt out of love and jealousy, Agatha Christie once again comes up with a solution that her devoted fans are the least likely to find.

As is the case with most of the passionate relationships leading to murder in Agatha Christie's novels, the love of Clotilde Bradbury-Scott and Verity Hunt is given minimal development and exposure. The element of suspense and the deliciously anticipated shock of expectations deceived which Christie's readers rely on her to provide in the final pages depend on our having no expectation that the striking and impressive Clotilde had been so moved by passion as to kill her beloved and charming ward, Verity. In her explanation of the crime and its motives, Miss Marple rigidly upholds the conventional view typical of her generation and class that passionate friendship between women is a phase, not uncommonly met with, which will inevitably end when one of the women, usually the younger one, discovers her true sexual destiny through contact with the male.

The Verity Hunt-Clotilde Bradbury-Scott relationship offers no insights into lesbianism, but it allows us to see with peculiar clarity how strange and unconventional were Agatha Christie's views on sexual relations between men and women. Fiercely convinced as she was of woman's sexual nature and of her imperative need for and right to full sexual experience, Agatha Christie seems not even to entertain the possibility that a lesbian relationship might allow an equal, or even possibly superior, sexual fulfillment. An Agatha Christie woman is a woman who has to have a man, who finds irresistible the charm, the looks, the company, and — by implication — the pleasure men can afford, and for whom the moral worth, social standing, and financial position of the target male are largely irrelevant. As Miss Marple freely acknowledges, Michael Rafiel has never been any good and probably never will be. Even Michael's strongest defenders — his father Jason Rafiel, psychologist of crime Professor Wanstead, and Archdeacon Brabazon — see little possibility that Michael Rafiel will be reformed by his love for Verity Hunt or hers for him. Yet despite all these shortcomings that Agatha Christie seems to delight in emphasizing, Michael Rafiel is The Man for the young, beautiful, innocent, and good Verity Hunt. His handsome looks and his charm have engaged her capacity for love, and he can offer her sexual fulfillment and children, should she want them. In the strange Christiean-Christian world view, marriage between Verity and Michael even receives the blessing of the church, as expressed by benevolent patriarch Archdeacon Brabazon. Only Clotilde Bradbury-Scott, a noble, intelligent, impressive woman who loves Verity more than anything in the world, including herself, and whom Verity has loved because she has proved worthy of love, cannot accept the logic of Verity's "natural" preference of Michael Rafiel to herself.

If *The Body in the Library* is constructed in doubles, *Nemesis* works mainly with threes. The essential love triangle between Verity Hunt, Clotilde Bradbury-Scott, and Michael Rafiel remains concealed until the last pages, but it is doubled by the hazier triangle of Michael Rafiel, Clotilde Bradbury-Scott, and Nora Broad. The sexy, working-class Nora Broad's disappearance is linked by rumor to her alleged relationship with Michael, who has a track record of liaisons with very young lower-class women. In fact, however, it is Clotilde, whose seductive gifts and acts of friendship toward the girl arouse no suspicions, who takes Nora off by car and brutally murders her. Nora's body is battered to impede recognition and then hidden in a place where it invites discovery. When Nora's body is discovered, it is linked to the case of Verity Hunt, the missing upper-class girl whom police still search for. Nora's disappearance has been dismissed as a case of a promiscuous girl going off with some man and not informing her family. As Verity's guardian, Clotilde Bradbury-Scott is asked to identify the body, and, to mislead the police and cover her criminal acts, she declares it to be that of Verity Hunt. As with Josephine Turner in *The Body in the Library*, the police have no reason to doubt that the person they have routinely and logically contacted to identify a body has any motive to make a false identification.

Nemesis is an unusually literary book, and the theme Agatha Christie develops most insistently is that of three sisters. With one of those excursions into Shakespearian interpretation which are fairly common in her later work and which reflect her growing fascination with the stage, Christie first refers to the three weird sisters from *Macbeth*. Miss Marple decides that if she were directing *Macbeth*, she would cast the three witches not as outrageous or eerie, but as very ordinary old village women, whose menace lies precisely in their ordinariness. Later, when Miss Marple finds herself staying the night in the dilapidated old home of the three Bradbury-Scott sisters, she is reminded of Chekhov's play *Three Sisters*. The Chekhovian Prozorova sisters, Olga, Masha, and Irena, look forward in vain to the move back to Moscow that they hope will redeem their sad, drab, meaningless lives. The Bradbury-Scott sisters, Anthea, Clotilde, and Lavinia, seem similarly to have been left behind by life and to watch helplessly as the fabric of their house and their lives falls in pieces about them. However, their forlornness has a subtly sinister atmosphere about it which Miss Marple's refined instinct picks up immediately, like a faint whiff of corruption arising out of the flowering mass of polygonum in the garden. The names of the Bradbury-Scott trio are carefully chosen to recall the Moirai — Atropos, Clotho, and Lachesis — the three fates of Greek mythology, who variously spin, allot, and cut the thread of life. If Lavinia has much of the commonsensical banality of Olga Prozorova and Anthea the slightly crazed sensitivity of Masha, Clotilde plays the role both of Atropos and Lachesis in the life of Verity Hunt, first helping her to weave the pattern of life and then cutting the thread off short.

The influence of drama on the novel *Nemesis* continues in the important references to Greek tragedy contained in text and title. In the summation of the novel, Miss Marple says that from the first she has seen a resemblance between Clotilde Bradbury-Scott and the Clytemnestra of Aeschylus's *The Agamemnon* that she had recently been taken to see in a boys' public school performance. Earlier in the novel, comparing Clotilde with her wild-haired, crazy younger sister, Anthea, Miss Marple muses, "Clotilde was certainly no Ophelia, but she would have made a magnificent Clytemnestra — she could have stabbed a husband in his bath with exultation. But since she had never had a husband, that solution wouldn't do. Miss Marple could not see her murdering anyone else but a husband — and there had been no Agamemnon in this house." It will take Miss Marple awhile to realize that she is seeing in Clotilde not a Clytemnestra, but a murderous Sappho.

The tall, handsome, compelling Clotilde is a brilliant woman whose longing to go to university was frustrated by family demands. As a scholarly spinster, Clotilde forms a sisterly trio with two other women deeply involved in young women's lives whom Christie introduces into her novel — Elizabeth Temple and Emily Waldron. Miss Elizabeth Temple is the retired headmistress of the very famous girls' boarding school which Verity Hunt attended — very much the brilliant, successful, attractive woman whom Agatha Christie has already portrayed in detail in the Miss Bulstrode of Meadowbrook in 1959's *Cat Among the Pigeons*. Miss Temple has long experience of girlish "crushes," and she understands and respects the emotional intensity possible in the relationship of young girl and older woman. Thus it is Miss Temple who tells Miss Marple that love was the reason why Verity Hunt died, who is on the trail of Clotilde Bradbury-Scott, and who must be killed before she discovers any more. When Miss Marple sees Miss Temple for the first time, she is reminded of another even more commanding and successful woman she had once met and never forgotten — Dame Emily Waldron, the principal of an Oxford women's college and a notable scientist. In *Nemesis*, this character is merely referred to, but Agatha Christie had painted precisely such a sympathetic and commanding woman in the Dame Laura Whitstable of the 1952 Mary Westmacott novel *A Daughter's a Daughter*.

It is interesting to see Agatha Christie at this late stage in her life experimenting with the character and role of the powerful, successful, professional older woman — a woman, that is, like herself, Dame Agatha Christie. Jane Marple, in her final mystery *Nemesis*, is heralded as having entered the ranks of such women. Jason Rafiel, a very shrewd and influential man, is so impressed by Jane Marple that he entrusts to her a problem that his own power and wealth and insight have been unable to solve. Miss Marple is recognized by the great financial expert as equally expert in her own field — the pursuit and confusion of evil. As a recognized expert with a recognized talent, Miss Marple will for the first time receive a handsome fee — 20,000 pounds — for her efforts. Henceforth she will be able to be charitable to others, as they have been to her, and to choose her own excursions to the theater and opera. More importantly, however, in *Nemesis*, Jane Marple, the frail, fluttery old lady in the pink woolly scarf, chattering on about her hydrangeas, achieves a kind of mythic dimension. She lays claim to that prepatriarchal authority held by the ancient female goddess Nemesis Adrasteia, virgin goddess of the sacred grove, who stands wheel in hand to symbolize the inevitability of divine anger.

In a celebrated essay, "The Simple Art of Murder," Raymond Chandler argues that detective fiction as perfected by the English writers of the Golden Age is intrinsically silly and second rate because there is no real connection between the crimes, usually murders, which form the genre's core, and the genteel, upper-class milieu ("a typical laburnum-and-lodge-gate English country house") in which the crimes occur. Modestly neglecting his own efforts in the same direction, Chandler singles out his contemporary Dashiell Hammett as that rare writer who has imparted to the detective genre some kind of realism and, therefore, some of that vitality which Chandler considers the essential quality of literary art. "Hammett gave murder back to the kind of people that commit it for reasons, not just to provide a corpse; and with the means at hand, not with hand-wrought duelling pistols, curare, and tropical fish. He put these people down on paper as they are, and he made them talk and think in the language they customarily used for these purposes. He had style, but his audience didn't know it, because it was in a language not supposed to be capable of such refinements." Chandler describes Hammett's audience as "people with a sharp, aggressive attitude to life. They were not afraid of the seamy side of things; they lived there. Violence did not dismay them; it was right down their street." For Chandler and for the "hardboiled" school he represents, murder is realistically to be found in large cities, on mean streets, committed by the bootleggers, mobsters, brothel owners, and crooked public officials whose business it is. Such men speak in their own language that the writer strives to capture and domesticate for a public that lives in fact in the kind of violent society portrayed in the fiction. The villains in such pieces are caught, as in real life, by the hard-working cop or else by the private detective, a man Chandler apotheosizes as common yet uncommon, "neither tarnished nor afraid," a man of honor, a poor man, a lonely man, a proudman, a hero.

Chandler's essay is still considered one of the most powerful indictments of the English tradition of detective novels, and his emotional rhetoric carries the reader along even today. Chandler is clearly right that in "real life," little violent crime occurs in English manor houses, bijou country cottages, or Chelsea flats, that it is rarely thought out in advance, that it is rarely elegant or recherché. As the most lastingly successful of the Golden Age generation of English writers, the reputed "Queen of Crime," Agatha Christie, seems particularly likely to stand condemned by the "realist" criteria Chandler invokes. The heart of a Christie novel is undoubtedly the puzzle, and the author is indifferent to establishing a well-researched milieu or a psychologically convincing portrait of the criminal mind. Never does Christie feature a murderer, and only very exceptionally a victim, from the classes Chandler considers to have "reason" for murder. Her private detectives, most especially Miss Marple, in no way resemble the romantic hero walking tall and proud through mean streets that Chandler introduces as the climax of his essay.

It is idle to deny that Christie's talent and craft as a novelist is quintessentially an artificial rather than a realist one. It is founded on the general fictional tradition of Austen, Trollope, Eliot, and Dickens and the specifically detective fictional tradition of Wilkie Collins, Anna Katharine Green, Conan Doyle, and Gaston Leroux. Today, however, even if one were to agree that the world of *The Maltese Falcon* or *Farewell, My Lovely* is, in fact, more realistic than that of *Trent's Last Case* or *Busman's Honeymoon*, or that the poor and criminal classes have provided the audience for detective fiction, it is no longer critically so self-evident as in 1944 that realism is an equivalent term for truth or for literary value. In her television interviews for the American Public Broadcast System's *Mystery* series, P. D. James argued convincingly that the very tension between the surface law and order of a traditional English village and certain violent passions below the surface is a potentially much more powerful and provocative motive for crime than a back-street tenement.

When Miss Marple comments quietly on the evil that exists in a small village, she is not simply making a justification for her creator's particular brand of escapist fiction. She is also making a statement about human nature, evil, and crime that is fundamentally much more radical than Raymond Chandler's. The murderers that Miss Marple brings to justice are from her own community or from a community just like hers. It is because the motives and psychological patterns leading to murder are sadly familiar to her that she can solve the mystery and unmask the criminal. Instead of placing violence outside the privileged world of the rich and respectable, among people whom "we" do not know, Christie places it in our midst, or in the midst of those just above us on the social scale, those who, perhaps, possess the rank and resources we aspire to and might possibly be willing to commit crimes to achieve. In the Miss Marple novels, the person who solves the crime is not a romantic hero, a lonely outsider who comes into a situation, uses his gun and his sex appeal to get the job done, and then moves on, gathering no social or psychological moss. It is a woman who expresses and represents those traditional values of nonviolence that the murderer has chosen to flaunt.

In the first Miss Marple novel, the narrator, the Reverend Leonard Clement, offers a classic justification for the existence of elderly amateur female sleuths such as Miss Marple. He tells Lawrence Redding, a recent arrival in St. Mary Mead, not to underestimate the detective instinct of a small village where people make it their business to know their neighbors' most intimate affairs. Elderly spinsters with nothing to do all day but ask questions and observe are, in the Reverend Clement's opinion, the ultimate detectives. In the Chandlerian world view, in the realistic world view, this is nonsense. Crimes are solved by the police, not by little old ladies, or even by retired officers of the Belgian Sûreté. The collaboration of amateur sleuth and professional detective that occurs in Christie mysteries is unknown in real life. If, however, one views the mystery novel in terms of transgression rather than crime, of ethics rather than law, of exposing truth and refusing violence its reward, rather than in terms of justice and punishment, the Miss Marple crime scenario takes on a logic of its own.

As is noted explicitly time and again in *Nemesis*, Jane Marple has an instinct for evil, of which crime is the active, social manifestation. Her mission is not so much to arrest, try, and punish the murderer as to expose his or her wrongdoing to society as well as to the murderer him- or herself, and thereby to lift the weight of false accusation. That such a high proportion of the murderers in Agatha Christie's novels die or commit suicide before they can be brought to trial is not simply a result of the lack of hard evidence against them, but of the author's fundamental world view. Even though Agatha Christie held traditional and conservative views on law and order and the rights of crime victims, her novels show that her essential preoccupation is not with human justice and legality, but with good and evil, with the supreme wrong of taking life. It is perhaps not by chance that, as Agatha Christie grew older and more reflective of the lessons of two world wars, she increasingly chose not Hercule Poirot, not some official representative of the law, but her women detectives, Jane Marple and Ariadne Oliver, to embody the values she wished to protect.

Afterword
The Secret of Success

The central facts of Christie's view of the world were her reluctance to give information, particularly about herself, her difficulty in expressing deep emotion, her belief that only through God and after death could one truly know another human person, and her feeling of closeness with the sensual world. The central fact of Christie's writing is that she has attracted millions of devoted fans all over the world and continues to do so through films and television as well as books and plays. What makes the created world of this eccentric and reclusive woman so popular?

Christie's fiction is unabashedly mass-market art, and on the surface the aim of mass-market art seems to be as simple as its techniques are sophisticated — to make money for the producer by giving the target audience what it wants. Yet even as this mass-market product aggressively defines itself as anti-intellectual and devoid of content, it attains a paradoxical importance as ideology. On a fantasy level, it is able to express, maintain, subvert, or advance powerful social and psychic movements. Structured into the plot of a novel, the images of a film, or the layout of an advertisement, is an expression of raw emotions, memories, and drives that tend to lose their motivating energy when they emerge into consciousness. It is popular art's ability to tap into the collective unconscious while bypassing the reason that accounts for the cultural significance of such apparently trivial subgenres as the Harlequin or gothic romance, cowboy books, mystery novels, spy fiction, and, in the visual field, television soap operas, private-eye series, horror movies, and commercials.

Sometimes characters or sets of characters created in popular literature transcend the texts which generate them and take on the quality of a modern myth. Crusoe and Friday, Dracula and his brides, Frankenstein and his monster, Tarzan and Jane, Holmes and Watson and Moriarty, Svengali and Trilby, the Phantom of the Opera and Christine Daaé — all are figures from popular art that crystallize a web of relations of such cultural resonance as to defy normal boundaries of time and place. Hercule Poirot and Miss Marple, those vigilant defenders of society against the evil ever within it, possess this mythic energy, which has little to do with conventional portrayal of realistic or "rounded" characters. Paradoxically for a writer so overtly committed to the superiority of the reason and the ego as epitomized by Poirot's "little grey cells," Christie's essential appeal as a writer is perhaps to the reader's unconscious.

That the unconscious is at work in Christie's fiction can be seen in the mirroring devotion of the writer to her writing and of the public to her work. Painstakingly, reliably, year after year, Agatha Christie built up a fictional world which three generations of men and women have turned to in search of that apparently simple commodity, "mere" entertainment. The progress of the writer herself through fifty-five years of writing and some eighty-six completed volumes indicates an authorial compulsiveness that goes beyond the simply financial motivations Christie avows. Had Christie really written her books for the practical and contingent reasons she admits to in her autobiography, had writing been as tiresome and nerve-wracking a job as she likes to tell us, she would surely not have continued writing until the very end of her life. After 1938, for example, when Max's career had taken off, Rosalind was grown up, Greenway was bought, and royalties from some thirty successful titles were rolling in, Christie had no practical need to keep writing. Dorothy L. Sayers at essentially this stage in her life did decide to write no more detective stories. Sayers felt she would be happier doing something else and had already published enough to keep her in comfort for the rest of her days. And just as Christie compulsively produced book after book, in good times and bad, whether she needed the money or not, so the public has responded to Christie's books, buying them in larger and larger numbers, regardless of "quality," apparently insatiable for plays and films based on her writing. Such compulsiveness in an international public over many decades demands more complex explanations than that people like a good yarn, or a neat puzzle.

Agatha Christie was herself a devoted reader of detective fiction. She remembers in her autobiography how fascinated she was at age eight when Madge read her *The Leavenworth Case*, and she refers to herself and Madge as connoisseurs of the detective story. Thus, when she came to write mystery fiction, Christie had not only expert knowledge but also a fan's intuitive understanding of the genre and the hold it had over the public. However, this empathy between Christie and her potential audience was built upon a rare and much more fundamental correlation between writer and target reader.

The public for the various subgenres of popular literature divides sharply into subgroups that find pleasure in subtle variations on an established formula. The detective-story readers, in contrast with devotees of romance or adventure, see themselves as intelligent realists, not romantic escapists, and they have a strong preference that message and meaning be presented implicitly through clues laid by an authorial voice that is trustworthy but never intrusive. This readership preference coincided to an almost unique extent with the psychic requirements of Agatha Christie. Agatha Miller had, from childhood, a quite extraordinary problem in speaking her inner world or giving even trivial information about what she thought and knew. This intense reserve was reinforced by the failure of her first marriage. In later life, Christie's exceptional success and happiness depended upon her rare freedom to structure a private and public realm in which she was not required to explain herself, even to friends, or to make speeches for the public. Consciously, her novels are an attempt not to reveal but to mask the self, yet even as she succeeds in eliminating personal opinions and autobiographical information, Christie thereby gives free rein to her unconscious. Hers is a fictional world in which the author is hidden, and which fixes readers' minds upon the analysis of emotionally neutral elements, such as cigarette butts and railway timetables, while sweeping their fantasies along on an effortless, unthinking race to the denouement.

It is no accident, then, that Christie never lost her childhood fascination with fairy stories — "fairy stories were her passion. Stories of real-life children did not much interest her," writes Christie of her alter ego Celia in *Unfinished Portrait* — and that fairy-tale themes ring out so insistently in her work. *Ten Little Indians; One, Two, Buckle My Shoe; Crooked House; Hickory Dickory*

Dock; Five Little Pigs; A Pocket Full of Rye; Three Blind Mice; Cat Among the Pigeons — how many of Agatha Christie's titles recall the world of childhood fairy tales, the world of Mother Goose and the Brothers Grimm? The fairy-tale world is today recognized as a vital expression of the collective unconscious, revealing a special kind of archetypal truth. Christie's writing has the sparseness, the directness, the narrative pace, and the universal appeal of the fairy story, and it is perhaps as modern fairy stories for grown-up children that Christie's novels succeed.

"I don't know anything about him," says the enigmatic Isabella of her lover John Gabriel just before her death. A scene later in *The Rose and the Yew Tree*, Teresa, while assuring Hugh Norreys that he is not responsible for Isabella's death, says to him, "You loved her enough to leave her alone." These two bald sentences are emblematic of Agatha Christie's strange and yet compelling vision of life. A woman of strong views, a woman convinced that there are eternal values and verities, Christie was yet singularly free of evangelical zeal and didactic purpose. If she had a message, it was that each person should and must make choices for himself or herself and should impinge as little as possible upon the choices of others. In the words of Thomas à Kempis, "You are not required to answer for others but you will have to give an account of your own life." Humility, tolerance, and acceptance are for Christie the essential virtues. She reserved her anger and condemnation not for the sinners of the flesh, but for those who see themselves as more than other men, who use their talent to bind others to their will and their strength to kill and maim.

Physical ardor, a passionate response to the whole world of the senses — to nature, to human beauty, to music, art, and literature, to good food — combined in Agatha Christie with a mental coolness to create a fictional world whose very reserve and refusal of allure constitute its greatest attraction. Agatha Christie makes no claim to know her readers, merely to respect and enjoy us. She loves us enough to leave us alone, and we love her for it.

BIBLIOGRAPHY

Aisenberg, Nadya. *A Common Spring: Crime Novel and Classic.* Bowling Green, Ohio: Bowling Green University Popular Press, 1980.

Arendt, Hannah. *The Origins of Totalitarianism.* New York: Harcourt, Brace & World, 1966.

Auden, W. H. "The Guilty Vicarage," in *The Dyer's Hand.* New York: Vintage, 1968.

Bargainnier, Earl F. *The Gentle Art of Murder: The Detective Fiction of Agatha Christie.* Bowling Green, Ohio: Bowling Green University Popular Press, 1980.

Barnard, Robert. *A Talent to Deceive: An Appreciation of Agatha Christie.* New York: Dodd, Mead, 1980. (Reissued in paperback by The Mysterious Press, 1987.)

Barnes, Melvyn. *The Best Detective Fiction: A Guide from Godwin to the Present.* Hamden, Conn., and London: Clive Bingley/Linnet Books, 1975.

Barzun, Jacques, and Taylor, W. H. *A Catalogue of Crime.* New York: Harper & Row, 1971.

Behr, Frank. *Studies in Agatha Christie's Writings: The Behaviour of a Good (Great) Deal, a Lot, Much, Plenty, a Good (Great) Many.* Göteberg: Universitetet. No. 19 in the Gothenburg studies in English, 1967.

Bettelheim, Bruno. *The Uses of Enchantment: The Meaning and Importance of Fairy Tales.* New York: Knopf, 1976.

Brabazon, James. *Dorothy L. Sayers.* London: Gollancz, 1980.

Brandon, Ruth. *The Spiritualists: The Passion for the Occult in the Nineteenth and Twentieth Century.* New York: Prometheus Books, 1984.

Bredin, Jean-Denis. *The Affair: The Case of Alfred Dreyfus.* Trans. Jeffrey Mehlman. New York: George Braziller, 1986.

Briggs, Julia. *A Woman of Passion: The Life of E. Nesbit.* 1858-1924. Penguin Books, 1987.

Brittain, Vera. *Testament of Youth: An Autobiographical Study of the Years 1900–1925.* London: Gollancz, 1933. (Reissued in paperback by Virago, 1978.)

Cassiday, Bruce, ed. *Roots of Detection: The Art of Deduction Before Sherlock Holmes.* New York: Frederick Ungar, 1983.

Cawelti, John G. *Adventure, Mystery, and Romance: Formula Stories as Art and Popular Culture.* Chicago and London: The University of Chicago Press, 1976.

Champigny, Robert. *What Will Have Happened? A Philosophical and Technical Essay on Mystery Stories.* Bloomington and London: Indiana University Press, 1977.

Chodorow, Nancy. *The Reproduction of Mothering.* Berkeley: The University of California Press, 1978.

Christie, Agatha. *An Autobiography.* New York: Dodd Mead & Co. 1977 (Reissued in paperback by Fontana in 1978 and 1989.)

Craig, Patricia, and Cadogan, Mary. *The Lady Investigates: Women Detectives and Spies in Fiction.* New York: St. Martin's Press, 1981.

Dinnerstein, Dorothy. *The Mermaid and the Minotaur.* New York: Harper & Row, 1976.

Eliot, T. S. *T. S. Eliot: The Complete Poems and Plays, 1907–1950.* New York: Harcourt, Brace & World, 1971.

Ellenberger, Henri. *The Discovery of the Unconscious.* New York: Basic Books, 1970.

Freud, Sigmund. "Mourning and Melancholia." *The Complete Psychological Works of Sigmund Freud.* Trans. James Strachey. 24 vols. London: Hogarth, 1955, Vol. 14, 239.

Gay, Peter. *The Bourgeois Experience: Victoria to Freud.* Vol. 1, *Education of the Senses.* New York: Oxford University Press, 1984.

——. *Freud: A Life for Our Time.* New York: Anchor Doubleday, 1988.

Gilbert, Sandra M., and Gubar, Susan. *The Madwoman in the*

Attic: The Woman Writer and the Nineteenth-Century Literary Imagination. New Haven, Conn.: Yale University Press, 1979.

——— and ———. *No Man's Land: The Place of the Woman Writer in the Twentieth Century.* Vols. 1 and 2. New Haven, Conn.: Yale University Press, 1988 and 1990.

Grossvogel, David I. *Mystery and Its Fictions: From Oedipus to Agatha Christie.* Baltimore and London: The Johns Hopkins University Press, 1979.

Hart, Ann. *The Life and Times of Miss Jane Marple.* New York: Dodd, Mead, 1985.

———. *Agatha Christie's Poirot.* London: Pavilion, 1990.

Hartmann, Mary S. *Victorian Murderesses: A True History of Thirteen Respectable French and English Women Accused of Unspeakable Crimes.* New York: Schocken Books, 1977.

Haycraft, Howard, ed. *The Art of the Mystery Story.* New York: Grosset and Dunlap, 1946. (Reissued in paperback by Carroll and Graf, 1983.)

Heilbrun, Carolyn G. *Reinventing Womanhood.* New York: W. W. Norton & Company, 1979.

———. *Writing a Woman's Life.* New York: Ballantine Books, 1988.

———. *Hamlet's Mother and Other Women.* New York: Columbia University Press, 1990.

Hitchman, Janet. *Such a Strange Lady: A Biography of Dorothy L. Sayers.* New York: Harper & Row, 1975.

Homans, Margaret. *Bearing the Word. Language and Female Experience in Nineteenth-Century Women's Writing.* Chicago and London: The University of Chicago Press, 1986.

Huhn, Peter. "The Detective as Reader: Narrativity and Reading Concepts in Detective Fiction." *Modern Fiction Studies*, Vol. 33, No. 3, Autumn 1987.

Keating, H. R. F., ed. *Agatha Christie: First Lady of Crime.* New York: Holt, Rinehart and Winston, 1977.

Klein, Kathleen Gregory. *The Woman Detective: Gender and Genre.* Urbana and Chicago: The University of Illinois Press, 1988.

Lambert, Gavin. *The Dangerous Edge.* New York: Grossman

Publishers, 1976.

Lehman, David. *The Perfect Murder: A Study in Detection.* New York: The Free Press, 1989.

Maida, Patricia D., and Spornick, Nicholas B. *Murder She Wrote: A Study of Agatha Christie's Detective Fiction.* Bowling Green, Ohio: Bowling Green University Popular Press, 1982.

Mallowan, Max. *Mallowan's Memoirs.* New York: Dodd, Mead, 1977.

Mann, Jessica. *Deadlier than the Male: Why Are Respectable Women So Good at Murder?* New York: Macmillan, 1981.

Masters, Anthony. *Literary Agents: The Novelist as Spy.* New York: Basil Blackwell, 1987.

Meade, Marion. *Madame Blavatsky: The Woman Behind the Myth.* New York: G. P. Putnam's Sons, 1980.

Miller, D. A. *The Novel and the Police.* Berkeley: The University of California Press, 1987.

Moers, Ellen. *Literary Women: The Great Writers.* New York: Anchor Doubleday, 1977.

Morgan, Janet. *Agatha Christie: A Biography.* New York: Knopf, 1984.

Most, Glen, and Stowe, William, eds. *The Poetics of Murder.* New York: Harcourt Brace Jovanovich, 1983.

Murdoch, Derrick. *The Agatha Christie Mystery.* Toronto: Pagurian Press Ltd., 1976.

Nevins, Francis M., Jr. ed. *The Mystery Writer's Art.* Bowling Green, Ohio: Bowling Green University Popular Press, 1970.

Osborne, Charles. *The Life and Crimes of Agatha Christie.* New York: Holt, Rinehart and Winston, 1982. (Reissued by Macmillan, 1990.)

Ousby, Ian. *Bloodhounds of Heaven: The Detective in English Fiction from Godwin to Doyle.* Cambridge, Mass.: Harvard University Press, 1976.

Petersen, Audrey. *Victorian Masters of Mystery from Wilkie Collins to Conan Doyle.* New York: Frederick Ungar, 1984.

Poovey, Mary. *The Proper Lady and the Woman Writer.* Chicago and London: The University of Chicago Press, 1984.

Radway, Janice A. *Reading the Romance.* Chapel Hill: The University of North Carolina Press, 1984.

Ramsey, G. C. *Agatha Christie: Mistress of Mystery.* New York: Dodd, Mead, 1967.

Reddy, Maureen T. *Sisters in Crime: Feminism and the Crime Novel.* New York: Continuum, 1988.

Riley, Dick, and McAllister, Pam, eds. *The Beaside, Bathtub, and Armchair Companion to Agatha Christie.* New York: Frederick Ungar, two editions, 1979 and 1986.

Rivière, François. *Agatha Christie: Duchesse de la mort.* Paris: Seuil, 1981.

Robyns, Gwen. *The Mystery of Agatha Christie.* New York: Doubleday and Company, 1978.

Ryan, Richard T. *Agatha Christie Trivia.* Boston: Quinlan Press, 1987.

Schweickart, Patrocinio P. "Reading Ourselves: Toward a Feminist Theory of Reading," in Elaine Showalter, ed., *Speaking of Gender.* New York and London: Routledge, 1989.

Showalter, Elaine. *A Literature of Their Own.* Princeton, N.J.: Princeton University Press, 1977.

Siebenheller, Norma. *P. D. James.* New York: Frederick Ungar, 1981.

Slung, Michelle B., ed. *Crime on Her Mind: Fifteen Stories of Female Sleuths from the Victorian Era to the Forties.* New York: Penguin Books, 1975.

Spacks, Patricia Mayer. *The Female Imagination.* New York: Avon Books, 1972.

Springer, Marlene. *What Manner of Woman? Essays on English and American Life and Literature.* New York: New York University Press, 1977.

Steinbrunner, Chris, and Penzler, Otto. *Encyclopedia of Mystery Fiction.* New York: Harcourt Brace Jovanovich, 1976.

Steward, J. I. M. *Myself and Michael Innes.* New York and London: W. W. Norton, 1987.

Stoppard, Tom. *The Real Inspector Hound.* New York: Grove Press, 1968.

Suleiman, Susan Rubin. *The Female Body in Western Culture: Contemporary Perspectives*. Cambridge, Mass.: Harvard University Press, 1985.

Symons, Julian. *Mortal Consequences: A History. From the Detective Story to the Crime Novel*. New York: Harper & Row, 1972. (Revised and updated as *Bloody Murder*. New York: Viking, 1985.)

——. *Great Detectives: Seven Original Investigations*. New York: Harry N. Abrams, Inc., 1981.

Symons, Julian, with Adams, Tom. *Agatha Christie: The Art of Her Crimes: The Paintings of Tom Adams*. New York: Everest House, 1981.

Thomas à Kempis. *The Imitation of Christ*. Trans. Ronald Knox and Michael Oakley. New York: Sheed & Ward, 1959.

Tomalin, Claire. *Katherine Mansfield: A Secret Life*. New York: Penguin Books, 1987.

Tompkins, Jane P. "Sentimental Power: *Uncle Tom's Cabin* and the Politics of Literary History," in Elaine Showalter, ed., *The New Feminist Criticism*. New York: Pantheon Books, 1985.

Tynan, Kathleen. *Agatha*. New York: Ballantine Books, 1978.

Wagoner, Mary S. *Agatha Christie*. Boston: G. K. Hall, 1986.

Watson, Colin. *Snobbery and Violence: Crime Stories and Their Audiences*. New York: St. Martin's Press, 1971. (Reissued in paperback by The Mysterious Press, 1988.)

Wilson, Edmund. *Classics and Commercials*. New York: Vintage Books, 1962.

Winn, Dilys. *Murderess Ink: The Better Half of the Mystery*. New York: Workman Publishing, 1979.

INDEX

trusts created to protect earnings, 247;

pleasures of old age, 248-51;

relationship with Mathew, 252;

international fame, 253;

DBE, 254;

preparations for death, 255;

and Abney House, Cheshire (home of the Watts), 91, 134, 142, 152, 170, 180, 209, 252;

and adoption, 7;

and agoraphobia, xviii;

and alibis, 38, 51, 273, 276;

and ambition, xvi, xxii, 15-16, 22, 23, 36, 65, 81, 103, 110-11, 125, 163;

and America, United States of, 8, 15, 111, 227;

and amnesia, x, 130-1, 147, 149, 152, 156, 157, 160;

and anti-Semitism, 119-27, 188, 226, 228;

and anxiety of influence, xii;

and archeology, 167, 168, 175, 176, 178, 180, 182, 215, 216, 218;

and Ashfield (the Miller home in Torquay, Devon), 1-10, 11, 14, 16-17, 28, 30, 32, 33, 35, 37, 85, 91, 92, 93, 102, 125, 134, 140, 142, 171, 179, 210, 248;

and Athens, 169, 175, 177;

and Australia, 88;

and autobiography, ix, xv, xvii, xix, xxii, 15, 23, 39, 63, 65, 69, 81, 134, 181, 219-20, 253-4;

and Baghdad, 121, 137, 164, 167, 169, 175, 176, 215;

and banality of evil, 11, 196, 288-96;

and beauty, xv, xvi, 16, 24, 84, 103, 135, 228;

and being a Victorian, 5, 10, 13, 14, 21, 110, 195, 197, 203, 259;

and Beverley, Yorkshire, 154, 155, 156;

and the black sheep of the family, 99, 101, 102, 273;

and the British Royal Family, 254;

and Bulawayo, 99, 103;

and "The butler did it", 188;

and Cairo, 25, 111, 180;

and Canary Islands, 150, 161;

and cars and motoring,

DATE DUE			
8/93			